Mysteries
of
Demeter

Mysteries of Demeter

REBIRTH
OF THE
PAGAN
WAY

Jennifer Reif

SAMUEL WEISER, INC.

York Beach, Maine

First published in 1999 by
Samuel Weiser, Inc.
P.O. Box 612
York Beach, ME 03910-0612
www.weiserbooks.com

Second hardcover edition, 2000

Library of Congress Cataloging-in-Publication Data
Reif, Jennifer.
    Mysteries of Demeter : rebirth of the pagan way / Jennifer Reif.
       p. cm.
    Includes bibliographical references and index.
    ISBN 1-57863-133-5 (alk. paper). —ISBN 1-57863-141-6
       (pbk. : alk. paper)
    1. Demeter (Greek deity)—Cult —Miscellanea. 2. Goddess
religion. I. Title.
BL820.C5R45 1999
299—dc   2199-29771
                                                        CIP

EB

Cover design by Ed Stevens
Typeset in 11/13 Minion

Printed in United States of America

The paper used in this publication meets all the minimum require-
ments of the American National Standard for Information
Sciences—for Permanence of Paper for Printed Library Materials
Z39.48-1992 (R1997).

This book is dedicated to the people of Eleusis. Their mar-
velous Temple of Demeter was and, in memory, is a symbol
for the spiritual life of the ancient world. It must be said that
the Great Mother is revered there still, as
"Mary, the Lady Inside the Seed."

CONTENTS

P R E F A C E

It was 1989 and I was right in the middle of Professor Shirley St. Leon's art history class, when I somehow ran headlong into Demeter and Persephone. The Celtic side of Goddess religion had held my interest for some time, but this was different. I'm not completely sure why I became so attracted to the subject of Demetrian Paganism. Perhaps I was drawn to the Holy Mother and Daughter because I sought an all-embracing and powerful Mother Goddess. Or perhaps I sought the image of a tender-hearted maiden, who would eventually transform into a queen. In the end, I found these sacred images, but I discovered much more along the way.

My journey into Demeter's temple began when I saw a photograph of the east-pediment sculptures of the Parthenon, a reconstruction from the Acropolis Museum in Athens. These exquisite images of the Greek Goddesses and Gods awoke something that had been sleeping within me. I saw tremendous grace and beauty in the figures, but there was another element present, something that had nothing to do with physical appearances. The figures of Demeter and Persephone seemed to emerge from the rest, calling me with very powerful voices, saying, "Look at me, find me, know me. . . ." I became intensely curious. Who were these Goddesses? What were their characteristics, beyond those found in common, general descriptions? I had to know.

I sought out books on the subject, anticipating each book as eagerly as the advent of some new culinary feast. And as I studied, their ancient religion began to rise up before me like a ghost out of the past. I felt that soon I was to discover something ethereal and precious. My spirit on fire, I became driven, like some insane banshee, to search out clues to unravel the mystery.

As I read, apparent images of the past began to show themselves. Whether they were memories of a past life or simply the musings of an active imagination, they were quite startling: visions of helping to put on festivals, of walking between the buildings of the sanctuary on various errands, of seeing exquisite statuary, of having an audience with a priestess high above me in rank, and much more. I saw these all as precious moments of beauty in a spiritual world that felt as though it would have no end. Then there were the visions of a glorious temple being destroyed—of men on horseback riding in, smashing statuary, taking precious objects, and setting fire to draperies and to carved wood decoration. Whether this was fantasy or memory, within a few months I was placed firmly on the road of discovery.

Because the myth of Demeter is based on a yearly agricultural cycle, I spent several seasons raising grain (with accompanying red field poppies) in the Mediterranean coastal climes of southern California. Learning about the Holy Mother and Daughter through the planting of grain revealed much about the internal life of the myth. Nature became an instructress, leading me to observe the Goddesses and Gods in their most primal elements of earth, seed, rain, sun, green growth, flowering, harvest, and fallow time.

The first evidence of Demetrian Paganism is found in the 15th century B.C.E. in Eleusis, Greece, where its first religious structure took shape. By the fifth century C.E., the Eleusinian temple to Demeter was destroyed. Its marble was used in the building of bridges, wells, and Christian churches. The exact theology and ritual practices of the temple were lost. My personal quest is now to bring forward a full interpretation of Demeter's rites, seasonal festivals, and mysteries.

It has been a long journey from my initial curiosity about Demeter to the completion of this book. Many years of research have finally resulted in a re-creation of the mystery religion of the Greek Goddess Demeter. From ancient Greece, to Rome, to North Africa and Macedonia, Demeter's temples were once important centers of Goddess worship. I believe that these centers presented a religion that celebrated, not only the Goddess and her seasonal themes of life, death, and rebirth, but also the mystery and divinity of the soul.

While the Holy Mother and Daughter are the focus of the myth and rites, many other Gods and Goddesses are also included. This book presents a rich composite telling of the myth and explains its mystical themes. The background and historical information given prepare the way for Demeter's yearly cycle of festivals and mysteries.

By experiencing the Demetrian Wheel-of-the-Year holidays, the reader can experience the archetypal forces of life and nature. Nature is sacred, containing magical forces that may be recognized, not only as guiding divinities, but as powers that live within us.

Every moment of our lives is a part of the sacred drama, the fore-word moving spiral of life, death, and rebirth. The Goddesses and Gods of Demeter's myth are powerful forces within this sacred drama. Through them and their mythic relationships, we may come to understand our own relationships to the natural and spiritual worlds. The rituals of Demetrian Paganism tell us a little about our-selves, our origins, and our relationship to the natural world. We can step into the myth and its rites, and learn something of the nature of the soul. The natural world then becomes the setting in which this jewel of a religion takes its place.

—*Jennifer Reif*

ACKNOWLEDGMENTS

I had been teaching the class "Demeter: Myths and Mysteries of Ancient Eleusis" for some time, when my friend, Laurie Miller, invited me to present it for Long Beach WomanSpirit. After the class, one of the students suggested that the material be taken further, that Demeter rituals be created. This enthusiastic woman's name is Maureen Cormier; I am eternally grateful to her for being the catalyst. I remember my original hesitation, and a feeling of the enormity of the work that might lie ahead. The following year, I felt ready to proceed.

By 1993, two students, Lisa McNabb and Darlene Levettre, were working regularly with me on the idea of reconstructing a temple of Demeter. Together we discussed many of the rituals, after which I would retreat to compose the rites. They became an administrative part of the temple, and worked to help present its services to others. In 1994, Lisa became the editor of the temple newsletter, *Mystica*. Much appreciation to them always, for their work and participation.

Many thanks to those who participated as clergy: Lisa, Darlene, Laura Janesdaughter, Russell Holster, Marline Haleff, Donna Albino, Kathleen Zundell, and Rita Winston, as well as to all those who were drawn to attend the rites.

I give heartfelt thanks to Laura, Kathleen, MaryScarlett Amaris and Lunaea Weatherstone for their thoughtful support in moments of challenge. Thanks and appreciation also to Sheila Bernard for her encouragement and proofreading assistance.

Many thanks to Susan Gray, Starr Goode, MaryScarlett Amaris, Jane R. Wheatley, and Judith Tolley (whose Demeter-Persephone ritual, which I attended in the late 1980s, was my first) for their generous contributions to Appendix 4. We benefit greatly from the sharing of their experiences. They illustrate for us some of the many ways that Demeter and Persephone's myth can be seen and understood.

My thanks to Professor Shirley St. Leon, of Santa Monica College, whose teaching inspired me and introduced me to the arts and ideas of ancient Greece and Rome, and to Professor Matthew Dillon, of Loyola Marymount University, whose knowledge of the ancient Greek language was invaluable. He generously gave of his time to translate from the Greek, and provide me with many of the meanings of the various names of Demeter used in this work. Thanks also to Michael DeHart, horticulturist of the J. Paul Getty museums in Malibu and Brentwood, who introduced me to the Mediterranean garden at the Malibu villa museum, and gave me my first lessons in planting grain.

Much appreciation to two authors without whom this work could not have been considered. The first is George E. Mylonas, who wrote *Eleusis and the Eleusinian Mysteries* (Princeton University Press, 1961) and who excavated the temple site at Eleusis. His important historical perspectives, information on the sanctuary grounds, and telling of specific elements of the mysteries were essential and a great inspiration. The second is Allaire Chandor Brumfield, whose dissertation, *The Attic Festivals of Demeter and Their Relation to the Agricultural Year* (Arno Press, 1981), gave me my first look at what I've come to call the Demetrian Wheel of the Year. Through her studies of ancient texts and her experiences of Greek farming life and village communities, she influenced my views of the Mediterranean yearly cycle. It was through Brumfield that I began to understand the world of nature, of which we are a part, as the source of the myth and its festivals.

PART I

A Passionate Theology

The Light of Ecstasy

Deo, divine mother of all, Goddess of many names,
august Demeter, nurturer of youths
and giver of prosperity and wealth . . . .
You yoke your chariot to bridled dragons,
and round your throne you whirl and howl in ecstasy . . . .
come, blessed and pure one, laden with the fruits of summer,
bring peace, together with the welcome rule of law,
riches too, and prosperity, and health that governs all.[1]

The mysteries of Demeter were among the most famous mysteries in the ancient world. Many of the wealthy traveled from as far as Egypt to attend them, and country folk saved their money for years just so that they could experience them once before they died. The Goddesses and Gods that are a part of Demeter's mysteries are certainly powerful, fascinating archetypes that have much to reveal to us. But this is only a part of their power.

Demeter's religion is one in which the various elements are knit together by the passionate drama of love flowing between divinities. It is, however, the human desire to be at one with the light of the soul that holds center stage as this religion's greatest drama. Here, the voice of the primal sacred marriage entices us with its alluring beauty. Glittering images flow from the font of creation. From

---

[1] Apostolos Athanassakis, trans., *The Orphic Hymns* (Atlanta: Scholars Press, 1988) p. 57. Reprinted by permission of Scholars Press.

within, an ancient longing arises, as we seek to understand the mystery. How did we come into being? What sustains us and what happens to us at death? What shall we name the source of life and how shall we image it? In Demetrian Paganism, I have found answers.

Demeter's myth is filled with many characters, divinities who portray the elemental forces within the sacred drama of life. The Goddess Demeter shows us the relationship between abundant harvests and barren sadness. She demonstrates the healing power of compassion, and also reveals the brilliant light of the infinite. The dual role of Demeter's Daughter, as both the Maiden of Spring and the Queen of Death, teaches us about the journey of the soul. The young demigod Triptolemos is a teacher and way-shower, and magical Hecate teaches us of life's transitions. These are but some of the archetypes of Demeter's myth.

Within my rendition of Demeter's holy day, the Greater Mysteries, is a sacred drama. Through myth, the drama tells the story of the agricultural year whose beauties, magic, crisis, and resolution reflect the phases of our personal lives. The mysteries teach us to see our lives through a more sacred vision. They tell us the story of our own creation, lifetime, physical passing away, and rebirth. An understanding of our birth from divinity, and the knowledge that we are a part of that divinity, is also established during the rites.

By experiencing life's holiness we can feel religious ecstasy. Children express this joy naturally. Adults find this feeling in love relationships where the spark of the divine is kindled in the heart. It is felt during high moments of creativity, or in the stillness of the moment when one experiences the beauty of nature. It can also be found by going back to the source, by experiencing devotion to deity.

Every cross-cultural deity that I know of exists within a mythic structure. Divine myths have developed to provide metaphors that illustrate the most esoteric questions we have about life. These myths can teach us about the light that lies beyond ordinary light, and about the love that is the source of all human love. Our questions are answered, not in scientific terms, but through the oblique perspective of poetic metaphor. Like an orchestrated hymn that takes a full year to be sung, Demeter's myth moves from joyful maiden-innocence to dark and barren sorrow, then to the awakening joy of compassion, and culminates in reunion and rebirth. All that appears to have been lost is returned. The climax forms a new beginning, a part of the forward-moving spiral of life.

Through Demeter's myth we learn that there is always reunion. That which we have loved remains a part of our soul. We live within the realm of time, but the divine exists beyond the form of time that it has created. When you are awake in devotion to divinity, you abide in the timeless. All of the cherished love that has blessed your soul is gathered in, and then you are given even more, as much as the beautiful chalice of your soul can hold.

In times of sorrow, when our passion for life seems lost, the Goddess is there to heal and bless with a mother's tender love. Whether through a simple prayer or a formal ritual, she will come to you. She is full of power and beauty. From the darkness of her womb has come light and life; all myriad forms of life are her creations. The Creatress brings comfort and spiritual sustenance. She can change what seems unchangeable. As you open your heart to her, you become one with the source, the spirit, the Mother, She embraces you and fills you with light.

In *The Madness of the Saints: Ecstatic Religion in Bengal,* by June McDaniel, we find many illustrations of divine passion, of inspirational fire. These kinds of personal experiences illustrate a sacred dimension. Often described with words such as sweetness, light, beauty, love, or a connection to all things, this dimension can be attained through the process of devotion, or through spiritual exercise. Spiritual exercises can include chanting, prayer, or other elements of ritual. Divine passion may also be brought about by chance, spontaneous events, or by sacred foods, which will be discussed in later examples. In the ritual ecstasy of India and Bengal, certain tried and true rituals are used by the devotee, having been learned from a teacher of accepted lineage. The rituals may include a combination of chanting, song, prayer, meditation, sacred poetry, ritual acts, and offerings to the deity.

The poet Ramprasad Sen was born in Halisahar, West Bengal, in 1720. He is famous in India and Bengal for his beautiful devotional songs to the Goddesses Tara and Kali. He was initiated into the Kali mantra by the family guru (teacher), Madhvacarya. Later, he was taught *Shakti* (Goddess) rituals by several other gurus. Throughout his life, he spent a great deal of time in ritual practice and meditation. He often experienced trances and visions that became the inspiration for his writings. "Blissful Divine Mother dwells in my heart, and always plays there," he tells us. "I never forget her name, in whatever condition I live."[2] And also, "Make me mad, O Divine Mother!

---

2   June McDaniel, *The Madness of the Saints* (Chicago: University of Chicago Press, 1989), p. 144. Reprinted by permission of the University of Chicago Press.

There is no more use for knowledge and discrimination. Make me intoxicated with the wine of Thy Love. O Mother! Enchanter of the devotee's hearts!"[3]

There are other poets from India who write about these kinds of experiences. From the poet Tirumantiram we hear, "Deep in the core of my heart She stood, in union with me, joined. I, in the rapture of an ascetic entranced, was drawn in by she, Shakti of Boundless Beauty. . . ."[4] "She is immaculate, bejeweled, and dances through *sushumna nadi channel* [Kundalini, divine energy that flows up the spine] as Jnani luminous She, beginning of universes all."[5]

Bengali holy woman Anandamayi Ma experienced spontaneous visions and trances as a child. She was born in 1896 in Kheora, East Bengal, and named Nirmala Sundari. During group singing of sacred songs *(kirtana)*, she often saw Goddesses and Gods, and experienced raptures and divine ecstasies. From 1918 to 1924, inner voices taught her what mantras to chant, what images to visualize, and what spiritual exercises to do. She initiated herself on the night of a full moon, with worship articles that were not visible in the physical world.

Anandamayi Ma described her spiritual ecstasy her *bhava,* as a wave of ecstatic emotion that rose up from within and flowed outward. When she became immersed in spiritual practices and exercises, she was possessed by this ecstasy. She stated that, at these times, sacred worship occurred within her whole body.[6]

There are also examples of spontaneous ecstasy occurring in the West. Although the following examples are not placed in any particular religious context, they portray some similar themes. From *The Relevance of Bliss,* by Nona Coxhead, we learn of the experience of medical journalist and psychotherapist Wendy Rose Neill of Buckinghamshire, Great Britain. While gardening, Neill noticed an unusual awareness of her surroundings. As she lay face down on the grass she felt an energy flowing through her, making her feel as though she were a part of Earth. The boundaries between her body and her surroundings began to disappear. In place of these boundaries came a feeling of peace and unity. She felt as though she had

---

3   McDaniel, *The Madness of the Saints,* p. 140. Reprinted by permission of the University of Chicago Press.

4   June McDaniel, "Shaktism" in *Hinduism Today* (Kapaa, HI: Himalayan Academy, Dec. 1991), p. 16. Reprinted by permission of Himalayan Academy Publishing.

5   McDaniel, "Shaktism," p. 16. Reprinted by permission of Himalayan Academy Publishing.

6   McDaniel, *The Madness of the Saints,* p. 200.

awakened from a long sleep and was now experiencing a real world. This experience impressed her memory with a lasting feeling of peace and joy.[7]

In another instance, author Claire Myers Owens was sitting in her Connecticut home, at her writing desk, when she noticed her surroundings changing. Somehow, everything in her physical field of sight had suddenly disappeared. Then, an even more dramatic change occurred. The concepts of time and space no longer existed for her. She describes the room she was in as filled with a wonderful golden light. What seemed to remain of her own personality was only a small piece of her consciousness. What she describes as a great, transcendent power became a part of her, flowing in a circular pattern with the universal force. This brought a mystical union with the infinite life-force. All fear disappeared. After this experience, she no longer feared death.[8]

Some ecstatic experiences may be brought about by the use of sacred food or drink, within the context of a religious rite. In Demeter's festival, the Greater Mysteries, a sacred drink was used. Some believe that it contained a psychotropic agent. At this festival, some kind of great vision was experienced by the initiates, often a vision of spiritual light and beauty. Most accounts agree that after the Greater Mysteries, the initiates no longer feared death. They had somehow become acquainted with the land of death, as well as with the mysteries of life. Through the rites, and most probably the sacred drink, the initiates became intimately connected to the Goddess and her Holy Daughter. Divinity became known to them as a personal, internal experience. The sacred drink was one of the elements that set the rites of the Greater Mysteries apart from the rites of the seasonal festivals.

Ecstatic experience can also be induced by the use of sacred food. In Mexico and Central America, peyote is used in ceremonial settings to commune with divine forces. This mescaline-producing crown of the cactus *Lophophora williamsii* is still used today by the Yaqui, Tarahumara, and Huichol Indians. It is eaten to gain guidance and knowledge directly from deities of the religious culture. It creates a state in which the votary is at one with the deity and gains knowledge of the mystical aspects of the world. The mushrooms of the Mexican highlands belonging to the genus *Psilocybe* are known to have been

---

[7]   Nona Coxhead, *The Relevance of Bliss* (New York: St. Martin's Press, 1985), p. 30.
[8]   Coxhead, *The Relevance of Bliss*, p. 35.

used ritually by the ancient Nahuatl Indians. They called this sacred food *Teonanacatl,* meaning "God's Flesh."

The sacred drink of Demeter's mysteries is the subject of much discussion in *The Road to Eleusis: Unveiling the Secret of the Mysteries,* by Swiss pharmacologist Albert Hofmann, together with Gordon Wasson and Carl Ruck. Here we find the ethnobotanist's view of the *Homeric Hymn to Demeter,* with additional information about related religious art and the various possible accompanying sacred drinks. A drink made from a strain of ergot (fungus) may have been used during the mysteries, the psychotropic *Claviceps paspali* being one possible variety. This wild variety grows on the local grass called *Paspalum dictichum.*[9] Perhaps this was the element in the drink that created the mystical state for Demeter's initiates. Ergot of wheat has also been suggested.

Architectural reliefs from Demeter's temple in Eleusis illustrate the *kykeon vessel* (pitcher that held the sacred drink), sheaves of wheat, and poppies. The drink was apparently a mixture of some sort, containing cooked barley groats and leaves of a member of the mint family (pennyroyal has been suggested). In addition, a psychotropic agent such as grain ergot was most probably a part of the drink, but this remains a subject of much discussion and speculation. Grain ergot creates an ecstatic experience, but is also a highly toxic poison. Without a refining process, grain ergot can cause gangrene of the limbs, delirium, and death.

The rites of the Greater Mysteries presented in this book do not propose a sacred drink. While the drink is a permanent part of the lore about the mysteries, the actual knowledge of its ingredients has been lost, and no experienced ministrants are here to guide us. However the seasonal festivals, mysteries, and other prayers and rites presented in the following chapters can open you up to a sacred dimension. The joys of divine passion may be experienced in Demeter's religion, just as they are experienced by the Goddess devotees of India and Bengal.

An attraction to Demeter and the development of a relationship with her myth can bring you a feeling of bhakti, of love, of ecstasy. The Demetrian rituals offered here use many elements that can bring ecstatic experience: sacred myth, invocation, prayer, poetry, and chanting. These bring union with divinity. An understanding of

---

[9]   R. Gordon Wasson, Albert Hoffman, and A. P. Ruck, *The Road to Eleusis: Unveiling the Secret of the Mysteries* (New York: Harcourt Brace Jovanovich, 1978), pp. 33–34.

Demeter's myth will illustrate, not only agricultural themes but the corresponding transcendent personal themes. You can gain these insights by becoming deeply aware of the interplay between Demeter's myth, the elements of the seasonal year, and the spiritual precepts that they offer.

You can also broaden your understanding by following the themes of the seasonal festivals throughout the yearly cycle. Ceremonial dedication to the Goddess is offered through the rites of the Lesser Mysteries. The Greater Mysteries are then perceived in this supporting context. Devotion becomes the catalyst that takes the rites from mental perception to spiritual ecstasy. Even though the magnificent temple of Demeter at Eleusis is lost, we may still resurrect her religion from its long absence.

The mysteries of Eleusis were centuries old by the first century B.C.E. Prospective initiates came from all over the Mediterranean. The initiation involved several fees: to the High Priestess of Demeter, to the High Priest, to the altar Priest, to the virgin Priestesses, and to the priest who read the sacred proclamations. Other costs included the several days spent in Athens prior to arriving at Eleusis, and the fees for the offerings.

At the height of the classical period, the large sanctuary at Eleusis, with its many buildings, courtyards, statues, reliefs, and surrounding lands, was governed and administered like a corporation. Funded in part by the various fees paid by initiates, Demeter's temple was also subsidized by the state. Beginning around 760 B.C.E., first-fruit offerings were provided by each Greek city-state. This practice of sending the first fruits of each crop to Eleusis began as an offering of thanksgiving at the end of a famine. During the eighth century B.C.E., a famine swept across Greece. The oracle at Delphi was consulted. Athens was advised to make a sacrifice to Eleusinian Demeter on behalf of all of Greece. The suggestion of the oracle was followed and the famine ended. This sacrifice evolved into the *Proerosia*, the preplowing rites during which prayers and offerings were given to Demeter and Zeus just before the planting season. An appreciation of Earth's sustaining powers had been renewed, and all of Greece learned of the mysteries of Eleusis.

After the Persian Wars, Pericles poured money into the sanctuary of Eleusis (and other civic and religious centers) as a part of his rebuilding program, creating one of the most beautiful temple sanctuaries in the Mediterranean world. Through the popularity of Demeter's mysteries, and the splendor of her sanctuary, her religion grew to have centers in other cities of the Greek mainland, in Asia Minor, Rome (Demeter-Ceres), North Africa, Egypt, and on the island of Lesbos.

The religion of Demeter was, at its highest point, a religion of ecstasy, utilizing a mythology that was reflected in the natural surroundings of the Mediterranean landscape and climate. Devotees were consecrated to the Goddess in the spring, during the Lesser Mysteries, and called *Demetreioi*, the Beloved of Demeter. Devotees were most probably taught to understand and observe the mythic cycle of the seasons. Eighteen months after consecration, they passed through a higher initiation, this one in the fall. This was the night of the Greater Mysteries with its experience of spiritual ecstasy. Having been taught and prepared by priestesses of temple lineage, the initiates experienced a night of prayer, invocation, song, secret rites, and the sacred drink. This, in some way, imparted to the initiate direct knowledge of the light of the soul, of soul origin, and of connection to the divine source.

The mysteries were said to bring greater joy in life, and also to remove the dread that some associate with the idea of death. In his work, *Eleusis: Archetypal Image of Mother and Daughter,* Carl Kerényi describes the experience of the mysteries as one that eliminated the fear of death from the minds of the initiates.[10] Of Demeter's mysteries, the poet Pindar states that those who have seen them before they die are blessed, because they understand death and the divinity of the new life yet to come.[11] Likewise, Plato describes the visions at initiation into these mysteries as including bright, shining beauty, a sense of soul-perfection, and a celebration of spirit.[12] From his work, *Phaedrus,* we learn that the initiates beheld a beatific vision of pure shining light, and felt themselves to be born of that same light. Plato ends by saying simply, "Let me linger over the memory."[13]

---

[10]   Carl Kerényi, *Eleusis: Archetypal Image of Mother and Daughter* (Princeton, NJ: Princeton University Press, 1991), p. 15.

[11]   Pindar, Sir John Sandys, trans., *The Odes of Pindar* (Cambridge: Harvard University Press; London: William Heinemann, Ltd., 1923), pp. 593–595.

[12]   Kerényi, *Eleusis: Archetypal Image of Mother and Daughter,* p. 98.

[13]   Plato, *Phaedrus,* in *Greek Literature in Translation,* Whitney Oates and Charles Murphy, trans. (New York: Longmans, Green, & Co. 1945), p. 503.

The Temple at Eleusis and Its Clergy

The Roman period was an era of further expansions of the cult and the extension of its benefits to the citizens of the Roman Republic first and the Empire later. This extension of the privilege of initiation was reflected in the construction of auxiliary buildings and in the multiplication of dedicatory offerings.[1]

The city of Eleusis (modern Elefsina) is about fourteen miles north of Athens. It lies at the end of a long valley and overlooks the Bay of Eleusis. According to Carl Kerényi, the name *Eleusis* means "place of happy arrival."[2] Author Katherine Kanta states that the word *eleusis* developed from the verb *elauno*, which means "I come."[3] This probably refers to Demeter's arrival at that sacred place where she first revealed the mysteries. *Eleusis* may relate to the word *Elysium*, the Greek paradise in the Underworld where blessed souls lived after death.

Once enemies, the city-states of Eleusis and Athens were eventually connected by a road named the Sacred Way (*Iera Odos*) that

---

[1] George Mylonas, *Eleusis and the Eleusinian Mysteries* (Princeton, NJ: Princeton University Press, 1961), p. 155. Reprinted by permission of Princeton University Press.
[2] Carl Kerényi, *Eleusis: Archetypal Image of Mother and Daughter* (Princeton, NJ: Princeton University Press, 1991), p. 23.
[3] Katherine Kanta, *Eleusis: Myth, Mysteries, History, Museum,* W. Phelps, trans. (Athens: n.p., 1979), p. 18.

linked the center of Athens with Demeter's sanctuary.[4] The Eleusinian sanctuary was referred to as "the sanctuary of Demeter" or "the
sanctuary of Demeter and Kore," rather than as the "sanctuary of
Demeter and Persephone." The great temple in which the rites were
conducted was called the Temple of Demeter, and also the
Telesterion. It is curious that the name Persephone was not used to
identify these structures, perhaps because Persephone, as the Underworld name for Demeter's Daughter, was reserved for use only in the
initiate's experience of the mysteries.

A large outcropping of rock and a cave underlie the natural setting of the sanctuary. The first temple was built in the 15th century
B.C.E. as a one-room structure. This later became the holy of holies,
the *Anaktoron*. The Anaktoron was approximately $47^1/_2$ feet long by
$11^1/_2$ feet wide. By the second century B.C.E., the Temple of Demeter
had been expanded and rebuilt several times. The Anaktoron always
remained within the temple, however, in the same location as
changes took place. The final temple was 58 yards square, with the
Anaktoron more or less in the center. By this time, many surrounding structures had become a part of the sanctuary.

One of the most important differences between Demeter's temple and other Greek temples was that it was used as a place of worship and ritual for votaries. Most temples were considered the dwelling
place of the deity, to be tended by priests and priestesses. Temples
were generally not used as places for worshipers to congregate and
celebrate their religion. Sacrifices and offerings were received by most
temples at outdoor altars. In the case of the Tele-sterion, however,
during Demeter's Greater Mysteries, votaries entered the dwelling
place of the deity to participate directly in ritual.

From author and archeologist George Mylonas we learn about
many details of the sanctuary. At its most fully developed, it contained the temple itself, living quarters for the clergy, a building to
house clergy vestments, granaries, a bakery, a kitchen, storehouses,
structures for administrative purposes, and courtyards. There were
several outdoor altars, including a fire altar that received some of the
animal sacrifices. In addition there was the Holy Well, the Plutonian
temple-cave, and a small temple of Hecate, which in later Roman
times, was replaced by a temple of Artemis and Poseidon. Many

---

4   W. Jones, trans., *Pausanias' Description of Greece* (London: William Heinemann; New York:
G. P. Putnam's Sons, 1918), p. 203. Pausanias cites terms after the war between Athens and
Eleusis: "The Eleusinians were to have independent control of the mysteries, but in all things
else were to be subject to the Athenians."

inner columns, connected by wooden architraves, lent support to the ceilings of the various rooms of the temple. A fountain house, with its brick-lined cistern, provided water year-round. There were several other cisterns. One underground cistern of the Roman period had vaulted ceilings and a stairway. Monumental gateways, plus much statuary and many reliefs lent elaborate decoration to the complex.

With a little theatrical embellishment, we can conjure up some of the architecture of the sanctuary and the customs of its initiates. Imagine that you have come for initiation into Demeter's mysteries. Yesterday, you made the traditional fourteen-mile walk from the center of Athens, down the Sacred Way to Eleusis. This all-day event had several rest stops. You enjoyed a good night's rest in one of the temple's outer auxiliary buildings. Today, you entered the gates into the sanctuary courtyards. You paid the proper fees and attended the various sacrifices and prayers, as you were instructed by temple clergy. You watched and participated as the priests and priestesses conducted the day's rites. Now you have returned to your lodgings in the outer auxiliary area to rest before tonight's ritual, the Greater Mysteries.

Evening arrives, and the herald calls out in his chanting voice for you and the other mystai to awaken and prepare for the Greater Mysteries. You rise and dress in a simple white *chiton*, draping a white *himation* over your shoulder. You do not wear any jewelry, as required by the rite. With other initiates, you exit the lodgings and walk around the short auxiliary road to the sanctuary entrance.

Dusk is descending. You enter the sanctuary grounds and are greeted with a warm welcome. Brightly lit torches lean out from the surrounding courtyard walls; the marble pavement gleams. Music drifts from an unseen source. Straight ahead, at the far end of the courtyard, is the holy well, where Demeter rested in her sorrows. Ahead and to the right is the little temple, belonging to Artemis and Poseidon. When all have entered the courtyard, the first outer gate is locked. A curving line of priestesses begins a special dance called the Dance of the Kernophoria. A small chorus sings of Demeter and of the God and Goddess of the Underworld. The dancers balance little flames on their heads in small offering pots.

When the performance is completed, you pass through the next gate, the Great Propylaia. After all have passed through, the heavy doors of the gate are locked. You find yourself in a small courtyard. You are guided to the next and last gate, the Lesser Propylaia. Gazing up at this third gateway, you see two 28-foot Corinthian columns flanking the entrance. Imposing in their great height and mass, the columns are decorated at the top with acanthus leaves and mythical winged creatures. The architraves running across the top of the entrance bear repeating designs of sheaves of wheat, stylized poppy rosettes, and the skulls of bulls. You see, by an inscription, that the gate was built by Consul Appius Claudius Pulcher to fulfill a vow made in 54 B.C.E. The ceiling of the gateway is coffered. The double doors swing open smoothly on rollers. You pass through and note that the marble pavement slopes upward.

Entering a third courtyard, you find yourself facing the side of the great Temple of Demeter. You turn back to look at the gateway through which you have just come. It is an impressive sight. In place of the two columns that were on the outside of the gate, there are two statue-columns (caryatids) on the inside. These are in the form of priestesses carrying the *cista mystica* on their heads.[5] The tops of the cista mysticas hold up the architraves. The cistas are cylindrical baskets, decorated with sheaves of wheat, myrtle, poppy pods, poppy rosettes, and the vessel for the sacred drink. These beautiful figures, powerful and elegant, wear chitons without the draping himation. The front of their wavy hair is pulled up and back; their serene gaze is leveled at the side of the temple.

In back of the temple and to the right, in a little rocky hill, is the cave entrance to the Underworld. There are two cave openings, one larger and one smaller. Within the larger cave entrance is a small temple to the God and Goddess of the Underworld. Earlier today, you witnessed a rite performed there. At that time, a child called the "Child from the Hearth of Athens" came forward with offerings. All congregated around the entrance of the cavern-temple. The Priestess of Plouton[6] came out of the temple and greeted the initiates. Another priestess guided the child to the cavern-temple entrance. Into the arms of the Ploutonian Priestess, the child placed gifts from the city of Athens: myrtle boughs and the pelanos offering loaf. The Priestess of Plouton then prayed to the Goddess to bless the initiates during their experience of the mysteries, and to bless Eleusis, Athens, and all

---

[5]   One of the two Cistophoros Caryatids is in the Museum of Eleusis, the other caryatid was taken by Edward Clarke and is now exhibited at Cambridge. Clark discovered the statue in a field of Eleusis in 1801 and took it even though it was still being venerated by the villagers. It had manure piled around it because the villagers felt that their beloved statue would bless the manure and increase its fertility-making properties.

[6]   Sterling Dow and Robert F. Healey, *A Sacred Calendar of Eleusis* (Cambridge: Harvard University Press, 1965), pp. 36–37. The authors describe the Priestess of Plouton, whose duties included preparing an altar "for the banquets of the Thesmophorian deities."

of Greece. Torches were lit and a tumultuous cheer rose up from the gathering.

Now, as evening falls, you face one side of the great Temple of Demeter, the Telesterion. (The Ploutonian temple-cave is on the right.) You see two doorways on this side of the Telesterion, flanked by statues of priestesses. You walk to the left and around the corner of the building, and face the temple from the front.

The front of the temple boasts a 58-yard-long colonnade, running its whole length. There are fourteen columns in the colonnade. Rams' heads are mounted on the corners of the roof. The roof is peaked, with an additional small raised roof at its center. Beautiful repeating reliefs run horizontally across the architraves, above the columns of the colonnade. You walk up the marble steps, passing through the columns, into the portico. Turning away from the temple, you look out past the columns to a small courtyard enclosed by a protective wall.

Facing the temple again, you observe that there are two front entrances. Between them is a beautiful marble relief of Demeter, Persephone, and Triptolemos, in high classical style (See figure 1, p. 16).[7] In this relief, Demeter is handing a young Triptolemos a golden sheaf of grain. Persephone is crowning him with a golden myrtle wreath. Lovely statues of priestesses holding lustration bowls, stand at the doorways.[8] The bowls contain water. You anoint yourself, as you were taught at the Lesser Mysteries.

Entering through one of the doorways, you are awed by what you see. Throughout the square interior, a forest of shining inner columns supports the roof. The ceiling is coffered, beautifully painted in deep blues and reds, and highlighted with glittering gold.[9] All of the walls are lined with rows of seats surfaced with fine marble and cushioned. In the approximate center of the massive room is the holy of holies, the Anaktoron, beautifully painted with the pomegranate trees of Elysium.[10] Now all of the participants are drawn into the temple. Lit by scores of lamps, the temple is scented with fragrant incense rising from brass thymiaterias. Slow and rhythmic music fills the chamber. The mysteries have begun.

---

[7] This relief is in the National Museum of Athens. Its actual placement at the temple site is not known. Although it is still in excellent condition, the assumed gold wreath and sheaf of grain are missing.

[8] One priestess-like basin-bearer statue is in the Museum of Eleusis. The other is in London.

[9] Remnants of sanctuary ceilings appear to have been coffered; the colors described here are typical.

[10] This idea of a painting on the Anaktoron wall is the author's invention.

Figure 1. The Grand Relief: Demeter, Persephone, and Triptolemos.
Relief from the Temple of Demeter at Eleusis, Fifth century B.C.E.,
National Archeological Museum, Athens, Greece.
Used by permission Alinari/Art Resource, New York.

The Eleusinian Clergy

The lack of a Priestess of Persephone in the listing below is not an
error. It is simply that descriptions of these clerical offices could not
be found (although I created the role for use in the reconstruction of
the rites). In Healy and Dow's *A Sacred Calendar of Eleusis*, a
Priestess of Athena and a Priest of Poseidon are briefly mentioned.
These offices, and many others, were most probably a part of the
Eleusinian temple hierarchy.

While Demeter's daughter is represented in this listing by the
Hierophantid of Kore, her Underworld name of Persephone may have
been reserved for special use in the Mysteries. In author-archeologist

George Mylonas' book, *Eleusis and the Eleusinian Mysteries,* he discusses references to Plouton and Persephone through the names *Theos* and *Thea* (God and Goddess). He states that he finds these names inscribed on their relief tablets and goes on to say that, as in other ancient cultures, in early Greek culture there was a sense of aversion to naming Underworld Gods.[11] However, a Priestess of Plouton was briefly mentioned in one source and this may have been a late addition to the clerical offices.

The Eleusinian clergy consisted of a complex hierarchy of clerical offices, each with specific and clearly defined roles. Together, these priests and priestesses conducted the rites and protected the mysteries of their patron Gods and Goddesses. Below is a list of these offices, along with descriptions of their functions.

Hiereia Demetros: The High Priestess of Demeter, sometimes referred to as the Priestess of Demeter and Kore, came from the family of Eumolpidae or Phillidai. She held office for life, and could marry and have children. She remained chaste, however, during the celebration of the mysteries. She resided in the sacred house within the sanctuary. Events at Eleusis were eponymous with, that is, dated by, her name. For example, an event could be said to have taken place in the third year of Klaudia Tatarion Menandrou.[12]

The High Priestess most probably took the role of Demeter at the sacred drama of the Greater Mysteries. She was responsible for performing sacrifices and sacred rites at all festivals and mysteries. She had a role in the rite of the Telete during the Greater Mysteries. All other priestesses were under her jurisdiction. As for all clergy, there were laws prescribing what her duties and rights of governing were.

The High Priestess received a payment from each initiate at both the Lesser and the Greater Mysteries. From this expense fund, some of the costs of administrating the rites were taken. In all religious matters, she and the Hierophant had final say, unless the matter was brought to trial. There are two cases known at which the High Priestess brought the Hierophant to trial regarding problems in conducting the rites. Little is known about one case, but for the other

---

[11]   Mylonas, *Eleusis and the Eleusinian Mysteries,* p. 198.

[12]   Kevin Clinton, *The Sacred Officials of the Eleusinian Mysteries* (Philadelphia: American Philosophical Society, 1974), p. 118. Clinton gives listings of clergy names in which Klaudia Tatarion Menandrou is listed as a Priestess of Demeter and Kore, having held office in the first or second century C.E.

there is documentation. The case concerned the Festival of Haloa, a woman's holy day. In the middle of the fourth century B.C.E., the Hierophant Archias insisted on performing the sacrifice to Dionysus at the Haloa. He was later convicted of impiety. We do not know the name of the High Priestess who brought him to trial, but a dedication was erected to her. Though her name is illegible, she was called the mother of Epigenes of Acharnae.

In another legal case brought in the fifth century B.C.E., a nobleman named Alcibiades was found guilty on a charge of impiety against the Goddesses of the mysteries. He had mimicked the Greater Mysteries with guests at a banquet in his home in Athens. This evidently included the sacred drink. How he obtained it is unknown. He was heavily fined and then banished. It was further decreed that all of the priests and priestesses of Eleusis were to curse him ritually. Theano Menonos Agrulethen, the High Priestess of Demeter at the time, refused, saying that she was a priestess who prayed, rather than cursed.[13] Seven years later, the courts of Athens were petitioned and Alcibiades was allowed to return to Greece, although the families of the Kerykes and the Eumolpidae tried to prevent it. Alcibiades was given his citizenship again, and the clergy of Eleusis were asked to rescind their curses. Theano had nothing to rescind.

Hierophant: The Hierophant was the High Priest and a member of the family of the Eumolpidae. He held office for life and could marry. Unlike the High Priestess, his name was completely replaced by his title (hieronymy). This custom was in force from the time of his investiture until his death. As a part of his ordination ceremony, his birth name was incised on a tablet and thrown into the sea. During the mysteries, the Hierophant displayed the hiera to the initiates, hence his title.[14]

The Hierophant could own and live in property in the city of Eleusis, outside the sanctuary. His hair was long, to the shoulder. As a part of his vestments, he wore the *strophion* (a twisted and coiled cloth crown) upon which was set a myrtle wreath.

Each initiate paid him a fee before attending the Greater Mysteries. He kept chaste during the celebrations. His duties were the singing of sacred songs, the performance of sacred rites, and displaying the hiera during the Greater Mysteries. Some of his duties were administrative, including any matters that had to do with the cultivation or use of the temple's sacred land.

One dedication to a Hierophant, erected after his death in 168–169 B.C.E., states how this priest was known for his wisdom and

---

[13] Clinton, *The Sacred Officials of the Eleusinian Mysteries,* p. 16.
[14] Mylonas, *Eleusis and the Eleusinian Mysteries,* p. 230.

his beautiful voice. He was described as having the beautiful voice of Eumolpos (one of Baubo's sons), and as singing and displaying the holy objects during the *telete* portion of the mysteries. In addition, he was known for having saved the hiera during an attack on the sanctuary by the Sarmations. He did this by escaping and taking the holy objects with him to Athens.[15]

Priestess of Plouton: No Priestess of Plouton is mentioned in Clinton's *The Sacred Officials of the Eleusinian Mysteries,* but one is mentioned in Sterling and Dow's *Sacred Calendar of Eleusis.* This calendar states that the Priestess of Plouton prepares an altar feast for the Thesmophorian festival deities. Sterling and Dow observe, however, that this Priestess is not mentioned in any other source. Outside this brief reference, we know nothing. Perhaps this office was a later addition to the clerical hierarchy, and included duties in the Ploutonian temple-cave.

Hierophantids: The Hierophantids were two priestesses who assisted in revealing the *telete.* It is possible that they assisted both the High Priest and the High Priestess in the performance of sacral rites. One was the Hierophantid of Demeter, and the other, the Hierophantid of Kore. They were members of the family of Eumolpidae. Investiture in their position was accompanied by hieronymy. They could marry and have children.

One Hierophantid of Kore is known from a monument erected by her son, Claudius Lysiades, after her death. In office during the reign of Hadrian, she became known for having the altar of Kore covered in silver.

Priestesses Panagia: The Priestesses Panagia (All-Holy) lived in the sacred house of the priestesses within the sanctuary. Hailing from the families of Eumolpidae or Phillidai, they remained virgin. They were sometimes called *melissa,* or bees. They were the many women ministrants of the cult who assisted in the performance of all festivals and mysteries. At Thesmophoria they were sent out to over thirty cities to assist in the celebrations and represent Eleusis. They were allowed to touch and care for the hiera, which they carried to and from Athens during the week of sacred activities before the Greater Mysteries.

Dadouchos: The Dadouchos was the sacred torchbearer. He held equestrian rank, was from the family of Kerykes, and held office for life. He could marry and lived inside the sanctuary grounds. His name became hieronymous. He could use the *fleece of Zeus* to cleanse those who, having killed in wartime as part of the military, were

---

15   Clinton, *The Sacred Officials of the Eleusinian Mysteries,* p. 38.

tainted with blood. He assisted in the sacrifices and also in conducting some of the rites.

Hierokeryx: The Hierokeryx was from the family of Kerykes. He was
appointed for life. He was the Sacred Herald, and read the sacred proclamations for the festivals. He wore the *strophion,* as described for the
High Priest. It was his responsibility to order the vow of silence regarding
the Greater Mysteries. He also introduced the initiates into the rites, perhaps by explaining a little of what they were about to experience.

Hiereuz 'epi Bomo: The Hiereuz was the altar priest. He was responsible for the altars in Demeter's sanctuary. He was always chosen from
the family of Kerykes. It is not certain whether his investiture was for
life, but he could marry. By 14–13 B.C.E., hieronymy was a part of this
office. He received a payment from each initiate.

Pyrphoros: This priest governed the maintenance of the fire altars.
His name became hieronymous at his investiture.

Hieraules: The Hieraules was in charge of the musicians and of the
sacred music. The *aules* was a long, double flute.

Phaethyntes: The Phaethyntes and his assistants were responsible
for cleaning and caring for the many statues throughout the sanctuary.

Hearth Initiate: The child from the Hearth of Athens was chosen by
lot from an Athenian aristocratic family and was initiated at the expense
of the state. From statuary, the child appears to have been somewhere
between eight and twelve years of age. Occasionally, a chosen child's par-
ent had, in her or his own childhood, been a hearth initiate. The position
was seen as a great honor, as the child was sent to gain the favor of the
two Goddesses for the initiates, the city of Athens, and all of Greece.

Iacchogogos: This priest accompanied the statue of the God
Iacchos in his carriage on his way to and from Athens during the
week of Greater Mysteries preparations. Iacchos appeared in every
way like a young Dionysus, long-haired and crowned with myrtle.
His presence represented great joy and celebration. As the initiates set
out from Athens to Eleusis, the torch of Iacchos was lit.

Hydranos Priestess: The Hydranos Priestess was responsible for
the water purifications of the initiates, probably at both the Greater
and the Lesser Mysteries.

Neokoros: The Neokoros was responsible for maintaining the decoration of the sanctuary.

C H A P T E R　3

The Myth of Demeter and Her Holy Daughter

But come, you goddesses, dwelling in the town of
fragrant Eleusis, and seagirt Paros, and rocky Antron,
revered Deo, mighty giver of seasons and glorious gifts,
you and your very fair daughter Persephone,
for my song grant gladly a living that warms the heart.
And I shall remember you and a new song as well.[1]

All was green upon the land. Kore, the lovely daughter of Holy Demeter, who brings us the fruits of the Earth, played on the woodland hilltops of pine and cypress.[2] She searched with her sacred companions for glens of violets, saffron crocus, and white narcissus. And lovely wreaths were made, with leaves of green thyme and wild parsley, upon which were laid the precious blossoms. Lush were these crowns of fragile beauty. When they were set upon the heads of fair Kore and the Daughters of Oceanus, the maidens became the enchantment of nature's great power.[3] The songs of birds rose in the air, and the Sun shone with a gentle and pleasant light.

From the hills, the maidens walked toward the sea, laughing and playing the mischievous games that maidens often play. They plucked the ripe apricot from the Mother's generous

> **The Festival of Chloaia:**
> A spring Festival of Flowers, and of the Verdant Mother and Maiden.

[1]　Helene P. Foley, *The Homeric Hymn to Demeter: Translation, Commentary, and Interpretive Essays* (Princeton, NJ: Princeton University Press, 1994), p. 26. Reprinted by permission of Princeton University Press.

trees, and smiled to see that the land was so glad. Where Kore walked, the grasses turned a deepening emerald, and purple lupines rose in vast seas of nodding blossom. This was their time of play, when all seemed an everlasting season of growth and blooming. There, beside the sea on the Nysian plain, the divine virgins picked flowers, and wove wild blue lupines and red poppies into garlands.

On the broad and fertile Rharian plain, the Goddess Demeter labored. She was tending the great fields of wheat and barley as she tended the life of her own Daughter. In joy, she watched the red poppies bloom among the stands of green grain now turning to gold. Here was her gift, precious food for the people of the world. Soon it would be harvesttime and Demeter's song flowed across the land.

On the verdant meadow of Nysa, beside the rhythms of the sea, the maidens rested from their play. In the sweet calm of the season, wreathed and garlanded, they slept upon the warm earth. With garments draped gently across their divine bodies, their rosy sleeping faces glowed in the sunlight.

---

2   This tale of Demeter and Persephone attempts to revive the myth as it was used in Eleusis. The story of mother and daughter takes place within the cycle of the grain, and pivotal points of this cycle become the Demetrian Wheel of the Year. "Stealing the bride," or *klepsigamia,* takes place without rape, though many aspects of the classical version are here. The myth encompasses the mysteries and, as in Homer, it ends with their origin in Eleusis. This version of the myth excludes the rape of the maiden by the God of the Underworld, as seen in Ovid's *Death and Proserpina* and in those writers who borrowed from him. See chapter 6 for themes of rape and abduction. Some of the texts that influenced the reconstruction of this composite myth were: *The Homeric Hymn to Demeter,* multiple sources—see Bibliography. *The Orphic Hymns: Text, Translation and Notes* by A. Athanassakis; *Hesiod and Theognis,* trans. Dorothea Wender, *The Road to Eleusis* by Wasson, Hofmann, and Ruck; Ovid, *The Metamorphoses,* trans. Horace Gregory; *The Greek Myths,* vol. I, Robert Graves; *The Attic Festivals of Demeter and their Relation to the Agricultural Year,* Allaire Chandor Brumfield; and *Eleusis and the Eleusinian Mysteries,* George Mylonas. The Arcadian myth was also an influence, see footnote 9. In addition were influences from the author's experience in the cultivation of winter grains and grain field poppies.

3   In *Art and Religion in Thera: Reconstructing a Bronze Age Society,* by Dr. Nanno Marinatos (Athens: D. & I. Mathioulakis, 1984), we find an Akrotiri fresco of maidens picking flowers (p. 62). They are picking lilies and crocus. There appears to be a divine transformation or initiation at hand. Perhaps the maidens are becoming priestesses serving the goddess, who appears enthroned. Marinatos considers a possible ritual transformation from maidenhood to womanhood.

4   Carl Kerényi, *Eleusis, Archetypal Image of Mother and Daughter* (Princeton, NJ: Princeton University Press, 1991), p. 171. Kerényi writes that Triptolemos, Euboleus, and Eumolpos are the sons of Eleusinian Baubo and Dysaules. Baubo and Dysaules appear to take the place of the king and queen of Eleusis (of the Homeric hymn) who receive the sorrowing Demeter into their home. In addition, Baubo takes the place of the serving maid, Iambe (of the Homeric hymn). Pausanias claims that Euboleus and Triptolemos were sons of Dysaules and that, because they gave Demeter information about her daughter, "the sowing of seed was her reward to them." See *Pausanias' Description of Greece,* W. H. S. Jones, trans. (London: Heinemann; New York: G. P. Putnam's Sons, 1918), p. 73.

Demeter's song flowed and time moved forward. The farmer Dysaules and his beloved wife, Baubo, watched as their fields turned to gold.[4] They knew this bounty as a blessing from All-Holy Demeter. At each New Moon, Baubo left an offering on the altar of the Goddess. Sometimes, she left flat cakes of barley, or fruit, or even cleaned, unspun wool. All were gifts from the Mother. Then, she lit Hestia's lamp and gave her heartfelt thanks.

Dysaules and Baubo had three sons: Eumolpos, Triptolemos, and Euboleus. Eumolpos cared for the sheep and had the talent of singing brightly and playing the sweet lyre.[5] Triptolemos cared for the cows, and also patiently tilled the land at plowing time.[6] Euboleus was a swineherd, with a gentle heart that led him to give good counsel to both friend and family.[7]

The family and the land thrived. Baubo knew the value of love and also of simple humor. And wisdom was hers in yet another way. She kept great stores of grain, beans and seeds, sweet dried fruits, olives in brine, wines and aged cheeses, salted fish, and the rich yellow first-pressed oil. Should famine ever arise, she and her family would be safe.

And so came the harvest. The family of Baubo and Dysaules, and those farmers on the plains of Thessaly and between the mountains, were hard at their labors. The scythe was raised and swung in measured cadence again and again, and the cut sheaves bound together. When the bound, sun-dried seed was gathered in, the gleaners came, finding plenty left on the dry harvest floor to sustain them. Then the farmers chose the best of the seed for the next year's planting and set it aside.

Thargelia: The Harvest Festival.
Kalamaia: The Threshing Festival.

The green of the season had passed, and Demeter reigned in her glorious ecstasy as the Great Harvest Mother. The meadows on the

---

5   Eumolpos means "he who sings beautifully." Eumolpidae was the name of the Eleusinian family who founded and ran the Temple of Demeter at its beginnings. The High Priest could only come from the family of the Eumolpidae.

6   The name Triptolemos has generally come to be accepted as meaning "thrice-plowed." In reference to the triple plowing in the rite Proerosia. It may also relate to the thrice-plowed field that Hesiod speaks of in his Theogony. It was to this field in Crete that Demeter wandered, inebriated with divine nectar. Here she made love with the hunter god, Iasos, and gave birth to Ploutos (wealth). Triptolemos is pictured on Roman and Greek vases and reliefs as Demeter's grain missionary, usually being sent off in her chariot. He was a deity worshipped particularly by farmers.

7   Euboleus means "good counsel." From a reference in the Orphic hymns, we find that Euboleus was tending his pigs when the earth opened and swallowed Persephone (Kore). A marble head of Euboleus, youthful and curly-haired, was found in the Ploutonian cave at Eleusis. He is considered a way-shower, because he saw where the maiden descended.

plains of Nysa turned yellow with age. Only the last of the poppies lent color to the land. The green grasses were gone and blood-red poppies gave out their last brilliant burst of life. The daughters of Oceanus rose once more from the sea, meeting Kore on the wide plains. Now the maidens crowned themselves with poppies and poppy pods, and little sheaves of dried grasses.

Gaily, the divine virgins danced and sang sacred songs. They sang of the Harvest Mother, of Delphi's Gaea, and of the beauties of the sea. They ate sweet fruit and drank from a sparkling stream. Then, upon fine woolen himations, they laid down to rest.[8]

As they slept, saffron-cloaked Hecate approached them. With the power of her immortal hand, a spell was laid upon the sleeping maidens. Whispering into the ear of Kore, she caused visions of the lands below to enter her dreams. She charged Kore to see what was transpiring in the dark of the Underworld, in Tartarus. And this is what Demeter's Daughter saw.

A great king was below, downcast and weeping in loneliness. On a throne of carved black marble, he sat in shadow, bent over as one who is forlorn and lost. Beside him was an empty throne. Upon it lay a jeweled silver crown. King Plouton, whose name means wealth, then began to sing. Low and omenous, the song bespoke such yearning that all of the souls below began to mourn with him. Their sounds rose up to the very gates of Tartarus, even to the cavern of Eleusis. Plouton sang and sang, until his deep and haunting sounds found the ear of fair Kore.

And in her dream, the Maiden Kore saw that the Lord of the Underworld could see her sleeping on the plains of Nysa far above. Kore saw his sadness, as well as his princely bearing. Her heart was flooded with love and compassion for the one who has been called the Unseen One. Her heart had awakened, it had opened to the Lord of Tartarus. Now her only wish was to join him, and to bring light and beauty to that dark place. She wished to bring him the essence of the Sun and of all the beautiful flowers that she had known in the bright world above. And she wished to bless the souls of the dead as well.

He had seen her. From his palace, whose lamps had grown dim, he went out to the grotto of the black stallions. And there, outside of Elysium he harnessed the steeds to their waiting chariot.

Above, the farmers, who had finished their work, spread flame across the crop's remnants. The fire burned, and in its wake lay

---

[8]   *Himations* were used as both veils and cloaks. They were of numerous lengths and weights and draped in many styles.

ember and fertile ash. It was time to let the land lie fallow. Demeter, her work completed, journeyed to Nysa to embrace and feast with her only Daughter.

Kore still dreamed. And in her dream, the Lord of the Dark called her by the name Persephone. Hearing the name, the Maiden stirred in her sleep. She awoke to find Hecate beside her and the daughters of Oceanus still asleep on their fine woolen beds. Hecate again raised her divine hand and, across the dry meadow of Nysa, there appeared flame. The poppies shone a deep blood-red before they were extinguished in the holy fire. And beyond the red and glittering flame, the Earth burst asunder. Great mounds of earth spewed out as the black stallions of Tartarus entered the world that had not borne them. The field became burning ember and flame and, beyond the field, the God of the Underworld drew up his chariot and waited.

Hecate raised Kore from the ground, as fear and courage awoke together in the Maiden's heart. Terror held her, but, in facing the unknown, she was steadfast. She removed the crown of poppies from her head and, with surety, cast it into the remaining flame. Her gaze was fixed upon the face of her beloved and, uncrowned, she walked across the field of ember and flame to descend with the Lord of the Dark. Her veil, embroidered with lilies, was left behind.

Around the shoulders of the Maiden was drawn a black himation, bordered with luminous silver threads and set with delicate patterns of precious gems. Then into the waiting chariot she fled, into the arms of Tartarus. The brilliance of passion filled her heart. Plouton drove the black steeds around Earth, and then down through the rocky chasm, into the lands below.

Skira Festival: Part A, Descent of the Maiden, Union of the Sacred Lovers.

As the Holy Daughter crossed over, the silver crown appeared upon her head. She had become Persephone, Queen of Tartarus and Elysium. Once entering the Underworld, she did not drink from the river of forgetfulness, the River Lethe. Instead, she drank from the shining silver spring of memory, from Mnemosyne. The voices of the dead rang out in jubilation. The Queen was received and celebration was at hand.

Above, the farmers, having chosen the seed for next year's crop, now stored it in burial urns. These were sealed with pennyroyal and wax, and set into pits lined with powdered lime and wormwood. Demeter of the Good Harvest was honored and a great feast was held throughout the

The Skira Festival: Part B, Underground Storage of the Seed Grain.

bright day and into the torchlit night. At the end of the celebrations, the pits were ceremonially covered and sealed with the sign of Hecate for safekeeping.

It was then that the powers of Aphrodite entered the Underworld. The lamps of the Tartarion palace were lit and the torches set blazing. But it was in the room of the sacred couch that Aphrodite, Goddess of Love, sent her great powers. As the lamps flickered their soft light, rose petals were showered across the bed of love. Glistening bowls of saffron crocus, lilies, and violets were set around the chamber. Myrrh, libanum, and cinnamon scented the air.

Into the palace Persephone and Plouton came, a fair light upon their brows. On the couch of Aphrodite they lay, entwining their jeweled arms in the fiery embrace of love and passion; he enamored of her beauty and light, and she, of his mystery and darkness. And so through the powers of love, did life become one with death. The pomegranate trees of Elysium burst into bloom, and flowers covered the broad meadows of the lands below.

In time, as Queen of the Groves of Elysium, Persephone came to receive the souls of the dead. Each drank of her cup, and rejoiced under the spreading pomegranate. In Tartarus, Persephone reigned with Plouton as Queen of Justice. She set herself to bring balance to the ledger of every shadowed soul who called out for her.

Then to the plains of Nysa Demeter came—she who is the Mother of the land, from whom all that is good and bountiful comes forth. Holy Demeter came in search of fair Kore. There, on the broad plains beside the sea, the scar of charred black remains was to be seen. The daughters of Oceanus had long since departed. The poppies and wild lupines had gone. Only the delicate veil, embroidered with lilies, was to be found, cast in haste upon the ground.

Holding the veil to her heart, the Goddess let out a mournful cry. To the edge of Nysa she went, calling out to the vast sea before her. But the sea was silent. She searched the mountain summits and the woodland meadows, calling for her Daughter. For nine days, she searched by the light of Helios, and at night by torchlight. She did not eat, nor did she drink of divine nectar. On the ninth day, she found Euboleus, the child of Baubo and Dysaules. He told the sorrowing Mother that, while he was tending his swine, he had seen the Maiden. He had seen her descend in the chariot of Tartarus.

The Divine Mother of all that grows upon Earth tore her golden diadem from her head and rent her flowing garments. She became Melaina the Black, full of anguish and sorrow.[9] In the guise of an old woman, she wandered the land. In her grief and anger, the land wasted away. No green vines or grasses flourished, no flowers bloomed. The farmers plowed the land, casting seed upon it again and again, but to no avail.

> **Proerosia:** This point in the myth evolved into the preplowing rites.

Demeter wandered until she came to Eleusis, where she sat at the well to rest. To this well Baubo came to draw water. Having pity on a weary traveler, she invited the old woman into her home. With no other road to follow, Melaina, dark and sorrowing, accepted this act of kindness.

Once in the farmer's home, Baubo gave Demeter a stool upon which to sit, covered by a soft sheepskin. She offered her wine, but the Mother refused. "Bring to me the Goddess' drink," she said, "of ground barley and sweet mint, and I shall be refreshed." Demeter took the drink from Baubo's kindly hands. Still the visitor was sad, with eyes cast to the ground. And so, Baubo danced for her and made licentious jokes, and lifted up her garments in the dance. Demeter laughed and, in those moments, her divine form was revealed. The home of Baubo and Dysaules was flooded with golden light. The Crone's garments were cast aside and the glo-

> **The Stenia Festival:** Through Baubo and the power of erotic humor, Demeter the Crone releases her dark aspect, and returns to the fertile Mother.

rious Goddess appeared, her golden hair in heavy long plaits, her flowing garments embroidered with red poppies and sheaves of wheat. Upon her head, the golden diadem was set, and from her very presence emanated a sweet and gentle fragrance.

The family of Baubo and Dysaules was honored and sanctified. The Mother went to the people of Eleusis and commanded that they build her a temple. There she stayed, the people bringing her offerings and lighting fragrant incense. But the land was still barren. Then Zeus, who brings the rains, sent Iris with a message for Demeter. Since the land had become barren, there were no gifts upon the holy

---

9   Arcadian Demeter took a very different form. Poseidon, in the guise of a mare, pursued Demeter. She changed into a mare and hid in a group of horses. Poseidon found her and a rape ensued. From this myth, images of her death aspect were created in Arcadian temples. In Phigalia, small figures of snakes and other small creatures flowed out from the mare-headed image of Demeter the Black. "Demeter Erinys" (angry and avenging) of Thelpousa was also portrayed with snaky locks. Joseph Fontenrose, *Python: A Study of Delphic Myth and Its Origins* (Berkeley: University of California Press, 1980), p. 369.

altars and famine threatened. He implored Demeter to make the land fertile again. She refused, saying that without her Daughter, she had no will to make the land bloom again.

It was then, deep in Tartarus, that Persephone heard the sounds of her Mother's weeping. And, from that moment, her heart was rent in two, one half for her Mother and one half for her beloved. From that day, she would neither eat nor drink, nor lie upon the sacred couch. Plouton, Lord of the Underworld, roamed the gemmed halls of his palace searching for a way to end the sorrow of his beloved. For, although Persephone was with him, she was no longer at peace. Restless and sorrowing, Plouton cried out, "Holy Mother of the Land, Great Demeter, beloved of all, Queen of the Fields and Meadowlands of Earth, hear my voice! Aphrodite, Goddess of Love and Compassion, I call out to you! And Hecate, who is wise and powerful in all matters, O come to the aid of the Dark Lord!"

And so, to Tartarus came Hecate and Aphrodite, bringing Gaea and also Dionysus. They entered Plouton's palace. Plouton was filled with hope, for Aphrodite at once gave them assurances that their love was pure and true. She offered her blessings upon the sacred couple, giving the red rose and the myrtle crown. Through the powers of Hecate, sanctity was pronounced upon the sacred marriage. Many gifts and blessings were given by Aphrodite, Hecate, Gaea, and Dionysus.

> **Festival of Arkichronia:** Before planting takes place, these gifts of the immortals will be commingled with the seed to create fertility talismans.

And then, a miracle occurred. A great light descended into the Underworld. From above, Demeter had seen Persephone's sadness. She had also seen the tender love that the Lord Plouton had for her Daughter. Descending through the rocky chasm of Plouton's gate, Demeter journeyed into the Underworld. Arriving at the palace of Tartarus, she filled it with rays that seemed of the Sun. Persephone was overcome with joy, as Mother and Daughter embraced once again.

Plouton spoke: "Welcome, Great Mother of the Land. Praises. You have heard my prayers and come to our aid."

Demeter responded: "Greetings, Lord Tartarus. Fear not, all will be well." Then she spoke gently. "Beloved Daughter, love has blessed your heart. And who am I to question the ways of Aphrodite? I know that nothing can stop the magic of her powers. Even I must bow to her, as I have done, in the gentle fields of Crete with fair Iasos. So, be at peace again, for I love thee as I ever have. You are still my child, but you are also a great queen, to whom I bow."

"Then, Mother, will you make the land bloom again for the people of Earth?"

"I fear that I have no will to make the land green again without the blossoming Maiden. Still, be sad no longer, for knowing of the love between you and Plouton, I do confer my blessings upon your sacred marriage."

Then another descended, the Goddess Rhea, who, leaving her lion-driven chariot at the gates of Tartarus, entered the deep of the Underworld. Full of wise council, she spoke with ancient Gaea and all her immortal descendants, saying this: "I was in Phyrgia, when your story came to me. And so I hastened my lions to Eleusis. Come now, and listen to my plan. Let fair Persephone stay with the Lord Plouton from the time the grain is stored to the time the grain is again planted. Then may Persephone rise to work with holy Demeter as before. Have pity on those above who cry out to Demeter to return the land's fertility. They cannot wait forever, else all will be below and none above."

Demeter was yielding and full of peace. At this outpouring of love and wisdom, Persephone rejoiced. Now there was a way for her to live both above and below, to be with those she loved, and to help serve those of the Underworld and Earth. The power of her Mother's love and understanding flowed through her heart, as did Rhea's perfect wisdom. Looking upon the face of her beloved, she saw that his mind was as hers. His heart at peace, Plouton acknowledged the freedom of the Holy Daughter to return yearly to her Mother above.

All partook of a great feast together, and Demeter added her gifts of sacred bread and divine ambrosia. From the groves of ripening pomegranate, Persephone set a basket of Elysium's fertile gift upon the table, so that all could partake of its red jewel-like seeds. Then pleasure and splendor reigned together at the feast in the palace of Persephone and Plouton.

Bright flowers bloomed on the banks of the River Styx, and the Underworld glowed with a mystic light of its own. All souls did dance and sing, celebrating the divine marriage and the powers of love and passion, placing the light and the dark into accord and in sacred union.

Returning then to the Middle World, Demeter went at once to Eleusis, to the family of Baubo and Dysaules. To them, she gave her blessings. She taught them the mysteries of sacred union both above and below. And she taught them of the sacred drink. She gave them the secrets of her temple's holy rites and charged them to found these as annual rites among the people. She conferred holy orders upon them all, each having a sacred duty. Having done all this, she retired to Crete until the time of her Daughter's return.

At the time of the Maiden's return, the silver crown of Tartarus was laid down. Persephone drank deeply from the River Lethe and crossed over to Earth. The Maiden was received by the Mother with great celebration, and crowned with evergreen and laurel. In her winged chariot, Demeter sent Triptolemos to let fall the precious seeds upon the earth. The rains of Zeus embraced the land, seed took root, and the earth became verdant once again. Then, the Mother and Maiden were seen in every green and growing thing, and in every pure and holy flower.

The Rites of Nestia: The Sadness. Persephone leaves Plouton and the Underworld.
Kalligenia: The Rejoicing. Persephone's ascent as Kore. Demeter and Kore are reunited. Planting may begin.
The Haloa: Celebration of Demeter and Kore at the beginning of the growing period.

This is the myth of Demeter and her Holy Daughter. May the Great Mother look upon my song with fair and kindly eyes, as I bow and honor her holy presence.

Theology and Spiritual Themes

Every God, every mythology, every religion
is true in this sense;
it is true as metaphorical of
the human and cosmic mystery.[1]

Religious myths contain images of divinity, that have evolved to help us understand life. Rita Knipe, in *A Jungian Journey Through Hawaiian Myth*, describes myths as expressions of the psychological patterns of societies. She further explains that mythology offers wisdom to societies, in the same way that dreams offer guidance to dreamers.[2]

Sacred myths carry universal themes that illustrate truths about life and death. They have been interpreted, reinterpreted, and fought over, as if they were concrete things rather than simply illustrations. They are not rigid territories, but moving internal experiences. Though they can be explained in a logical manner, they are best understood by intuitive perceptions.

---

[1]   Bill Moyers, video interview of "Joseph Campbell and the Power of Myth," vol. VI, *Masks of Eternity* (New York: Mystic Fire Video in assoc. with *Parabola Magazine,* 1988). Printed by permission of Mystic Fire Video.
[2]   Rita Knipe, *The Water of Life* (Honolulu: University of Hawaii Press), 1989, p. 15.

One predominant theme that crosses over into many religions is that from death arises rebirth—the process of eternity. The birth-life-death-rebirth theme is universal. It is seen in Egyptian myth, as Isis, with her magical powers, brings Osiris back from the dead. It is seen again in the triumph of Sumerian Inanna as she returns from death, in the return of Christ after the crucifixion, and in the power of Hindu Kali, who dances on the body of Shiva, returning Him to life. The same theme is repeated in Persephone's return from the land of death into her Mother, Demeter's, waiting arms.

The theology of Demeter's religion is learned through a reading of the myth, and by experiencing the seasonal festivals and the mysteries. One of the most important ideas in this theology is that the Goddess who gave birth to you, who created your life, made you a part of her divinity. As Demeter has given birth to Kore, so you have come into existence through divine birth. The Maiden is new life. She is representative not only of the soul, but of its journeys. She is the child of divinity, and so are you.

The myth reveals the divine light that resides behind the external image of the Goddess Demeter. This is seen during the revelation of her true form in the house of Baubo and Dysaules, and in her aura of light as she descends into the Underworld. In the same way, your own body and personality are a mask behind which lies the divine light of your soul. It awaits, glowing and glittering behind your reflection in the mirror, the divine light of the Great Creatress, of whom you are a part.[3]

Through the experiences of Demeter's Daughter, we learn about the cycles of the soul. The experiences of the Holy Daughter, from spring Maiden to Underworld Queen, are like the cycle of the seed. Both are Demeter's creations, her children. The daughter and the seed both spring forth from the earth to grow, flourish, and mature. Then, at the end of their cycle they pass into death. Later they arise and are born into life again. This pattern is symbolic of our own cyclical and continuing nature.

The Holy Daughter returns (is reborn to life) during the Nestia-Kalligenia portion of the Festival of Thesmophoria. This occurs at a time when the dry, parched, and yet fertile Earth awaits the rains.

---

3   Carl Kerényi, *Eleusis: Archetypal Image of Mother and Daughter* (Princeton, NJ: Princeton University Press, 1991), p. 145. Both women and men identified with the Goddess. Initiates became one with her, and the search for her daughter. Kerényi states that, following initiation, Roman Emperor Gallienus Augustus had a coin minted in which his image appeared crowned with grain, and his name appeared in the feminine form of "Gallienae Augustae" (p. 211, note 222).

The Earth Mother is prepared to receive the fructifying moisture. The Queen of the Underworld lays down her crown, drinks from the River Lethe (Forgetfulness), and returns to Earth as Kore. The veil of forgetfulness sets itself upon her divine being. The seed grain for planting is brought up from its storage chamber. Not long after the Daughter's return, the grain is planted. Then, nourished by the rains of fall and winter, the green fields of wheat and barley emerge. The Maiden is once again the young child, and the herald of spring. This portion of the myth is the prototype for our own physical rebirth into the world.

The harvested seed, which is both food and the source of the next crop, demonstrates the eternal cycle. The plant is cut and dies, yet it is the source of its own regeneration. The death was only an appearance. This parallels the Holy Daughter-soul, who is born, lives and dies to her maidenhood, and then descends into the dark unknown, the Underworld. Through passion, there is a mystical union with death. In death, she leaves her name, Kore, behind and becomes Persephone. She has matured to adulthood. Through her sacred marriage *(hieros gamos)* with Plouton, the lands below are infused with light, life, and beauty. Persephone brings the mysteries of the soul to Elysium, and perfect justice to Tartarus. So, what has appeared to be the Maiden's journey to death, is actually a journey to another kind of life. The parallel is that, when your physical body dies, the spirit that is you does not die, but continues in another kind of life.

In the beginning of the myth, Kore (the child of life) lives in a beautiful, lush, and harmonious springtime. Passion calls her to Tartarus, seeking union with her sacred lover. The Mother deeply mourns the loss of her Daughter and brings famine. This is a collision of life and death, creating pain. When later reconciled, this brings awareness.

After the loss of her Daughter, Demeter demands that we honor her with a holy temple. The people of Eleusis build her a temple and bring her sacrifices, hoping to end her grief. They have now learned to appreciate the bounty that they had previously enjoyed and its source. Later in the myth, Demeter's Daughter is returned to her and the balance is restored. As human beings, we have a tendency to take our blessings for granted.[4] It is restoration after a loss that brings the

---

[4]   In human experience, not every crisis is easily reconciled. The tragedies of war, the loss of a loved one, or the results of illness, sometimes create great difficulty for the individual to restore a balance. The time required for healing may vary, and we must respect that time, however long or short.

additional wisdom of appreciation. This creates a new feeling of contentment and happiness, one we may not have had before the crisis.

From the myth and mysteries, we learn that divine understanding (religious ecstasy) is experienced when we move beyond the world of time. The Maiden has grown to know the land of life that the laws of time control. But she will also know the land of death. There, she finds the paradise of Elysium, a place of the eternal. She also finds the spring Mnemosyne (the spring of memory). As she drinks from the spring, all of the cycles that have gone before are made known to her. It is then that she is crowned and takes her place as Queen of the Underworld. As Queen, she is emblematic of the union between life and death. The awareness that she has gained occurs outside of time and is experienced as passion, love, and ecstasy. It is in moments of love and ecstasy that our experience of time stands still, so that the divine may be made known to us.

Through both Persephone and Demeter, we learn lessons of compassion. When Demeter experiences the loss of her beloved child, she changes from a loving fertile giver of abundance to Melaina, the dark sorrowing Mother, and Erynis, who brings avenging famine. Through the observation of Persephone's love for Plouton, and an understanding of the power of love, Demeter shows compassion, forgives, and bestows her blessings upon the sacred marriage.

Persephone also teaches compassion. Plouton and the souls of the dead cry out for the light and beauty of the Goddess, for the Holy Maiden. When Persephone descends, her presence brings great joy. Later, compassion calls her back to the world above. Demeter and the people of Earth need her powers as well, the blessings of the verdant and blossoming Maiden. The Holy Daughter has chosen to serve in two worlds. She is called both noble and royal. Her titles have emerged because of her desire to serve.

The power of humor is another important part of the myth. It is Baubo, a beloved erotic clown, as well as a fertile wise mother, who turns the tide of this tale. Earlier, the momentum of the myth is fixed, stuck and unmoving because Demeter is closed in on her grief. Through the powers of Baubo and the erotic humor that she expresses, Demeter breaks through her grief. She discards the mantle of the Crone and reveals her form as Mother Goddess. The reawakening of her divine fertility is what sparks the cycle of life to move forward into creation. And yet, one more thing is needed to fully mend the cycle and get life really going again. This is insight, Demeter's own wisdom and compassion regarding her Daughter's journey to the land of death. So it is humor, and in this case erotic humor, that breaks through the rigidity of grief after the mourning period. Then it is insightful understanding that can return life to fertile creativity. In this example, the Mother reawakens, just as we do, to the powers of creation and the ability to live in a joyful state. Even after experiencing a loss, we may once again partake of divine ambrosia.

We can cultivate an awareness that includes some of these themes. The seasonal festivals and mysteries impart this awareness. From them, we gain an appreciation of life, self, and the source. It is easy, in all of the trials and decisions that must be made during a lifetime, to forget what has been given. The gift is life. As newborns, we *are* the gift, the Maiden. As adults, we can become aware of what we are, and choose to honor the gift and its source. Many people who have come close to their own death emerge with a new approach to life. As a result of surviving the accident, illness, or injury, we perceive life differently. Each moment is a joyful blessing. We can strive to be awake and aware of the gift we have been given.

Demetrian Paganism has at its very heart something that an urban world needs—that is, the knowledge that nature and its divinity creates and supports our lives. In addition, it is nature that teaches us about our souls and their journeys. Our lives have been made more comfortable with the modern tools of communication and transportation. Human ingenuity is admired for the creation of these tools, but we must remember that every physical element of their creation comes from Earth's resources. We do not ourselves create the building blocks of creation, however finite; we only work with them. Our resources are divinities to be honored, rather than simply used. We can maintain a conscious sense of appreciation.

In chapter 9, you will find the Thesmophoria complex of holidays. In the Thesmophoria Proper, the thesmoi (sacred laws) of Demeter are honored. As these laws are a vital part of the theology of the Demetrian myth, they are also listed here:

The Thesmoi of Demeter

> Give praises to the Holy Mother—all that is
>   born rises from within her.
> All that sustains thee flows from her body.
> The wise and Holy Mother pleasures
>   in peace and honest labor.

Tend to your life with gentle wisdom, and to
 your days with love's compassion.
Honor the Goddess' rites and mysteries—to bring
 justice, peace, and the nation's fertility.
Know the cycle of the blessed seed as the mystery
 of the soul, revealed.
Honor the pure and Holy Maiden, whose power
 is joy ever-reborn.
Praises to Royal Persephone, who at thy death
 will welcome thee.
Praises to the Holy Mother, whose song
 is the light of eternity.
May you know your immortal being and
 drink of her cup everlasting.

There are many religions and these provide the necessary variety of myth, symbol, and ritual for the people of the world. They have been born in certain times and places and have changed as time has moved forward. One must look to the universal themes as the common denominators. If we are fortunate enough to find a religious myth to which we can relate, then we have also found a way of perceiving our divine identity.

PART II

Facets of the Jewel

Demeter—Holy Names of the Great Mother

Sacred Prayers and Chants

*She has many names; call out to her. Let fragrant
smoke from the glistening censer rise, as soft
candlelight fills the sacred halls of prayer.*

The name Demeter means "Earth Mother," or "Grain Mother."
The Latin title *Dia Mater* (Mother Goddess) was used to
describe Demeter in Rome, as was the title *Megali Mater*
(Great Mother). Demeter was also called Ceres by the Romans, a
name from which we derive our word "cereal." To the Greeks,
Demeter was the Mother of all that lived and grew on the blessed
Earth. As land meant wealth, by extension, she governed prosperity
(see figure 2, p. 40).

In the Homeric "Hymn to Demeter," the Goddess tells the
daughters of the ruling family of Eleusis that she has just returned
from Crete. It may be that the myth of Demeter and Persephone is
rooted in the mythology of Minoan Crete.

The Cretans valued their Mother Goddess as a source of life and
fertility. Her priestesses were often depicted with snakes, also a
symbol of Demeter. Snakes were imaged with Demeter on the

Figure 2. Demeter of Cnidus.
Marble statue of Demeter from Cnidus, 330 B.C.E.
Used by permission, British Museum, London.

cista mystica (mystery basket), on Demeter's lap, and powering her chariot. The snake as the child of the Earth Mother is the Underworld offspring of the Goddess. The child, in this case, is she who is born of Earth, who descends, transforms, and is eternally reborn through the shedding of the skin.

In Cretan art, flowers such as lilies, crocus, and poppies were used to denote aspects of both the myth and seasonal year. Spring flowers are also a symbol of Demeter's Daughter. Poppies were an important Eleusinian image and were illustrated on the exterior of Demeter's temple and on the outside of the cista mystica.

In Mediterranean matristic society, the hero-hunter archetype revered women as the source of life and love.[1] From Hesiod, we read that Iasion and Demeter made love on the island of Crete ("joined in love").[2] This took place on a fallow field that had been plowed three times. From this union of Demeter's own free will, the Goddess gave birth to wealth and riches, to Ploutos.

There is a patriarchal version of the Demeter myth from Arcadia, a region located in the Peloponnesus, a rugged mountainous peninsula in the southern portion of the Greek mainland. In the myth of that region, Demeter is raped by Poseidon (both are in the form of horses). She becomes the Erinys (Angry One) and gives birth, not only to Despoina (the Mistress), but also to the winged horse, Areion (Orion).[3]

Black Demeter, Demeter Melaina, was worshiped with Despoina in Phigalia.[4] In a Phigalian cave on Mount Olive there existed an image of Black Demeter, portrayed with a mare's head, her hair decorated with snaky locks, and holding a dolphin and a dove. Demeter and Despoina were enthroned together in their temple in Lykosoura.[5] Despoina held the cista mystica and was draped in a mantle covered with earth and sea creatures. Beside Demeter and Despoina stood a statue of Artemis, holding two snakes in one hand and a torch in the other.

---

[1]   Carl Kerényi, *Eleusis: Archetypal Image of Mother and Daughter* (Princeton, NJ: Princeton University Press, 1991), p. 30. Kerényi describes Iasion (Iasos) as a hunter.

[2]   Dorothea Wender, trans., *Hesiod and Theognis* (London: Penguin Books, 1973), p. 55.

[3]   Joseph Fontenrose, *Python: A Study of Delphic Myth and Its Origins* (Berkeley: University of California Press, 1980), pp. 367–368.

[4]   Fontenrose, *Python: A Study of Delphic Myth and Its Origins*, pp. 368–369.

[5]   Kerényi, *Eleusis: Archetypal Image of Mother and Daughter*, pp. 31–32.

Long before the Greco-Roman period, women's ability to gestate and birth new life came to be identified with the earth, and with the growth and harvest cycles of agricultural produce. Agriculture brought a new kind of security, the storage of dried grain being the equivalent of money in the bank. The Mother of abundance was fertile and generous. The Goddess and women were seen as sacred, able to bring life and riches out of their bodies. This created a deep social awareness of women's connection to the Goddess. Today, social consciousness is reaching back in time, bringing forward an awareness of women's connection to the Great Mother.

For Eleusis, Demeter was the Earth Mother who provided for all humankind. In addition to her temple in Eleusis, there were Demetrian sanctuaries in Locri (a Greek colony in Italy), in Corinth (on the Greek mainland), in Myteline (on the island of Lesbos), and in Cyrene (a Greek colony in North Africa). The priestesses of Eleusis were much in demand all over Greece. At the fall festivals of the Thesmophoria, they were sent out from the Eleusinian temple to many cities to conduct Demeter's holy rites.

Many are Demeter's gifts. Two are most renowned: cultivated grain, by whose power civilizations have risen and are sustained, and the mysteries, which bring an understanding of our divinity here and in the hereafter. The mother of both life and death turns the seasons and bestows life-giving foods upon all. She has had many names. Her titles, as they are used in this work, are listed below.

Demeter Panagia *(Pan-ah-gee´-ah):*   Demeter Panagia means All-Holy Demeter. Panagia is also a title used today in the Greek Orthodox Church for Mary.

Demeter Chloaia *(Chlo-ah-ee´-ah):*   Demeter Chloaia describes the verdant aspects of the goddess. This name was used particularly at the Festival of Chloaia in early spring. At this time, she represents the green of cultivated fields and wild nature.

Demeter Antaia *(An-ta-ee´-ah):*   Demeter Antaia means Demeter Besought by Prayers. She is called, in the Orphic hymns, "Mother Antaia." With this name, one calls out to her for assistance and also finds the Mother of the Gentle Heart.

Demeter Melaina *(Meh-lay´-na):*   Demeter Melaina is the dark sorrowing Mother. This is the blackness of her grief and loss. As

Melaina, she is the Crone, bringing the barren aspect to the cycle of the seasonal year. In her dark grief, she is also Erinys, the Angry One. Later in the cycle, during the sacred drama of the Greater Mysteries, she transforms. Out of her dark aspects are born compassion and understanding.

Demeter Thesmophoros *(Thez-mo-phor′-ose):* Demeter Thesmophoros is Demeter of the Sacred Laws (Thesmoi). This title was used for Demeter during the Thesmophoria festivals that include fertility rites, a celebration of sacred law, and the return of the Maiden, Kore.

Demeter Chthonia *(C-tho-nee′-ah):* Demeter Chthonia is Demeter of the Below, of the deep earth, and also of the Underworld. In her journey below, she becomes reconciled with the sacred lovers, Persephone and Plouton. She also brings her gifts to the land of Death.

Demeter Evalosia *(Ev-ah-lo-see′-ah):* Demeter Evalosia is Demeter of the Good Harvest. As the harvest Mother, she is celebrated at the harvest and threshing festivals of Thargelia and Kalamaia.

Dea Mystica *(De′ ah My′-sti-ca):* Dea Mystica is the Goddess of the Mysteries. This is Demeter's form as the universal aspect of the divine and the unseen world of spirit. Dea Mystica is the great light that lies beyond ordinary light, and the depths of her love that has birthed our souls and our world.

The following prayers and chants will take you more deeply into the essence of Demeter. Use one of the prayers as a short candle-lighting rite, or create a short ritual using the following outline:

1. Be seated at the altar.
2. Light the incense.
3. Perform the Rite of Lustration (see chapter 7).
4. Use one of the short chants to deepen your state, letting the rhythm of the chant become smooth and flowing. You may do the chant in monotone, let your voice rise and fall, or add a simple melody.
5. Read one of the prayers (either a Demeter prayer from this chapter or a Persephone prayer from chapter 6).
6. Light a candle for the Goddess.
7. End the rite by saying: *"Blessed, by her Mystery."*

Prayer to Demeter Panagia

All Holy Demeter,
Pure luminous Mother of Creation,
With Your great powers
You turn barren lands into fields rich with wheat and barley.
You entice orchards to grow lush and green,
And to bear their weight of sweet fruit.
In Your name, meadowlands are covered with brilliant flowers,
As in its time, the patient ewe gives milk for the lamb.

Panagia,
Come to me, shining Your beauty upon my heart.
Goddess of ever more than harvest time,
But of all life's seasons,
O hear my prayer.

Beautiful One,
Bring rapture into my heart,
Rising as divine ecstasy,
And I become Thine.
Let Thy radiance flow upon me,
Until my heart is full of light.
May Your blessings flow upon my body,
My soul, my house, and my life.
Hail Panagia!
Hail!

[Light the candle.]

Prayer to Demeter Chloaia

Verdant One,
When the first green leaf of the hyacinth
Rises from the damp soil,
There is the sweet whisper of Your return.
As beneath the cool shadows of the clouds
You labor,
So that beauty may return to Earth.

And in the month of Anthesterion,
The hillsides and meadowlands appear
Dressed in emerald once again,
As the verdant Goddesses reign,
Jeweled in larkspur, lupine,
And blood-red poppies.

The spirits of the running stream,
The pine and the cypress,
All rejoice in the glory of the season,
For under the sea-blue skies,
Your song resounds across the land.

The lush green stands of wheat and barley
Bend and sway in the winds,
And it is You, Chloaia,
In Your Dance of Creation,

To You
I offer the gifts of the heart,
Of love, beauty, and reverence.
O grant me the season's bright benedictions
As I honor the Great Mother of the land.

[Light the candle.]

Prayer to Demeter Antaia

Mother of Fair Blessings,
When sorrow or lack has flooded the soul,
Then we cry out for Your aid,
And You, oh loving and generous Mother,
Are there to embrace the tender heart.
Amid the storm,
Small tender crocus rise from stony soil.
The light breaks,
As pale lavender petals open to winter sun,
And we may begin again.

Antaia,
Great is Your strength and compassion.
Into Your hands I place my needs and sorrows,
And there,
In the fires of the divine crucible,
Shall transformation take place,
As all the while, good and holy blessings
Fall radiant about my shoulders.

I listen, and hear Your song flowing across my soul,
And in the magic of its power and sweetness,
I rise on the broad winds.
With Your wisdom,
Come and bless the patterns of my life,
Bringing peace, well-being, and joy to my soul.
Hail Demeter Antaia,
Beloved Mother of Prayers Answered.
So be it.

[Light the candle.]

Prayer to Demeter Melaina

The land lies barren
As You search, dark and sorrowing,
For your Maiden Daughter.

Your great powers of creation drawn inward
As field and meadow lie fallow, You mourn.
For She who was born from Your womb
Has descended into Tartarus,
And is no longer at Your side.

But from Thee, Melaina,
And Thy shadows
Shall compassion arise.
In the darkness of Your solitude,
You dwell alone in Your fragrant temple,
And life gives birth to divine understanding.
Then, one who once raged in sorrow
As the Erinys, finds tenderness being born
In Her Divine Being.

In compassion,
You descend into the Underworld
To give Your blessings
To the royal Queen and the ancient King
Of Tartarus,
And in so doing heal all the worlds,
Teaching understanding to
Tartarus, Earth, and high Olympus.

O blessed art Thou, Holy One.
Great praises to both the fallow and the dark,
All Honor to Demeter Melaina.

[Light the candle.]

Prayer to Demeter Thesmophoros

You rose from the precious Earth,
Fair wisdom in Your hand,
The gifts of Your bounty even then taking shape,
Imparting to Eleusis and all the world,
The honorable way to live,
To bring sustenance from Earth
With simple honesty.
And also of the soul's Mysteries You have taught us,
Of our own divinity,
Which is the greatest beloved.

Thesmophoros,
Through the journeys of Your Holy Daughter
Do we learn of the Sacred Marriage,
That Life is wedded to Death,
Each a part of the whole of being.

Blessed art Thou who has born us,
For, as every woman gives birth to her child,
So You labored to bring us into being.
We honor and praise You,
Lighting candles and fragrant incense,
Offering flowers and sweet fruit.
But it is the pure and sincere offerings of the heart
By whose devotion we may embrace Thee
And our inherited divinity.

O Thesmophoros,
Bless me with Thy wisdom,
And with a life that is just and full of bounty.
May the richness and beauty of Thy presence
Remain with me always,
For I am Thine.

[Light the candle.]

Prayer to Demeter Chthonia and Dea Mystica

Deep, dark soil and its alluvial riches
Are the blessed remnants of Death,
As the green and fruit-bearing seasons of Life
Follow unseeming decay.
From the ashes of Death
Do You, Chthonia, forge new Life,
So that Being never ceases, but only changes form.

You are the magic of creation,
Never ending and always changing.
And with this power You have entered below,
Bringing the gifts for which You are renowned.

To the table of the King and Queen of Tartarus
You have brought the pelanos.
And bread was broken,
A sign of accord between Life and Death.
The Mysteries of Being You have also brought,
So that all who are below
Rejoice and are awake in the Mystery.

Chthonia,
Teach me hope when it is dark,
And patience when all is fallow.
May I learn to take pleasure in both
The stillness of the moment
And in the dance of change.
May wisdom and freedom reign in my heart,
Now and forevermore.
So be it.

[Light the candle.]

Prayer to Demeter Evalosia

Holy One,
All the world is filled with Your treasures.
Not the gold and silver of the dusky cavern,
But the myriad forms of teeming life that thrive under the Sun.
And when we bring in all that we need to live,
We partake of You, Evalosia.

The harvest is a grand thing,
For we have worked and labored hard
To bring the field to fruition.
And all that we do,
That is planting, weeding, and tending,
Leads to the joy of harvest day.

The ripened grain, the sweet apricot, and the pungent herb
Are but a portion of Your great bounty.
For pleasant satisfactions may arrive at the human soul
Through dreams found, as well as through dreams intended.
The basket of wild berries is as sweet as the cultivated apple,
And we give thanks for Your bounty as we find it.

All honor to the Mother of the Good Harvest,
Full of splendor and crowned with grain.
The beauty of the forest and the broad meadow,
The great mountains and shimmering silver lakes,
The rose, the lily, and the wild starlike anemone
Have all been bestowed by Thy gracious powers.
The riches of life, streaming from the palms of Thy hands
Bring us joy and sweet pleasure.
Great praise and thanksgiving do we offer Thee,
Hail Demeter Evalosia!
Hail!

[Light the candle.]

Chant for the Holy Mother

Panagia,   *(Pan . . . ah-gee-ah,)*
Holy Mother of Life,   *(Ho-ly Mo-ther of life,)*
Panagia,   *(Pan . . . ah-gee-ah,)*
O Lady divine.   *(O La-dy di-vine.)*

Chant for the Verdant Empress

Chloaia,   *(Chlo . . . ah-ee-ah,)*
Verdant Empress   *(Ver-dant Em-press of*
   of the Earth,   *the Earth,)*
Chloaia,   *(Chlo . . . ah-ee-ah,)*
In beauty mine.   *(In beau-ty mine.)*

Chant for the Goddess of the Mysteries

Dea Mystica,   *(De . . . ah Mys-ti-ca,)*
Brilliant light divine,   *(Brill-iant light di-vine,)*
Dea Mystica,   *(De . . . ah Mys-ti-ca,)*
Mother I am Thine.   *(Mo-ther I am Thine.)*

Her White Dove

With fluttering wings,   *(With flu-tter-ing wings,)*
Comes the Queen   *(Comes the Queen*
   of Creation,   *of Cre-a-tion,)*
Her white dove rising   *(Her white dove ri-i-sing)*
In sacred devotion.   *(In sa-cred de-vo-tion.)*

Enter Grace

Enter grace,   *(En-ter grace,)*
Enter beauty   *(En-ter beau-ty,)*
Enter the heart   *(En-ter the heart*
   into ecstasy.   *in-to ec-sta-sy.)*

Mother of Life

Great Mother of Life,   (Great Mo . . . ther of Life,)
Creatress, O blessed   (Cre-a-tress O bless-ed
   Lady,   La-dy,)
Great Mother of Life,   (Great Mo . . . ther of Life,)
In rapture come to me.   (In rap-ture come to me.)

Scarlet Alchemy Chant

On fiery golden wings,   (On fiery golden wings,)
Scarlet alchemy risen.   (Scarlet al-che-mee ri-sen).
Red the rose of   (Red . . . the rose of
   Her heart,   Her heart)
And the Womb   (And the Womb
   of Creation.   of Cre-a-tion.)

Dea Orea

Ela . . . Dea   (Eh-la . . . Deh-ah
   Orea.   Or-ay-ah.)
                                 (Come . . . Beautiful
                                    Goddess.)

Harvest Mother Chant

Demeter,   (De . . . meter)
Mother Demeter,   (Mother De . . . meter,)
Demeter Goddess   (Deme-ter Go-ddess)
Of the golden grain.   (Of the gol-den grai-ain.)

Power of the Queen

The power of the Queen   (The power of the Queen
   shall rise,   shall rise,)
Rise, rise within me.   (Rise . . . rise within me.)
In luminous silver   (In lu-min-ous silver
   shall rise;   shall rise;)
In magic, Her Spirit   (In ma-gic her Spir-it
   flows free.   flows free.)

Bless My Path

Bless my path, Great Mother of all things.
Weave for me the elements I need
For a pure and simple life.
Take beauty and reverence,
And weave them together with health and joy.
Remind me also of Your compassion,
That I may assist others as I can
In this journey of life,
And that I may forgive self as a blessing,
Knowing that nothing is perfect,
Until we arrive in fair Elysium.
O Holy and gentle Mother,
Come, and bless my life.

Evening Prayer

Evening falls,
And honoring the gift of life,
I give thanks for another day.
As the Sun descends below the horizon,
I pause to remember Her,
The Great Creatress.
O Beloved Mother,
You who have birthed all things,
Thank You for creating me.
Come, and bless my night's journey,
As I in peaceful sleep
Ascend in spirit,
Into the Holy Realms.
So be it.

CHAPTER 6

Persephone
Ancient Origins, Modern Views, Sacred Prayers

Born from her fertile womb, you grew from Maiden to Queen.
Venturing into the unknown, over dark fear were you victorious.
Come noble and bright Persephone, be with me,
That I may prevail.

Like her Mother, Demeter, the holy Daughter is a many faceted Goddess. On Earth, she is Kore (the Maiden) who, with Demeter, brings the spring. In the Underworld, she is Persephone, her Roman name being Proserpina. While the name Persephone has been translated as Destroyer, the destroyer persona of the Demetrian seasonal cycle belongs to Demeter Melaina (the Black) and to Demeter Erynis (the Angry One). It is she who brings the barren part of the agricultural cycle to Earth. Persephone, as Queen of the Underworld, receives the disembodied souls, but does not destroy them, or any other aspect of life.

After Kore's fearful descent, and the death of her maidenhood, the Holy Daughter transforms and becomes Queen Persephone. She is Plouton's bride and sacred lover, and a radiant source of life and light for the Underworld. In this reconstruction, she brings light to a dark God and to a dark realm. Persephone introduces the newly dead to the beauties of Elysium, and shows them the knowledge of their own divinity.

If Persephone destroys anything, it is the initiate's fear of death. She is the example of one who has overcome fear, descended into death, and yet lives. One of the primary points of the mysteries is that death is not an end. Initiates into the mysteries did not see the Underworld as a place of darkness, fear, or destruction, but as a place of light and joy. As far as they were concerned, they were initiates and, as such, they were headed for Elysium. That is part of what made the mysteries so popular.

While Persephone is Queen of Elysium, in shadowy Tartarus she brings justice. In the Orphic hymns, Persephone is called Mother of the Furies. It was the task of the Furies to exact divine retribution for crimes such as perjury and murder. Though Gaea (Earth) is considered to be the Mother of the Furies, here Persephone is named as the Underworld form of the mother of divine retribution. The Orphic hymns also give Persephone the title Praxidike (Prax-i-dee-kay), Goddess of Divine Action, who dispenses justice.

As Queen of the Underworld, Persephone's sacred union with the God of Death is essential to the continuation of the seasons, and therefore to the continuation of life. She is the power that balances the forces between Earth (life) and the Underworld (death). Though Kore becomes Persephone, within the heart of the Underworld Queen there always remains the spring Maiden, the flowering youthful Goddess of balmy sunlit days.

The rape of Persephone as a part of the myth most probably did not have its origin in Eleusis. We think of Persephone as being abducted against her will, primarily because of two literary works (and their descendants). These are the Homeric *Hymn to Demeter*, attributed to the Greek, Homer, possibly ninth to seventh century B.C.E.[1] and *Death and Proserpina* by the Roman, Ovid (43 B.C.E.-17 C.E.).[2] Homer says that the Maiden was seized and carried off

---

[1] R. Gordon Wasson, A. P. Ruck, and Albert Hofmann, *The Road to Eleusis*, Danny Staples, trans. (New York: Harcourt Brace Jovanovich, 1978), pp. 59–73. Also Marvin Meyer, *The Ancient Mysteries: A Sourcebook*, David Rice and John Stambaugh, trans. (San Francisco: HarperSanFrancisco, 1986), pp. 21–30; Helene Foley, *The Homeric Hymn to Demeter* (Princeton, NJ: Princeton University Press, 1993), 2–26.

[2] Ovid, *The Metamorphoses, Death and Proserpina*, Horace Gregory, trans. (New York: Viking Press, 1960), 149–159. Also *The Metamorphoses*, Mary M. Innes, trans. (New York: Penguin Books, 1955), pp. 125–133.

unwillingly, while Ovid says that the Underworld God "ravished" her and that she wept for the loss of her virginity. College students around the world have read these works, which have also inspired much art and literature, making the plight of Demeter's Daughter a well-known theme of the myth.

In the Orphic hymns, there is no mention of abduction or rape. The "Hymn to Persephone" makes no reference to it, while the "Hymn to Plouton" states only that the God took Demeter's Daughter away from the meadow to make her his bride.[3] Apollodorus (first to second century C.E.) states that Persephone was secretly carried off, but does not claim rape.[4] Nor does Callimachus (third century B.C.E.).[5]

What we don't have is the original Eleusinian full-length version of the myth that was used as the basis for the temple's yearly calendar of festivals. There does not appear to be evidence in the art works of Demeter's Eleusinian temple that illustrates a rape of Demeter's Daughter. In *Eleusis,* by archeologist Katherine Kanta, each item in the Museum of Eleusis is listed. None depicts a rape.[6] There is one statue of a fleeing Maiden, but this is considered to be one of the daughters of Oceanus. It is assumed that she is running at the moment of Persephone's descent. There are also fragments of a red-figured vase on which Plouton's head is clearly shown, but the rest of the pieces remain subject to speculation.

Author Allaire Chandor Brumfield writes of the Greek custom of *klepsigamia* (stealing the bride) in her book, *The Attic Festivals of Demeter and Their Relation to the Agricultural Year.* Klepsigamia was a practice, in ancient Greece, for the purpose of marriage, either against the bride's will, or with her permission.[7] The custom could be invoked for several reasons: it could force a wedding agreement onto an unwilling bride, between opposing families, onto disapproving parents, or it could occur as a mutual elopement. Regardless of

---

[3]   Orphic hymn 29, "Hymn to Persephone," in *The Orphic Hymns: Text, Translation and Notes,* Apostolos Athanassakis, trans. (Atlanta, GA: Scholars Press, 1988), p. 41. Orphic hymn 18, "Hymn to Plouton," in *The Orphic Hymns,* p. 29.

[4]   *Apollodorus, The Library,* Vol. I, Sir James George, trans. (London: William Heinemann; New York: G. P. Putnam's Sons, 1921), pp. 35–41.

[5]   A. W. Mair and G. R. Mair, trans., *Callimachus and Lycophron—Aratus* (London: William Heinemann; New York: G. P. Putnam's Sons, 1921), pp. 125–135.

[6]   Katherine G. Kanta, *Eleusis: Myth, Mysteries, History, Museum,* W. W. Phelps, trans. (Athens: n. p., 1979).

[7]   Allaire Chandor Brumfield, *The Attic Festivals of Demeter and Their Relation to the Agricultural Year* (Salem, NH: Arno Press, 1981), p. 225.

intent, the result was that the maiden, no longer virginal, had to marry her abductor.

It is important to note that the Greek marriage ceremony could include a mock abduction. It is highly possible that a mock abduction of the Maiden by Plouton became a part of the sacred drama of Demeter's mysteries. This may have evolved by the time of Homer, while it may not have existed in Eleusis centuries earlier. If it became a part of the myth and rites (as abduction for the purpose of elopement), the dramatic purpose of this element may have been to force Demeter to concede to a marriage of which she disapproved. Some believe that a remnant of klepsigamia has carried over into the modern traditions of marriage as the custom of carrying the bride over the threshold.

The myth and theology of Demeter-Persephone sanctuaries most probably included a dramatic portrayal of klepsigamia for the purpose of elopement. There is a terra-cotta relief from Locri (a Greek colony in the southern tip of Italy) that illustrates this.[8] Fragments of the relief are missing, but the surviving pieces depict Plouton in his horse-drawn chariot. A young man, curly-headed, beardless, and short of stature (perhaps Euboleus) stands beside the chariot. He has lifted the Maiden up and is in the process of placing her in the chariot. She does not appear to be struggling or leaning away. The relaxed faces of Plouton and the Maiden are in profile, and they face each other on an equal level in the design of the relief. It is interesting that museum curators have titled the relief "The Rape of Persephone," because, in actually looking at the image, there is no element of the work that illustrates rape, violence, or klepsigamia against the Maiden's will.

A very beautiful relief-tablet from Locri depicts a well-known and important image of Persephone and Plouton enthroned (see figure 3, p. 58).[9] The deities are seated in profile, and both are smiling. Persephone is the predominant figure in the foreground. A rooster is seated comfortably in the palm of Persephone's right hand. In her left hand, she holds a sheaf of grain. Plouton's head leans forward slightly. In his right hand is a bowl, perhaps a libation bowl or a wine

---

[8]   Carl Kerényi, *Eleusis: Archetypal Image of Mother and Daughter* (Princeton, NJ: Princeton University Press, 1991), p. 173.

[9]   Hector Williams, "Secret Rites of Lesbos," in *Archaeology Magazine* (New York: Archaeological Institute of America, July–August 1994), pp. 34–38.

Figure 3. Plouton and Persephone Enthroned.
Terra-cotta votive relief from Locri, 470–450 B.C.E.
Museo Archeologico Nazionale Reggio Calabria, Italy.
Used by permission Scala /Art Resource, New York.

cup. In his left hand he holds a five-petaled flowering plant. Another rooster stands on the floor, directly beneath the throne. This appears to be a scene of Underworld marital felicity.

In additional terra-cotta images from Locri, a connection of Persephone with Aphrodite is represented. This may seem unusual, but Persephone and Plouton are the sacred lovers who possess the *hieros gamos* or sacred marriage. Love, an aspect of Aphrodite, is the force that draws Persephone and Plouton together. In these reliefs from Locri, Persephone is sometimes shown with doves, sometimes with Eros, and sometimes with an ointment jar. Gunther Zuntz, in his work *Persephone,* states that these are emblems of the Daughter's power.[10] The doves and Eros may show the importance of Aphrodite's influence on the sacred marriage. Or, they may show that, at some point, there was a merging of Aphrodite's qualities with those of Persephone.

Regarding the portrayal of the narcissus, Homer and Ovid connect spring flowers with the abduction of the Maiden. In Homer, the Maiden picks narcissus that have been set as a trap. When she reaches down to pick it, she is abducted by the God of the Underworld. In Ovid, the Maiden is picking lilies and violets when Death takes her. Initially, narcissus and lilies were symbols of the Maiden and of the seasonal return to growth and blooming. Through Homer and Ovid, they became symbols of abduction.

I believe that Kore of Eleusis did not descend into the Underworld with the fear of rape, but with the fear that always accompanies a transitional descent into a dark unknown, into that which has been hidden. It is probable that one reason why the Eleusinian mysteries needed to remain secret was that they held to a matristic focus throughout the Greek patriarchal period. We must remember that, even though Demeter's festivals and mysteries are available to both men and women through this book, the majority of the seasonal festivals (though not the mysteries) of Eleusis were celebrated exclusively by women. This included the five holidays of the Thesmophoria, as well as the Skira and Haloa festivals. This was the last holdout of matristic religious society in the Mediterranean, even into our era. Rape is a tragedy, and I find it highly unlikely that women would use the model of a relationship based on violence as the foundation of their theology.

---

10 Gunther Zuntz, *Persephone* (London: Oxford University Press, 1971), p. 166.

The works of Homer, Ovid, and others were written in tune with the patriarchal times in which they were completed. Homer and Ovid could not have (particularly if they were initiates) have reflected the full matristic myth as I believe it was portrayed in Eleusis. Initiates of Demeter's mysteries were sworn to secrecy both through respect for the two Goddesses and under the threat of legal punishment, the inner secrets remained undisclosed. Not many were willing to go to trial over this, risking confiscation of personal property, banishment from Greece, or public cursing by Eleusinian clergy, just so that they could tell all. Risking the wrath of the Goddess of Good Fortune and Abundance probably didn't seem like a wise choice either.

Regarding the use of the pomegranate, both Homer and Ovid present it as a device to control Demeter's Daughter. The God of the Underworld tricks Persephone into eating from the pomegranate in order to force her to remain below against her will. Here again, we find coercion and a continuation of the abduction concept. This is far from the pomegranate's original meaning.

The dark-red jewel-like fruit of the pomegranate is symbolic of the magic and fertility of the Goddess. It flowers in early summer when the grain ripens. The pomegranate ripens in the fall, after the threshed grain has been stored. This occurs during the grain field's fallow period, the mythic time when Persephone reigns in the Underworld. On Earth, Demeter mourns as the barren Crone. The magic of the pomegranate in the Mediterranean cycle is its demonstration of ripeness when most of the landscape lies fallow. The flowers of the countryside are gone, the meadows have died in the intense heat of the Mediterranean summer, the grain fields lie dry and barren, but autumn comes and the pomegranate ripens, breaks open, and reveals its scarlet seeds.

There are modern authors who view the Maiden quite differently than Homer and Ovid. Author Clarissa Pinkola Estés states that, in older matristic tales of the East, the Maiden has a desire to descend below in order to find her bridegroom.[11] The author suggests that, in myths such as those of Inanna, the Maiden knows her destiny and chooses to meet it of her own free will. At some point in the mythic evolution of the Maiden and her relationship to the Underworld, the

---

[11] Clarissa Pinkola Estés, *Women Who Run with the Wolves* (New York: Ballantine Books, 1992), p. 412.

themes of abduction and rape took hold. Previously, Estes states, during the time of the matriarchies, women were guided to the Underworld by deep feminine powers.

E. O. James states that behind the Homeric "Hymn to Demeter" lies a long history of "ancient seasonal rustic rites."[12] The author suggests that the descent of the Maiden, Kore, may have begun as a part of a Minoan Goddess rite that equated her descent with the storage of the grain in underground grain silos. James suggests the Greek Persephone, as Queen of the Underworld, may have united with the Minoan Maiden as the abduction concept formed. Likewise, author Charleen Spretnak finds evidence that the myth underwent a change that began to include rape following a movement from matriarchal to patriarchal society. She further states that the original mythology did not contain rape.[13]

In the myth presented in chapter 3, there is a point at which Persephone becomes sorrowful. Here, she is torn between her love for her Mother, and her love for the God of the Underworld. This crisis, added to that of barren Demeter Melaina, leads to a resolution. In the end, Demeter (life) and Plouton (death) break bread together at the table of the immortals. Now the forces of life and death have been brought into accord. Ultimately, the Holy Daughter is loved by all, and all are willing to come into compromise for her. This compromise is the miraculous power that propels the cycle of life forward again.

---

[12]   E. O. James, The *Cult of the Mother Goddess* (New York: Barnes and Noble Books, 1994), pp. 153–155.
[13]   Charlene Spretnak, *Lost Goddesses of Early Greece* (Berkeley, CA.: Moon Books: 1978), pp. 100–101.

Prayer to Kore

Fair Kore,
Full of grace and light and beauty,
O my soul and my heart,
In purity were You born of the Great Mother.

All that glistens as new life,
The babe fresh from the womb,
The green grasses that rise after the barren time,
The saffron crocus and the white narcissus,
And every bud that breaks into bloom
To create a glorious Spring,
All, all are Thee!

It is You, lovely Maiden,
Who, living within the realm of time,
Make the long journey.
And within the season of the Crone on Earth
Do You dwell in the deep Below,
Where, as Persephone, You reign over glorious Elysium,
In union with Your Great Beloved.

O You who are as my very soul,
May I learn Thy divine wisdom.
From the patterns of the seasons,
And from You who are the
Living, changing, and eternal soul.
So be it.

Prayer to Persephone Praxidike

Fair Praxidike, Goddess of Courageous Action,
You looked beyond the burnt and barren field,
And crossed the black bridge into Your destiny.
Letting go Your white lily-veil,
You overcame the darkness of Your fear
And faced Death in Your truest moment.
O beloved Persephone, grant that I, like You,
May be filled with wisdom and courage,
For these are the true gifts of the Queen's crown.
Hail Persephone!

Invocation of Persephone

Hail Queen of Tartarus and Elysium!
Generous Lady who has brought light to the realms below,
Beauty You have brought to Elysium,
And perfect justice to the realm of Tartarus.
You are the Beloved of Death, who brings joy
To the King of the Underworld.

In rich robes, jeweled and crowned,
Wise and full of loving kindness,
You reside in Tartarus' palace,
Enthroned with the Lord Plouton,
Dispensing in compassion Themis' law.

And in Elysium,
Wreathed and garlanded in fragrant flowers,
You welcome the dead under the spreading pomegranate tree
Where You prepare them for another way of being;
One in which divinity is awake in the heart.
O fair Persephone, Mistress of Beauty and Light,
Come and bless Your pure-hearted initiate.

To Noble Persephone

Born from Her fertile womb,
You grew from Maiden to Queen.
Venturing into the unknown,
Over dark fear, were You victorious.
Come, noble and bright Persephone,
That I may prevail
When challenge is laid in my path.
Be with me, in body and heart,
And bless me,
O fair offspring of the Great Mother.

O Goddess of Delight

Joy is always in Your heart,
Written upon Your enchanting face,
Or deep in the realms of Your soul.
O Goddess of delight,
In Your Maidenhood,
Your Queenly joys, or in Your sorrows,
Always resides the beauty of Divine Spirit.
O fair Mistress,
I honor and praise You,
For You are perfect and precious unto me.

At the Altar, Lustration, and the New-Moon Ceremony

Let your altar be a place where time is suspended,
where beauty and peace mingle and the spirit
soars through the infinite realms
of the Great Mother.

Your altar should be in a place that is comfortable for you as a permanent setting. Any small table will suffice. Altars have been made atop a chest of drawers or even on small bookcases. At Greek temple sites, the word for altar meant simply the place where sacrifices and offerings were received. These were located outside the temple. The phrase *sacred table* was used to describe what we think of as an altar today. (See color insert between pp. 144–145.)

Here are some suggestions for setting up your altar. Place an icon, statue, or other image of Demeter in the center of a table, against a wall. I use a copy of a photograph of a statue of Demeter, placed in a standing frame. To the right and left of the icon are white taper candles. In front of the icon is a votive candle. Above, on the wall, I have placed a photograph of a relief of Demeter and Persephone. On the altar is a vase of fresh or dried flowers, and a terra-cotta vase of wheat. Wheat can be grown (see chapter 19), purchased in craft stores, or, in the fall, in florist shops. My altar also holds an incense burner, a bell, a ceramic snake, a bowl of mixed seeds, and a seashell filled with water.

In addition, I have draped some necklaces of red carnelian beads over the icon. Red is the color of Demeter's poppies and of menses (fertility). Items you add to the altar later for other rites (such as a dish of salt, or anointing oil) may remain, if you wish.

LUSTRATION: A RITE OF SELF-BLESSING

The Museum of Eleusis contains a relief of a Hydranos priestess holding a lustration bowl and purifying an initiate, as well as a priestess statue, called "the basin bearer," that has a square hole in the lower abdomen, which once held a marble basin.[1] This statue, and another just like it, stood beside the doorways of Demeter's temple, inviting those who entered to perform a lustral rite.

The lustration rite presented here may be used as a way to start the day, bringing the Goddess into your mind and heart as a self-blessing. For your lustration bowl, you may use a large seashell, or any bowl set aside for this purpose. You may choose to scent the water with a few drops of fragrant oil.

Altar Items
Icon or image of Demeter and a lustration bowl.

The Words and Actions
1. Dipping the fingers of your right hand into the lustration bowl, bring them to the center of your forehead and say:
    Eye of spirit where wisdom enters,

2. Extend your right arm out toward the right saying:
    May her good enter from the right hand,

3. Extend your left arm out toward the left saying:
    May her good enter from the left hand,

4. Bring both hands to your heart (mid-chest), and say:
    For she dwells within . . .

---

[1]   Katherine Kanta, *Eleusis: Myth, Mysteries, History, Museum,* W. W. Phelps, trans. (Athens, n. p., 1979), p. 84.

5. Bring your forearms down, palms up, and say:
    And without,

6. Bring your hands again to your heart, as before, and say:
    In beauty . . .

7. Bow your head and say:
    And honor,

8. Raise your arms up, hands upward, and say:
    Hail!

THE NEW MOON CEREMONY

This rite begins a new lunar cycle, taking place as the first little crescent is seen, just after the dark of the moon. Combining a house
blessing, a self-blessing, and a prayer, the New-Moon Ceremony also
includes a dedication, or rededication, to the Goddess.

Set the altar and have your offerings ready. Cleanse your living
space, in a way that feels renewing to you. Bathe or shower. Dress in
clean, comfortable clothing. Arrange to have no interruptions, such
as the telephone ringing. Create ventilation in your altar area, especially if you tend to become sensitive to the smoke from the censer.

Altar Items

An icon or image of Demeter, two white taper candles (one to the right and one
to the left of the icon), a votive candle, matches, a lustration bowl, a bowl of
wheat, barley grains or other mixed seeds, myrrh or sandalwood incense, a
censer and a self-lighting coal (if required), a dish of salt, and a vase of fresh or
dried flowers.[2] In addition, bring an offering for Demeter: bread, fruit, honey,
wine, sweet cakes, or whatever food you wish. At the end of the rite, you will
partake of the offerings, sharing a repast with the Goddess.

The Words and Actions

In the ceremony that follows, step 9 involves an anointing that combines fire
and water in a self-blessing. Practice this anointing in the following way: dip the
fingers of one hand into the water of the lustration bowl. Pass the fingers of the
other hand quickly across the flame of the votive candle. Then bring both hands

---

2   See chapter 18, "Icons."

together, the fingers of one atop the other, palms facing toward your body.
Anoint your body as directed, with your fingers.

1. Light the incense.
2. Light the votive candle or oil lamp and say:
   Hail Hestia!
   Ancient Hearth Mother,
   And Goddess of the Spiritual Flame,
   Come, and enter herein.

3. In an inward manner, ask Hestia to make your altar a place of spiritual
   focus. Ask her to bless your home with peace, safety, and beauty.
4. Pick up the censer and Hestia's flame. Go to each room of your home,
   always moving in a clockwise direction. Walk around the periphery of each
   room. Bring Hestia's light and power as you go.
5. Return to the altar. Set things down, saying:
   Hail Hestia!

6. Sprinkle a little salt into the bowl of water. Place a hand into the water and
   say:
   I call to the Mother of the Sea,
   To Daira of deep oceans and bright dolphins;[3]
   As Demeter is to the vast Earth,
   So You are to the primordial sea.
   Come Lady, and refresh my spirit,
   Filling my soul with peace.
   May Your waters bless me
   In this time of the new crescent.

[Anoint the top of your head, your heart, and any other area you wish with
water.]

7. Hold the bowl of grain on your lap, and say:
   All-Holy Demeter,
   Pure luminous Mother of Creation,
   With Your great powers
   You turn barren lands into fields rich with wheat and barley.
   You entice orchards to grow lush and green,
   And to bear their weight of sweet fruit.
   In Your name, meadowlands are covered with brilliant flowers,
   As in its time, the patient ewe gives milk for the lamb.

---

[3] See Appendix 2, "Daira."

Panagia,
Come to me, shining Your beauty upon my heart,
Goddess of ever more than harvest time,
But of all life's seasons,
O hear my prayer.

8. **Say:**
Great Mother,
Enter now, into the house of Your votary,
Come and bless me,
As the iridescent Moon
Begins her cycle once again.

[Set the bowl of grain down and light the two taper candles.]

9. **The Fire and Water Anointing [See instructions on page 66]:**

Anoint your lower abdomen and say:
May my actions begin in wisdom.

Anoint your upper abdomen and say:
May strength serve me, as is my need.

Anoint your heart and say:
May I practice compassion for myself and others.

Anoint your throat and say:
Great Mother, may Your wisdom bless my words.

Anoint the center of your forehead and say:
Great Mother, with Your eyes, may I see divinity in all the world.

Anoint the top of your head and say:
May your light stream from this vessel of the Great Mother.

Now bring your hands up and out. Allow your arms to fall gracefully downward to your sides and say:
Hail Panagia!

After the rite, partake of some of the offerings, feasting with the Goddess. Then place a portion of the food offerings outside on the earth. Allow the candles to burn fully.

PART III

The Seasonal Festivals

CHAPTER 8

The Demetrian Wheel of the Year
An Introduction

*Take heed when you hear the voice of the crane
from high in the clouds, making its annual clamour;
it brings the signal for ploughing
and indicates the season of winter rains. . . .* [1]

The Demetrian holy days mark special moments of the seasons with agricultural rites, festivals, and mysteries. These rites developed under the influence of a Mediterranean climate (mild, wet winters and hot summers). Much of Greece's soil is poor, the richest soil being that of the coastal lowlands and the plains of Thessaly. The principal Greek rainy seasons are fall and winter. Most of the few rivers in peninsular Greece are dry by summer.

In the Demetrian cycle, the planting of grain takes place in the fall in order to take advantage of fall and winter rains. Harvest takes place at the end of spring and in early summer. The month of Hecatombaion (August-September) was a month of leisure for farmers. During Hecatombaion, the great festival of Athens, called the

---

[1] Hesiod, *Theogony, Works and Days,* M. L. West, trans. (London: Oxford University Press, 1988), p. 50. Reprinted by permission of Oxford University Press.

Panathenaia, took place, and many from the countryside attended. Now as then, summer drought causes the countryside's wildflowers and grasses to disappear, and the trees to take their moisture from deep in the earth, awaiting the rainy season.

While the holidays of Celtic paganism revolve around a fallow period that occurs during winter's freezing cold, Demetrian paganism revolves around a fallow period that occurs during summer's drought. At about the time when winter covers the land with its blanket of snow in northern of Europe, renewing rains arrive in the Mediterranean. Central and coastal southern California, central Chile, western Cape Province in South Africa, western and southwestern Australia, and the coastal regions and islands of the Mediterranean Sea, all have Mediterranean climates, one that supports the production of grain, barley, grapes, figs, olives, citrus, and many varieties of fruits and vegetables.

Wheat and barley are planted in Greece today "from the middle of October to the end of December, depending on the rains," according to Brumfield.[2] Hesiod, in *Works and Days*, advised planting before the Winter Solstice. By February, the grain fields have become a carpet of emerald green. By March, the fields are lush and the grain has flowered, the barley first, then the wheat. The field poppies bloom in April. By May, the grain has matured.

In *A Sacred Calendar of Eleusis,* by Dow and Healey, the preplowing rite of Proerosia is listed in the month of Pyanopsion (roughly mid-October to mid-November). The calendar, examined by Dow and Healey in August of 1963, is not dated, but the authors place its creation as early as 330 B.C.E.[3] Fragments of it tell us of the many festivals that occurred in the month of Pyanopsion. The information, incised in marble, was found in an epigraphic storeroom in Eleusis.

In the Demetrian Wheel of the Year, more festivals occur in the month of Pyanopsion than in any other month. In addition to the preplowing rites, there are the five festivals of the Thesmophoria, occurring on consecutive days. It is a busy month. These holidays are

---

2   Allaire Chandor Brumfield, *The Attic Festivals of Demeter and their Relation to the Agricultural Year* (Salem, NH: Arno Press, 1981), p. 20.

3   Sterling Dow and Robert F. Healey. *A Sacred Calendar of Eleusis* (Cambridge, MA: Harvard University Press, 1965), p. 2.

dedicated to the magical activities required to assure a good planting season and are intended to honor Demeter's gifts. The preplowing rites invoking Demeter and Zeus, the festivals of fertility, the public honoring of Demeter's laws, the call for Persephone's ascent, the Maiden's return, and the sacred bestowal of Demeter's blessings all fall within this portion of the calendar. These rites begin the agricultural year.

The yearly cycle also contains the Haloa festival, a winter fertility festival honoring Mother and Daughter. The Festival of Chloaia, in early spring, celebrates the Green Mother, the Maiden Daughter, and the God Dionysus. The harvest festivals of late spring to early summer include Thargelia (the harvest), Kalamaia (the threshing) and the Skira festival celebrating the Maiden's descent, the union of Persephone and Plouton, and the storage of the seed grain.

Other holidays that are not included in this reconstruction of the Demetrian holy days include the Eleusinia, a festival of competitions (gymnastics and music) that took place in the month of Metageitnion (August-September). Winners of the competitions received grain from the temple's sacred Rharian Field. Another holiday not in this reconstruction is the Sacrifice to Daira (an Attic Sea Goddess), which took place in the month of Gamelion (January-February).

Animals were sacrificed to Demeter and Persephone, as well as to other Olympian deities. In the records kept of the kinds of animals used for the festivals, pigs are mentioned most frequently as a sacrifice to Demeter. Meat was an expensive luxury for most Greeks. Everyday meals did not include it. The basic Greek diet was barley, wheat, sheep and goat cheese, onions, garlic, olives, wine, beans and seeds, fish, and fruits and vegetables (dried or in season). Only the wealthy ate meat frequently, lamb and pork being the most common. An animal sacrifice was thus equal to a gift of a luxury. It also represented life being sacrificed to life so that it could continue. Sacrifices offered to deities of the Underworld were set on the fire altars and consumed by flame. Animals that were sacrificed to Olympian deities could, for the most part, be received by temple clergy for their own use, or for use at public feasts following holiday celebrations.

There were also bloodless sacrifices. These were ritual offerings of honey, wine, grains, breads, sweet cakes, fruit, and flowers. For festival offerings, we should not ignore the significance of the pig, an animal sacred to Demeter. The pig is a hardy and prolific animal that produces an abundance of offspring in a relatively short period of

TABLE 1. **The Greek Calendar.**

MODERN CALENDAR	GREEK CALENDAR	MODERN CALENDAR	GREEK CALENDAR
September-October	*Boedromion*	March-April	*Elaphebolion*
October-November	*Pyanopsion*	April-May	*Mounichion*
November-December	*Maimakterion*	May-June	*Thargelion*
December-January	*Poseideon*	June-July	*Skirophorion*
January-February	*Gamelion*	July-August	*Hecatombaion*
February-March	*Anthesterion*	August-September	*Metageitnion*

time, in comparison with other animals. The pig thus became a symbol of the fertility and abundance of the goddess, and its image in art and ritual was a useful one.

Today we can only approximate the dates of the holidays. See table 1, where the original Greek dates are given. The difficulty comes in moving the Greek holidays out of their lunar calendar and into our solar calendar. Each Greek month began on the new moon and lasted for one lunar cycle. By the fifth century B.C.E., a thirteenth intercalculary month was being used to advance the year to the proper solar timing. The Greek lunar-calendar date for each holiday may have varied in solar timing by as much as several weeks. Of course, agricultural activities occurred as the individual farmer's wisdom dictated. Some of the solar-calendar choices below were made for modern convenience (see the individual chapters on the festivals for more information.)

The Demetrian festival season can be divided into the Season of Planting, the Season of Growth, the Season of the Harvest, and the Season of the Fallow Period. Because of climate and temperature differences, these do not exactly fit into the spring, summer, winter, and fall patterns into which the Celtic-Wiccan seasonal festivals fall. However, Demeter's festival seasons can be shifted in order to fit non-Mediterranean climates (see p. 79).

Tables 1 and 2 give the Greek months and Demeter's holy days. You will find introductions to each holy day, along with their seasonal and transcendent themes and their full liturgy, in the subsequent chapters.

TABLE 2. **The Demetrian Wheel of the Year.**

MODERN DATE	GREEK FESTIVAL AND DATE	FESTIVAL DESCRIPTION
October 7th	RITES OF PROEROSIA —Pyanopsion 5	Preplowing rites. Blessings and magic to prepare the sacred field.
October 15th	STENIA FESTIVAL —Pyanopsion 9	Bawdy humor, sacred sexuality. Barren Demeter becomes Fertile Mother.
October 16th	RITES OF ARKICHRONIA —Pyanopsion 10	Creation of fertility talismans. Combining Earth and Underworld powers.
October 22nd	THESMOPHORIA PROPER —Pyanopsion 11	Celebration of Demeter's sacred laws. Remembering our divinity.
October 23rd	RITES OF NESTIA —Pyanopsion 12	The Sadness. Queen Persephone leaves her beloved Plouton and the Underworld.
	RITES OF KALLIGENIA —Pyanopsion 13	The Rejoicing. Ascent of the Maiden. Reunion of Demeter and Kore. Planting.
January 10th	FESTIVAL OF HALOA —Poseideon 28	Celebration of new green growth in both cultivated field and wild nature.
March 1st	FESTIVAL OF CHLOAIA —early Anthesterion	Festival of flowers, of Verdant Demeter and Kore, and of the green Earth.

TABLE 2.   The Demetrian Wheel of the Year (cont.)

MODERN DATE	GREEK FESTIVAL AND DATE	FESTIVAL DESCRIPTION
April 12th	THE LESSER MYSTERIES —mid-Anthesterion	Ceremony of the whole festival cycle. Purification. Consecration to Demeter.
May 15th	THARGELIA —Thargelion-Skirophorion	The Harvest. Demeter, the Harvest Queen. The seed and the Maiden are matured.
June 7th	KALAMAIA —Thargelion-Skirophorion	The Threshing. Freeing the seed grain from the chaff. Honoring Triptolemos.
June 28th	SKIRA FESTIVAL —Skirophorion 12	The Maiden's descent. In love, Plouton and Persephone unite. The grain is stored. The fallow period begins and, in the following months, Demeter becomes Crone.
September 20th	THE GREATER MYSTERIES —Boedromion 20–21	The Sacred Drama. The reconciliation of Demeter, Plouton, and Persephone. The Rite of the Cista Mystica. The Thanatos Rite. The Crowning.

ADAPTING THE HOLY DAYS FOR NON-MEDITERRANEAN CLIMATES

Although the Demetrian rites evolved from a Mediterranean climate and its seasons, they may be adapted for other climatic locations by referring to their themes of planting, growth, harvest, and fallow time. Following Persephone's descent, the fallow time begins. It ends with the Greater Mysteries.

Proerosia, the preplowing rites come just before the Thesmophoria holidays that begin the new agricultural year. The seasonal cycle moves from fallow time to one of planting time, when rain is prayed for in Mediterranean climes. In more northerly regions, the warmth of the spring Sun is invoked. Because of this, some changes in liturgy may be required. For example, in the Stenia festival (the beginning of the Thesmophoria holidays), which occurs in October, rain is one of the elements needed to awaken Earth. For those in more northerly areas, the heat and light of the Sun is an additional aspect of awakening Earth, so blessings from the God Helios (the Sun) may be needed.

Proerosia and Stenia will occur in late February or early March in those regions where which winter is harsh. The remainder of the festivals will follow in order, with those of planting in spring, of growth in summer, of harvest in fall, and of the fallow time in winter.

CHAPTER 9

The Fall Festivals
The Planting Season

Triptolemos, child of Dysaules and Baubo
Wise son of a noble family,
Impart to all, the arts of planting and cultivation.
Give to the people of Earth, the knowledge of agriculture.

The season of Planting contains both the end of the old agricultural year, as well as the beginning of the new year. After the hot Mediterranean summer, this is the season of welcome rains. Fall crocus rise up from the earth, their blooms proclaiming a change in season. For northern climates, the holidays of the Planting Season, would be appropriate in early spring.

Fall celebrations begin with *Proerosia*, preplowing rites that bless the land for the new planting season. Following come the five holidays of the Thesmophoria. First is *Stenia*, a bawdy and raucous festival in which the humor of Baubo transforms Barren Demeter into the Fertile Mother. Next is *Arkichronia*, a festival of magical rites that combine both Earth and Underworld powers into precious fertility talismans. Then comes the reverent *Thesmophoria Proper*, a celebration of Demeter's sacred laws. *Nestia* follows and this tells the story of Persephone's ascent from the Underworld. And last is the celebratory festival of *Kalligenia*, the reunion of Demeter and Kore, and their blessings upon all, who are the fair offspring of the Great Mother.

THE RITES OF PROEROSIA—OCTOBER 7TH

> ## Seasonal themes
> Preparing the field for cultivation with preplowing rites. Honoring and invoking the blessings of Demeter the Earth Mother, Zeus the Rain God, and Demeter's emissary Triptolemos, teacher of the arts of agriculture.
>
> ## Transcendent themes
> Preparing for a goal, considering not only the practical preparations, but also honoring the forces of divine power that are in play. Sacred prayer at a time of new beginning. Study, education, learning new skills, procuring resources.

The Proerosia *(Pro-e-ro-see'-ah)*, a part of both the Athenian and Eleusinian calendars, took place on Pyanopsion 5. The Hierokeryx of Eleusis (the priest who made the sacred proclamations) made the traditional announcement in Athens, inviting all to the Eleusinian celebration. The Eleusinian clergy, the Athenian clergy, and the participants would then proceed to Eleusinian lands, the rites taking place in the temple's sacred field.

Here in southern California, I have celebrated Proerosia anytime during the first two weeks of October. In northern regions, begin in March, or as soon as the ground is warm enough to be worked. For preplowing (and planting) ceremonies, a small piece of earth or even a large pot of soil, will suffice. Different ways to grow grain are given in chapter 19.

Proerosia is the preparatory rite for the new agricultural year, the time when seed (Maiden) and Earth (Demeter) will reunite and begin the fertile season. At the planting, which takes place in the following weeks, the Maiden will again reside in the body of Mother Earth. Later, as the seed sprouts, the Maiden is reborn from the earth. The young shoots are called Korai.

During Proerosia, a ritual blessing of the land occurs, with offerings and an invocation for rain. Prayers are offered for the return of life and new growth via invocations to Demeter, Zeus, and Triptolemos. Triptolemos is seen as a teacher who has been empowered by Demeter. He teaches us, at this time of new beginnings, that the process of agriculture contains ideas that can guide us in living.

Ritual Outline

I.   Welcome
II.   Chant for the Lady of Life
III.   Invocation to Demeter
IV.   Invocation to Zeus
V.   Invocation to Triptolemos
VI.   Instructions of Triptolemos
VII.   Ritual Plowing
VIII.   Closing Blessing

Clergy

Priestess of Demeter
Priestess of Hecate
Hierophant
Priest of Triptolemos
Priestesses Panagia

The Field Altar

A small table, a censer, incense, two hand-held bells, rattles, or tambourines, a bowl of barley, a bowl of water with a straw or leafy spurge, a myrtle or green leafy crown, a crown of wheat or barley with decorative ribbons (see chapter 18), and two cups or chalices of water.

Preparation

Prior to the rite, the area of earth to be blessed should be weeded, turned over once, and raked flat. You may also prepare soil in a large pot (see chapter 19). If a large area is to be used, participants may want to wear clothes suitable for gardening. The draping *himation* (chapter 18, "himation") may be used for the dramatic portions of the rite. The rite can be followed with a potluck feast.

Staging

Adjacent to the altar are a plow, a pickax, or some other tool with which to "plow" the soil, and shovels or trowels with which participants can turn the soil over.

The Rites of Proerosia
I. Welcome

All form a circle in the field, or around the area to be planted. Light incense. **Priestesses of Demeter** and **Hecate** ring hand bells or shake rattles or tambourines three times.

Priestess of Hecate:
> Welcome to the rites of Proerosia!
> We are here to prepare the sacred field,
> To bless the Earth in the name of Holy Demeter,
> And to learn the arts of cultivation through Triptolemos.
> Zeus Epakrios we will also invoke,
> Bringer of thunder and rain from on high,
> That He may bless the coming season.
>
> When the soil is prepared, and in its time the seed planted,
> Then the fertile Mother will bring forward Her green fields
>   once again,
> As the Maiden, child of Holy Demeter and Blessed Zeus,
> Lifts Her face to the shining Sun.

II. Chant for the Lady of Life

Priestesses Panagia/All [Chant or sing]:
> O Holy Mother we honor Thee,
> Thy power and Thy mystery.
> O Lady of Life, of fruit and seed,
> All reverence and praise to Thy beauty.

III. Invocation of Demeter

Priestess of Demeter:
> Demeter Panagia,
> Pure and Holy Mother of Creation,
> Goddess of the Blessed Seed and of the Great Mysteries,
> We call to You!
>
> Beloved Mother of the Earth, fertile and full of power,
> With reverence we ask for Your blessing on this holy day.
> O Verdant and Fruitful One,
> Spin out Your magic from the richness of the Earth.
> And in this new planting season,
> Let the seedlings rise young and green.
> Sustain them until the flowering, and from flowering
> To the golden fruit of harvesttime.
> O Mother of Life,
> Come, and bless our labors here.

Priestesses Panagia:
> So be it.

Priestess of Demeter: The Priestess of Demeter then takes the bowl of barley and blesses the earth in the name of Demeter, asking that the sacred field and
surrounding countryside grow verdant and fruitful. She then scatters barley as an
offering and passes the bowl to others, so that they may offer blessings.

Priestesses Panagia/All: All bless the earth by scattering a little barley
and stating their blessing.

IV. Invocation of Zeus

Hierophant:
> Hail Zeus Epakrios!
> Great Father of the thundering skies,
> Let Your blessed rains flow
> Upon the Mother's fertile body.
> May the powers of the infinite sky
> Bring blessings to Earth.
>
> O Benevolent One,
> Call Your fire unto the ethers,
> And gather the forces of the darkening clouds.
> Let fall both potent and gentle rains upon the land,
> Blessing the Mother and Maiden
> Once again.
> So be it.

The priest takes the bowl of water and blesses the earth by scattering water
with the spurge and stating a short blessing for rain. The bowl is passed to others and all offer the same kind of blessing.

V. Invocation of Triptolemos

Priest of Triptolemos:
> Hail Triptolemos, son of Eleusis,
> Treasured God of plowing and sowing.
> Beloved of all farmers and of all those who work the land,
> We call to You.
>
> Honorable servant of the Great Mother,
> Today we remember how You were first crowned,
> How the wisdom to plant the seed and bring it to harvest
> Was given to You by Holy Demeter.

O chosen One,
Come and bless our plowing today,
And all that we will soon plant.

VI. Instructions of Triptolemos

Priestess of Hecate:
We remember
The crowning of Triptolemos . . .

Priestess of Demeter: The Priestess reenacts the ritual crowning of Triptolemos. First, she takes the crown of wheat in her hands and silently invokes Demeter, before placing the crown on her own head. She then picks up the myrtle (or green leafy) crown and faces the Priest of Triptolemos.

Triptolemos,
Child of Baubo and Dysaules,
Wise son of a noble family,
Impart to all, the arts of planting and cultivation.
Give to the people of Earth
The knowledge of agriculture.

Teach them the wisdom of right timing
And remind them to honor the land.
Show them the benefits of a loving approach
To the arts of cultivation.
Reveal to them that within the patterns of cultivation
Are lessons for living
A just, honorable, and successful life.

Come Triptolemos,
I give you this knowledge
And send you in my winged chariot of gold
With its bridled serpents,
So that you may carry this charge
To the people of the world.
Do you accept this charge?

Priest of Triptolemos:
Yes Panagia, with honor, I do.

Priestess of Demeter: She then crowns him with myrtle while speaking the following words:

Then this crown is laid upon Your brow.
It is an emblem of Your ministry;
A sign of Your art and Your wisdom.
Teach all the manner in which
To raise food from the body of the Earth,
For in this resides the art of living also.

The Priestess of Demeter recedes into the background, as the Priest of Triptolemos pauses, and then steps forward to speak.

Priest of Triptolemos:

The Great Mother has imparted to me
The wisdom inherent in seed and soil.
She has taught me of life and death;
That the spark of new life
Feeds from the remnants of yesterday.
Nothing is lost, and death
Is never an ending in the cycles of creation,
For decaying leaves feed the roots
Of both the great oak and the sweet narcissus.

At the beginning of each season,
Pray to Holy Demeter for the fertility of the land,
And to Zeus to bring the rains.
Plant the seed, and to this new life
Bring the blessings of Persephone's journey.
These are a passionate and tender love for the work you do,
Generosity of spirit, and mindful caretaking.

Priestesses Panagia:

As the young green Korai sprout and grow,
Nourish them with sacred prayer,
For the grain is holy
And grows from the body of the Great Mother.

Priest of Triptolemos:

As the season of life moves forward,
You must weed the sacred land.
For weeds steal fertility and moisture from the growing
    Korai.
Remove what you do not want from the cycle of creation.

But always with compassion,
And in so doing, you strengthen the crop for all.

Priestesses Panagia:
As the lush green of Anthesterion springs forward,
Rejoice and celebrate the good harvest to come!
When the green Korai flowers and turns gold,
Do not mourn the loss of the Maiden,
But be content that the field has grown to maturity,
And rejoice with the Harvest Mother in the good that has been
    created.

Priest of Triptolemos:
When Hecate wields Her sickle at the harvest,
It will appear that the field has become barren,
And that in the fallow is death.
But do not grieve overlong, for death is not an end,
But a part of the song of eternity.
And so, be at peace.
Know that all that has gone before
Creates the new life that will come again.

VII. Ritual Plowing

[The Priest of Triptolemos picks up the plowing tool and says]:
It is time for the thrice-fold plowing.
I will plow, seeing the seed of the future crop
Rise green from the earth,
Seeing the roots descend into Her body;
Seeing even unto the golden harvest.

He digs three long furrows in the field.

Priestesses Panagia/All [Chanting/singing repeatedly as the Priest of
Triptolemos plows]:

Roots journey deep	*(Roots jour-ney deep)*
As the grain rises,	*(As the grain ri-ses,)*
Green the Korai	*(Green the Kor-eye)*
As the Maiden arises	*(As the Mai-den a-ri-ses.)*

Each participant then plows the field once across while the above chant continues. When all have plowed once, it is time to turn the field over. The field is

turned over with shovels and raked over at the end. When finished, all circle in/around the field.

VIII. Closing Blessing

The Priestess of Demeter takes her cup of water from the altar. The Hierophant takes his cup of water from the altar. The Priestess of Demeter walks to the center of the sacred field. She raises her arm, beckoning the Hierophant to join her. He enters and faces her. Holding their cups, the forearms of each extend toward the other, then cross. Their hands are comfortably positioned so that they will easily be able to pour out the contents of the cups onto the earth. They are focused on each other's eyes.

Hierophant: The Hierophant raises his arm that is not holding the water up to the sky. He draws the energy of the sky downward, through his hand and arm, with a breath. Then, as he says the word "Flow," he pours his water onto the earth. All the time, his gaze is not removed from the eyes of the Priestess of Demeter.

Priestess of Demeter: She then extends her hand that is not holding the cup downward toward the earth. She draws the energy of the earth upward, with a breath. Then, as she says the word "Conceive," she pours the water onto the earth. All the time, her gaze is not removed from the eyes of the Hierophant.

Hierophant and Priestess of Demeter: They touch their empty cups, release their gaze, and face the participants, saying together:
> The field has been prepared, consecrated, and
> > blessed.
> In the names of Demeter and Zeus,
> May all come to fruition.
> So be it.

Priestesses Panagia/All:
> So be it!

The Priest and Priestess exit the center of the consecrated space. They place their empty cups on the altar and then rejoin the circle.

Priestesses Panagia/All [Chanting or singing in melody several times, in circle)]:
> Demeter, Mother of the grain,
> Come birth the Maiden once again!
> And the Wheel turns 'round.
> The Wheel turns 'round.

Priestesses Panagia/All:
> These are the Rites of Proerosia.
> This temple rite complete,
> In grace and in joy,
> May Her blessings proceed unto all!
> To the feast!

THE STENIA FESTIVAL—OCTOBER 15TH

Seasonal themes

With the powers of humor, the garments of the Crone fall away from the Mother as her fertile forces are reawakened. Through Baubo, sacred sexuality and humor are celebrated with rites of invigoration. This is the opening festival of the Thesmophoria holy days. At its completion, the old year is ended.

Transcendent themes

The sacred aspects of sexuality, and the renewing powers of humor are part of the creative process of life, not purely of its physical reproduction, but of its joy. Personal identification with Earth, and the creative powers of the Goddess.

Stenia *(Ste'-nee-ah)* began the five consecutive days of the Thesmophorian holidays (Stenia, Arkichronia, Thesmophoria Proper, Nestia, and Kalligenia). It took place, in the old Greek calendar, on Pyanopsion 9, four days after the Proerosia. Stenia is a bawdy and energetic festival, in contrast with the highly magical, stately, and reverent themes of the other Thesmophorian holidays.

For convenience, I have celebrated Stenia and Arkichronia (the following festival) on one weekend, and the rest of the Thesmophorian holidays on the following weekend. Originally, all of the Thesmophorian holidays were conducted and celebrated by women only. In practice, I have experienced Stenia and Arkichronia as women's holy days, and Thesmophoria, Nestia, and Kalligenia as celebrations for both women and men.

Stenia celebrates the power of humor to transform loss, sadness, and infertility. It uses sexual humor and rites of fertility to bring a return of fecundity. It celebrates the power of the Great Mother to gestate and give birth to life. There are personal identifications with both Baubo and Demeter during the rite.

Stenia included sexual humor, rites of invigoration, wine, and the making of pastry representations of parts of the body, such as breasts, pudenda, etc. During Thesmophoria, there was also a rite called the Penalty. I have included an interpretation of these ceremonies in this re-creation of Stenia. Another traditional rite included is the Rite of the Morotton, a rite similar to an African women's fertility rite in which the body is gently paddled with an image of the Goddess to increase fertility. To this I have made one change. The Morotton or paddle, was traditionally made of woven bark. Here, the slightly cupped palms of the hands are used instead, in an alternating tapping motion on the back, reminiscent of a motion in Japanese massage.

At this time, the fields and meadows are dormant. The Holy Daughter has not yet returned. The Barren Mother has no will to make the land fertile again. By the bawdy, sensual, and humorous powers of Baubo, fertility begins to return to the Mother. Humor is restorative, and the creative and invigorating rites of the women at Stenia are in alignment with the mythic needs of the season.

Baubo is needed to lighten Demeter's heart as the Mother waits for her Daughter's return. Through the Rites of Stenia, Demeter's heart is prepared for the Maiden's restoration. This will come during one of the later Thesmophorian festivals. Through the renewed fertility of Earth, and the fall rains, the land will become green again. The Wheel will turn, and the cycle of creation will move from the fallow time toward birth and flowering.

Ritual Outline

I. Preritual Activities
II. Invocation to Hestia
III. Invocation to Demeter
IV. Invocation to Baubo
V. Myth of Stenia
VI. Chant for Stenia
VII. Baubo's Delight; the Penalty Game
VIII. The Mother is Cheered
IX. Honoring Dionysus
X. Rites of Invigoration
XI. Earth Mother Blessing

Clergy

Priestess of Demeter
Hierophantid of Demeter
Priestess of Hecate
Priestess of Baubo
Priestess of Hestia
Priestesses Panagia
A Priestess Panagia

The Main Altar

A side altar against a wall, an icon or image of Demeter draped with a small black veil or scarf, two red taper candles (one on either side of the icon), a white votive candle (in front of it), a vase of flowers, a small bowl of barley, a censor, incense, and a small green palm fan or other fan, a pomegranate (or red apple), an oil lamp or candle for Hestia, another votive candle for Baubo, two bowls or baskets, one for the pomegranates or red apples and the other for flower petals that the participants will bring.

The Altar of Baubo

A large cloth is laid in the center of the room. There are percussion instruments (rattles, drums, etc.) laid out around the edge of the cloth. In the center is a large bowl of earth, in the center of which is set the sculpted image of Baubo, or the image of some other wide-hipped fertility Goddess (see chapter 18, "Baubo"). There are candles set into the earth around the Baubo statue, at the bowl's edges. A wine glass or chalice and a bottle of wine or grape juice are set on the table. You will be making "bawdy" marzipan candies or "bawdy" cookies. (See recipes in Appendix 1 for Stenia candies and pastries). Have the dough for the cookies, or the paste for the marzipan, and the edible decorations ready in bowls and set around the bowl of earth. Have the cookie sheet (or sheets) ready for your creations.

The Blessing Areas

These three areas are for the rites of invigoration. For the Earth Mother Blessing, you will need an area with two seats, facing each other. Over the seat for the participant is laid a gold or yellow cloth. There is a small bowl of earth and a bottle of anointing oil on or below the priestess' chair, ready for her to use. For the Rite of the Morotton you will need a bench or couch on which the priestess and the participant can sit. For the third, the Rain Blessing, you will need an area of the room in which the priestess and participant can stand. Place a bowl of water and a spurge here (see chapter 18, "spurge").

Preparation

Each participant brings flower petals, a pomegranate (or a red apple), something for the potluck feast, and a lewd, but not in-completely-poor-taste, joke. If pillows are not available at the ritual location, each woman should bring a pillow for the resting portion prior to the guided visioning at the end of the ritual. Clergy and participants wear festive, comfortable clothing. You may consider wearing full Greek costume, or simply add the draping himation (see chapter 18).

THE FESTIVAL OF STENIA

I. Preritual

When they arrive, participants place their pomegranates and their flower petals in the baskets/bowls provided on the altar. The Stenia pastries or candies are then made in a relaxed manner. These edible effigies are decorated with nuts, chocolate, and dried fruit. Try some instrumental music in the background while you create your masterpieces! The candies can be eaten at the end of the feast, or the cookies baked and then eaten.

All circle in the center of the room, around the Baubo altar. The incense is lit. All begin a humming, "MMM," chant.

Hierophantid of Demeter: She takes up the incense and fan. Moving in a clockwise direction, she censes the participants.

Priestesses Panagia/All [Chanting or singing]:
> O Holy Mother we honor Thee,
> Thy power and Thy mystery.
> O Lady of Life, of fruit and seed,
> All reverence and praise to Thy beauty.

II. Invocation of Hestia

Priestess of Hestia [At the main altar]:
> We call Hestia,
> Goddess of hearth and temple fire,
> Of the spiritual center of our world,

And of all sacred places.
Hestia, beloved Goddess of the spiritual flame,
Come, and enter this temple.
Make all that is here holy and sacred in Your name.
Bring to us the peace and sureness
Of that place which is home and hearth.
Bring Your purity and beauty to us
As we honor You,
Who are the center of the spiritual flame.
So be it.

She lights the Hestia lamp or candle, raises it up, and says:
Hail Hestia!

Priestesses Panagia/All:
Hail Hestia!

III. Invocation of Demeter
Priestess of Demeter [At the main altar]:
Holy Demeter,
Great Mother of the land,
Goddess of wealth, plenty, and regeneration,
Of all the world's beauty and of the Spirit's
     Mysteries,
We call to You!

Demeter Melaina,
Dark are You in Your sorrows,
For You await the day when the Sun will shine
Upon the face of Your beloved Daughter.

Panagia,
In these, Your Holy Women's Rites,
And through the powers of Baubo,
May Your heart be lightened.
May You rise in Your ecstasy
And awaken to Your fertile powers once again!
Hail Demeter!

The Priestess of Demeter lights the candle in front of Demeter icon.

Priestesses Panagia/All:
> Hail Demeter!

IV. Invocation of Baubo

Priestess of Baubo [At the main altar]:
> Baubo, gentle and kindhearted,
> You have the power to bring laughter to the face of
>   sorrow.
> You have known the sensual and joyful ways
> Of the sacred couch,
> And perhaps also of field and sandy shore.
>
> Your love, joy, and sexuality are simple and unfettered.
> With licentious and joyful dances,
> You bring laughter to the heart of Melaina.
>
> And so, Holy One,
> We ask that You dance and jest with us tonight!
> Hail Baubo!

The Priestess lights the Baubo candle.

Priestesses Panagia/All:
> Hail Baubo!

V. Myth of Stenia

Priestess of Hecate:
> The fields and meadows lie dormant,
> So lies the end of summer's fate.
> The Mother is barren and sad,
> For the Holy Daughter has not yet returned from Tartarus.
>
> Below, Persephone lives with the God of Death,
> The God and Goddess of the Underworld
> Reigning, united in loving Sacred Union.
> The seed grain is also below,
> Stored by Persephone in the regenerative depths.

Priestesses Panagia:
> As Demeter yearns for the Maiden's return,
> Baubo comes to lighten Her heart,

Bringing the Rites of Invigoration.
It is through these rites and those of bawdy humor,
That the Mother's powers will awake.
Prepared for the rains of Zeus and the return of the Maiden,
The Mother will become verdant once again.

VI. Chant for Stenia

Priestesses Panagia: The Priestesses Panagia light the candles that are set into the earth around the Baubo statue saying "Hail Baubo," at each lighting. All join hands and chant the following, shifting their weight from side to side, with the rhythm of the chant.

I come to the dance,
Magic set us free.
I Come to the dance,
Her fire in me!

VII. Baubo's Delight: The Penalty Game

Priestess of Demeter: The Priestess asks each woman to take a pomegranate (or apple) from the bowl. Then participants stand in a circle around the Baubo altar, placing their pieces of fruit on the ground. This creates a circle of pomegranates around the altar. The Priestess removes one pomegranate from the circle. She takes the bowl of flower petals and fills in the area of the missing pomegranate with petals. The petals should cover a partial outline of the circle. This line represents the "penalty area."

Priestess Panagia: The Priestess explains the game. After circling with the following chant, the participant who stands in front of the flower petals, will pay the penalty. All join hands and move in a circle, clockwise, rhythmically chanting:

Baubo's great delight!   (*Bau-bos great de-light!*)
Laughter in the night!   (*Laugh-ter in the night!*)
How She breaks the rules!   (*How She breaks the rules!*)
Skirts fly in the wind!   (*Skirts fly in the wind!*)
Pretend! . . .   (*Pre-tend! . . .*)
To show! . . .   (*To show! . . .*)
The Queen's jewels!   (*The Queen's jewels!*)

At the word *"jewels,"* all stop. Whoever is standing in front of the flower petals must pay the penalty. She must act the part of Baubo by telling a lewd joke, lifting her skirt, or by some other bawdy words or actions. When the fun and silliness die down a bit, the game repeats itself, until all get a chance (or two).

VIII. The Mother Is Cheered

Priestess of Baubo: Standing at the main altar the Priestess of Baubo prepares to light the red taper candles on either side of the Demeter icon. She reverently removes the black veil from the Demeter icon and says:

> The Mother is cheered.
> Her heart has been blessed
> By the joys of Baubo!

She lights the red taper candles and says:

> Awake . . . Awake again.

IX. Honoring Dionysus

Priestess of Hecate: She instructs the participants to be seated around the Baubo altar. She goes to the main altar where she retrieves the chalice and the bottle of wine or grape juice. She then takes her seat in the circle and says:

> Now we take up the chalice of wine,
> And honor another.
> We give thanks to Dionysus,
> The God of the Vine.
> His warming draught
> Slakes the thirst, yet lends fire to the spirit!
> Just as the Mother's seed brings forth ripe fruit,
> So do the roots of the vine bring forth the vintage.
> Let us praise the Lord of woodland revels
> As we say: Hail Dionysus!

Priestesses Panagia/All:

> Hail Dionysus!

The chalice is passed around, and around again, if needed.

X. The Rites of Invigoration

Priestess of Demeter: She explains the Rites of Invigoration. There are three rites. First, the participants will go to the area set up for the Earth Blessing from the Priestess of Hecate. Then they will be guided to the next area, for the Rite of the Morotton with the Priestess of Baubo. Next, they will be guided to the area set up for the Rain Blessing with the Hierophantid of Demeter.

Hierophantid of Demeter:

> Now, with Baubo's gifts,
> Demeter's fertile powers begin to flow.

Rising like fragrant incense,
Her powers begin to move across the land.
We rise on the wings of Her heart.
She is red poppies, red pomegranates, and red roses,
And so we sing of Her Mysteries . . .

Priestesses Panagia/All [Singing, or chanting voice]:

On fiery golden wings,	*(On fie-ry gol-den wings,)*
Scarlet alchemy risen.	*(Scar-let al-che-my ri-sen.)*
Red the rose of Her heart,	*(Red the rose of Her heart,)*
And the Womb of Creation.	*(And the Womb of Cre-a-tion.)*

Priestess Panagia:
She awakes. At one with Her,
We will perform the Rites of Invigoration.
The Rites of the Morotton, and those of Earth and Rain.
Each participant begins with the Priestess of Hecate,
Who stands by the golden chair.
When you have completed the three rites,
Be seated or recline, as you wish,
In silence, and feel Her awakened powers.

Priestess of Hecate, Priestess of Baubo, and Hierophantid take their positions.
You may choose to play a soft, slow drumming tape to add a hypnotic mood.
You may also wish to lower the lighting in the room. One by one, participants
experience the three blessings.

XI. Earth Mother Blessing

The participant is seated on the golden chair, facing the Priestess of Hecate, who
is also seated. The participant is asked to hold a small bowl of earth. She is
then asked to close her eyes and repeat the following lines, one by one, after
the Priestess.

Priestess of Hecate:
Holy Mother,
You who birth all of life,
I am Thee.
I am the rich fertile plains,
The small stones,
And the great mountains.
I am the curling vines and the blessed trees.
I am Goddess,
Ready to receive the seed

And bring forth fruit.
I am the All-Holy One,
And I await the rain.

The participant is next guided to walk to the area reserved for the Rite of the
Morotton.

XII. Rite of the Morotton

Priestess of Baubo: The participant sits on the bench or couch, with her
back to the Priestess of Baubo. The participant is instructed to close her eyes.
With the slightly cupped palms of her hands, the priestess gives a gentle but
invigorating massage over the back of the participant. She alternates hands,
using a tapping rhythmic motion. At the same time that this action is being performed, she says the following words, slowly:

The blood flows,
The heart is cheered;
Baubo warms the heart of the Earth.
Cast the old year aside!
The Sacred Field is prepared.
O Fertile Mother,
We bow to You!
Hail!

Participant is guided to stand and go to the next station.

XIII. Rain Blessing

Hierophantid of Demeter: The participant stands facing the Hierophantid
of Demeter. She is instructed to close her eyes. The Priestess dips the spurge into
the bowl of water and gently sprinkles the participant on both front and back
while saying the following words:

In the warmth of the new year, gentle rains
Will fall upon Your Holy body.
The planted seed will become the green Korai,
And, with the rains,
The fields and meadows will become verdant once again.
All reverence and praise to the Holy Mother!
Hail!

The Priestess instructs the participant to sit or recline, and wait for all to finish
the ceremony.

XIV. Guided Visioning

Priestess of Demeter: The participants are instructed to stand in a circle around the Baubo altar, eyes closed. The soft drumming music in the background continues. All join hands. The Priestess of Demeter calls for a visioning of the coming year, of a world blessed by the abundance of the Great Mother. All are invited to give their blessings. Then the Priestess guides the following vision:

Here is the Wheel of the Goddess.
The Wheel has turned and the Mother is awake.
Her powers call out for the seed and the rain,
And You are She.
And you are awake.
You yoke Your chariot to bridled (serpents),[1]
And round Your throne You whirl and howl in ecstasy!

Come, Blessed and Pure One,
(May You become) laden with the fruits of (the harvest),
As the fertile body of the world flourishes,
Lush and green,
As all manner of fruits ripen in the blessed fields
And on Your generous trees,
O beautiful Mother!
May the people of the Earth live in joy and plenty!
Bring peace . . . prosperity, and health that governs all[2]
As You rise in power once again!
So be it. Hail Panagia!

Priestesses Panagia/All:
Hail Panagia!

The Priestess of Demeter then guides the participants to raise a scream of ecstasy, as joined hands are also raised. All are then guided to ground the energy, using the breath. All lay on the floor. Breathe in, exhale, and, on the exhale, release energies and relax deeply into the earth below you.

XV. Closing Words

Priestess Panagia guides all to stand in a circle and directs participants to repeat each line:

Here is Her wisdom,
For She is within

---

[1]   This and the three lines that follow are from *The Orphic Hymns*, Apostolos Athanassakis, trans. (Atlanta, GA: Scholoars Press, 1988), p. 57. Reprinted by permission of Scholars Press.
[2]   This line is from *The Orphic Hymns*, p. 57. Reprinted by permission of Scholars Press.

And without,
In beauty
And honor,
Hail!

Priestesses Panagia/All:
These are the Rites of Stenia!
This temple rite complete,
In grace and in joy,
May Her blessings proceed unto all!
To the feast!

THE RITES OF ARKICHRONIA—OCTOBER 16TH

Seasonal themes
Time out of time, the day between the old and the new year. With fertility magic, the seed grain is mixed with the remnants of prior offerings to Persephone and Plouton. Talismans are made from the mixture, and will be used to bless the seed and bring the success of future harvests.

Transcendent themes
There is a magic that is born from the union of life and death, of past and present. Allowing the highest influences to combine with your ideas and goals. Know that creativity has been influenced, even fed, by the barren times. Realizing the effects of the past on the present.

The Rites of Arkichronia are celebrated on the second day of the Thesmophoria complex of holidays. They may be celebrated the day after Stenia, as part of a Saturday-Sunday weekend, the fertile energies of Stenia influencing the creation of fertility talismans. The talismans are composed of two parts: the remnants of prior offerings to the God and Goddess of the Underworld, and a portion of the seed grain for the next planting.

Less is known about this festival day (Pyanopsion 10), than about any of the other Demetrian holidays. Fertility talismans were made during the Thesmophoria holidays, although it is not known with certainty on which day. There is no ancient name specifically given to the second day of the Thesmophoria. I have chosen

Arkichronia as the name for this day after a modern custom of that name celebrated by Greek farmers on the island of Rhodes. On September 1st, the farmers make a fertility talisman to bless their planting. Into a bag they place stalks of wheat from the past harvest, walnuts, an onion, garlic, a rose, millet, cotton seeds, and grapes. The bag is censed, hidden, and brought out several months later. It is then kept to be used at the next sowing. In a different version of the ceremony, a part of the seed is simply kept in a church for forty days prior to planting.

The making of fertility talismans by drawing up the contents of the *megara* (a sacred pit or chamber containing the remnants of earlier offerings) was definitely an important part of the Thesmophoria holidays. This sacred activity has been placed on this day because it works, in practical terms. Although some authors consider that the making of the talismans may have been a part of the Thesmophoria Proper itself, it is not a certainty. The making of the talismans on this day leaves the rite of Thesmophoria Proper, concerned with Demeter Thesmophoros, as a celebration exclusively of the Goddess' sacred laws.

When you perform this ritual, you are entering into a continuous cycle of connected holidays for which some special preparation is needed. For the rite, you will need a megara (a sacred pit or chamber). This is a place from which you will draw up some of the talisman contents. An indoor megara altar may be used, or an outdoor megara, a covered pit lined with brick will do as well. In my interpretation of this section of the Thesmophoria holidays, the megara contains remnants of the *hiera* (the holy objects.) (For more detailed information on the megara and the hiera, please read the introductory paragraphs to the Greater Mysteries, pp. 220–221).

Through Brumfield, we learn of a scholion to Lucian's *Dialogues of the Courtesans* that describes bringing remnants of sacrificed pigs, pine, and wheat cakes up from the megara. It tells of the women mixing the megara remains with the planting seed in order to bring the blessings of a good harvest.[3]

In the ceremonies contained in this book, the offerings are placed into the megara during the Greater Mysteries, several weeks earlier. The sacred drama of the Greater Mysteries (see chapter 15) provides the mythic and practical reasons for these offerings. The offerings were gifts given to Persephone and Plouton at a mythic time

---

[3]   Allaire Chandor Brumfield, *The Attic Festivals of Demeter and their Relation to the Agricultural Year* (Salem, NH: Arno Press, 1981), pp. 73–74; excerpt from H. Rabe, *Scholia in Lucianum* (Leipzig: n. p., 1906).

of reconciliation. Remnants of the offerings are brought up during Arkichronia as a gift from Persephone and Plouton. The seed grain for the next planting is also brought up from its storage area. The offering remnants and the seed grain are mixed together to create fertility talismans. The passionate energies of the God and Goddess of the Underworld infuse Demeter's seed with additional power. Through magic, the powers of the land of life and death are combined for our use.

If you have not celebrated the Greater Mysteries, you will need to create the megara contents (the hiera) prior to enacting Arkichronia. For these contents, use snake effigies (see chapter 18), a pine branch or pine needles and a few small pine cones (if available), a sheaf of wheat or a small loaf of well-dried bread (use the oven on low for several hours), myrtle, two red roses, a pomegranate or red apple, and a little bit of saffron-and-rose scented oil that you can sprinkle over all (see chapter 18). Place these onto a large purple cloth, then tie it up like a bag. Cense the bag and wrap it in black fabric. Set the black parcel in a place that you identify as the megara (see chapter 18, "megara," and also "megara" listing in the Glossary).

If you need to set up the hiera, do so as a separate preparatory rite ahead of time. I suggest that you state the meanings of these items as you place them onto the purple cloth, using the words of the Hierophant from the Greater Mysteries (see chapter 15, "The Rite of the Cista Mystica"). When you are done, place the wrapped hiera into a small covered basket, and then place the basket under the megara altar.

Ritual Outline

I.   Preritual
II.   The Welcome
III.   Procession to the Megara
IV.   Entering the Precinct of the Cavern
V.   Invocation to Hestia
VI.   Myth of Arkichronia
VII.   Invocation to Persephone
VIII   Unsealing the Megara
IX.   Creating the Fertility Talismans
X.   Closing

Clergy

Priestess of Demeter
Priestess of Persephone
Priestess of Hecate
Hierophantid of Demeter

Priestess of Hestia
Priestesses Panagia

For the Procession

A lidded basket lined with plastic, a censer, and a hand bell. This basket will receive the contents of the megara.

The Precinct of the Cavern

This mythic area includes a pathway to the cavern. It is created by marking a doorway through which priestesses and participants will pass (such as two plaster columns, two stacks of bricks, or two small tables). One side of this doorway is used for a water blessing and has a lustration bowl. The other side of the doorway will hold the censer, after all have walked into the precinct. Four candles mark the corners of the cavern precinct. The precinct includes the pathway to the cavern and the indoor megara altar (or the outdoor megara). Unfortunately, our megara cannot be in a cave, as it traditionally was. Alas, so few caves are readily available!

The Megara Altar

The megara altar is either an altar set up indoors, or is created atop an outdoor megara pit. This is symbolically within the Ploutonian cavern and leads to the Underworld. If you are not using an outdoor megara, then use a small table covered with black and/or purple cloth. Beneath it, place the covered basket that contains the hiera. You may want to cover all of this with an extra black cloth.

Set up a small shrine on the megara altar. This may include an oil lamp or candle for Hestia, an image of Hecate or her symbol (such as a sickle), images of snakes, and a dish of white flower petals. Have matches available. Lay rattles around the megara. During the ritual, the megara will be opened, and the hiera remnants retrieved and taken to a sorting area.

The Sorting Area

Here, the megara contents are sorted and refined. You can use a table for this, or simply a sheet laid out on the ground. Have scissors and knives available. The small bowls that the women will bring are set in this area. Wear gloves, particularly if your megara is outdoors. The remains, after being sorted and refined, are crushed or cut into small pieces. Later they will be mixed in a larger bowl with fresh rose petals.

The Altar for Demeter and Persephone

This altar is used for the ritual mixing of the contents of the megara with the seed. Here, the talismans will be made. The altar holds images of Persephone and Demeter. (These can be framed pictures, clay or plasticene [4] statues, or simply sheaves of grain tied with fresh or dried flowers.) There is a bowl of pomegranates (or red apples). There is an urn or vase of the seed grain to be used for planting (following the Thesmophoria holidays). The urn of seed is covered with a cloth, which is then tied. This is hidden in another room, or placed a distance away from the megara.

The altar also contains 8-inch circles of green cloth with which to make the talismans, and 10-inch lengths of green ribbon with which to tie them. There is also a bowl of fresh rose petals. The fertility talismans will be given as gifts at the end of Kalligenia, the last celebration in the Thesmophoria complex of holidays. The primary purpose of the talismans is to bring a good harvest. Their contents will be sprinkled over the field after planting, and/or mixed with the rest of the seed before planting. There can be additional uses for the talismans, including personal magical rites for prosperity, fertility, and abundance.

Preparation

Each participant brings a rattle, food for the feast, and a small bowl. The Priestesses of Demeter and Persephone bring offerings of bread and fruit for the two Goddesses. All wear clothing that is festive but comfortable. The precinct, altar, and work areas are prepared. Items are made ready for the procession.

Staging

Create your cavern entrance, megara, sorting area, and altar. If you have performed the Skira festival during the prior June, the Priestess of Gaea takes the urn of seed from its storage area prior to this rite. She buries the prayers that were stored with it and hides the urn in the place from which it will be taken for this rite. If you have not performed the Skira festival, create an urn of seed by purchasing whole wheat sold at a health food store for sprouting purposes, or procure your grain by mail from a farming supply company and place it inside a vase.

THE RITES OF ARKICHRONIA
I. Preritual

The four candles are lit at the four corners of the cavern precinct, enclosing both the megara and the cavern entrance. Outdoor candles need glass chimneys or other protection so that the flames will not go out in the breeze. The Priestess of Demeter lights the incense and holds the censer, the Priestess of Hecate holds the bell, and the Priestess of Persephone carries the basket lined with cloth. The Priestess of Demeter instructs all to form a circle.

---

[4]   Plasticene is a plastic-based product available in art stores. It looks and works like clay, but bakes in your home oven.

II. Welcome

Priestess of Hecate [Rings bell three times]:
> All welcome to the Rites of Arkichronia!
> The Wheel turns.
> Through the powers of Baubo,
> The Mother is awake in Her ecstasy.
> She is prepared for the return of the Maiden.
> Today the Holy Daughter offers Her fertile gifts
>   from below.
> She also sends up the seed grain,
> Which is the herald of Her return.
>
> Together, the gifts of Demeter, Persephone, and Plouton,
> Will be conjoined in the enchanted creation
> Of the fertility talismans.
> With the power of the talismans,
> The fields will be blessed at the planting,
> As will our city,
> With plenty, abundance, and well-being.
> So be it.

III. Procession to the Megara

Participants and clergy proceed to the megara. The Priestess of Demeter goes first, carrying the smoking censer. The Priestess of Persephone is next, balancing the lidded basket on her head using both hands. Clergy and participants follow.

Priestesses Panagia/All [Chanting as they walk]:
> We retrieve from the Lands of Death,
> Fertile gifts that will feed Life.

All proceed to the precinct of the cavern.

IV. Entering the Precinct of the Cavern

The Priestess of Demeter sets the censer down onto one of the cavern entrance pillars. The Priestess of Hecate moves to the other pillar to perform the water purification. The Priestess of Persephone is the first to be anointed. She then enters, placing the basket next to the megara.

Priestess of Hecate: The Priestess places her fingers in the water, and then on the center forehead of each participant, saying:
> She dwells within.

All clerics and participants are anointed in the same way they. They enter the precinct. The Priestess of Persephone guides all to stand around the megara.

V. Invocation of Hestia

Priestess of Hestia [Facing the megara, she invokes Hestia]:
> We call Hestia,
> Goddess of hearth and temple fire,
> Of the spiritual center of our world,
> And of all sacred places.
> Hestia, beloved Goddess of the spiritual flame,
> Come, and enter this temple.
> Make all that is here holy and sacred in your name.
> Bring to us the peace and sureness
> Of that place which is home and hearth.
> Bring Your purity and beauty to us
> As we honor You,
> Who are the center of the spiritual flame.
> So be it.

The Priestess of Hestia lights the lamp or candle. She picks it up and turns, to face the women. She raises it and says:
> Hail Hestia!

Priestesses Panagia/All:
> Hail Hestia!

VI. Myth of Arkichronia
Priestess of Demeter:
> Today we bring up from the Megara,
> Potent gifts of magic.
> From the Tartarion Palace of Persephone and Plouton,
> We receive those gifts which have been empowered
> By the deep magic of the Sacred Lovers.
> With Plouton's blessing,
> Persephone offers these gifts to us
> As She prepares to ascend;
> To return to Earth and to Holy Demeter.
> Now listen to the words of the Hierophantid,
> As she tells us of the gifts from the Underworld.

Hierophantid of Demeter:
> During the time of the Greater Mysteries,
> The gifts to the Sacred Couple were many.
> Pine was given to Persephone and Plouton by
>   Dionysus,
> For wildness and joy.
> Myrtle and roses were given by Aphrodite, for sacred love.
> Hecate anointed and blessed them with a sweet-scented oil.
> Gaea offered Her serpent, to teach of primeval change.
> And the sacred grain, was given by Holy Demeter
> As She imparted Her blessings,
> And the powers of rebirth, to the lands below.
> Persephone added the pomegranate;
> The sign of the fertile Mother of Life,
> And of Rebirth in the Lands of Death.
> Listen as we invoke Persephone
> Before opening the Megara.

VII. Invocation of Persephone

Priestess of Persephone:
> Hail, Persephone, Queen of Tartarus and Elysium!
> Generous Lady who has brought light
> To the Realms of the Dead.
> Wedded to Death,
> Your presence has brought great joy to the King,
> And to all the souls of the Underworld.
> As the herald of Your return,
> You offer Your gifts to Earth.
> The seed grain, too, that you have kept stored,
> You now release.
>
> Persephone, it is Your fate
> To move from life to death, and back again,
> Balancing the powers of Above and Below.
> In beauty and compassion does the Queen
> Dispense light and joy in Elysium,
> And perfect justice in the shadowy realms of
>   Tartarus.
> And so we praise You, saying:
> Hail Persephone!

Priestesses Panagia/All:
> Hail Persephone!

Priestess of Demeter:
> We will journey below to touch the Underworld,
> Moving through the Megara,
> Down, down, down. . .
> Sinking into the soft darkness.
> We journey to Tartarus
> To receive the gifts of Persephone and Plouton.
> We will chant, and each in turn,
> Will place their hands upon the Megara,
> Making a connection to the powers below.

VIII. Unsealing the Megara

Priestesses of Hecate and Hestia: Remove the items on top of the Megara (if outdoors) and set them behind the cover. If the hiera are indoors, below the megara altar, they bring them forward so the small covered basket holding the black parcel can be reached.

Priestesses Panagia/All: Start a slow steady beat with the rattles (a low-toned drum is an option). They chant or sing, repeatedly.
> Journey deeply to Death's domain,
> Where the Lady of Tartarus reigns.

As the chanting goes on, each places hands on the megara or on the black cloth covering the basket of the hiera. After all have made a connection, it is time to open the megara. All participants pick up their rattles.

Hierophantid of Demeter:
> Grandmother Gaea,
> We honor You as we open Earth.

The Hierophantid sprinkles white flower petals around the megara opening.

Priestesses Panagia/All: Shake rattles and create hissing snake sounds.

Priestesses of Hestia and Hecate: The priestesses open and uncover the contents of the megara. The rattles and hissing sounds continue.

Hierophantid of Demeter:
> We enter the Underworld,
> To receive the gifts of Persephone and Plouton.
> She faces all and says:
> The Megara is open!

Priestesses Panagia/All: Surround the megara and shake rattles over the opening. One by one, each takes out a part of the megara contents, placing the objects into the basket brought by the Priestess of Persephone. Wear gloves, particularly if the contents have been underground. When done, close the megara.

Priestess of Persephone: Prepares to process out of the megara precinct by placing the basket on her head, supporting it with her hands. She leaves the area and proceeds to the sorting area. All follow.

Priestesses Panagia/All: Processing and chanting repeatedly.
> From their Underworld domain,
> Where the Sacred Lovers reign,
> We bear gifts . . .

Priestess of Persephone leads all to the sorting area. She pours the contents of the basket into the center of the area, saying:
> From the Land of Death will come Life!

All: All are seated or stand around the sorting area. The sorting and refining process begins. Each participant places a portion of the contents into a small bowl and works. The snake effigies and any pine cones are placed on Demeter and Persephone's altar. Any large stems, branches, or stalks are discarded or cut up. If the hiera have been underground since the Greater Mysteries, they will include bread offerings. Expect the unexpected and do this outside. Anyone may take up the following chant, on and off, as they work:
> Gifts from the Land of Death,
> Fertile, these gifts feed Life.

Priestess of Persephone: When the sorting is complete, the Priestess of Persephone pours red rose petals on top of the refined contents. Then she mixes them together. The mixture is put into a large bowl. She walks over to the Demeter-Persephone altar and pours the mix in a pile on the altar table, saying:
> Hierophantid of Demeter,
> Retrieve the seed!

IX. Creating the Fertility Talismans

Hierophantid of Demeter: She retrieves the hidden urn of seed, bringing it to the altar saying:
> I bring the seed grain from Tartarus.

Priestess of Demeter: She takes the cover off the urn, and removes the grain that is within it. She pours the seed into a separate pile on the altar, next to that of the megara contents.

Priestesses of Persephone and Demeter/All: Two participants at a time mix the megara contents and the seed together. As an example, the Priestesses of Demeter and Persephone may go first. They stand very close together, facing the altar. Together, they place their hands over the megara contents and seed, saying:

> In the names of Demeter and Persephone,
> May Death feed Life.

Then they begin mixing the two piles with both hands (consider using gloves). Two by two, the participants come to the altar saying,

> May Death feed Life.

Seed and megara contents are conjoined by envisioning the two elements blending in harmony. The mixing process continues until all have had a hand.

Priestess of Demeter: She puts the total mix back into the bowl. Then she takes up one of the small cloth circles and a ribbon. She makes a talisman by putting some of the mix onto a piece of cloth and tying it into a little bag. She then invites all to do the same. When the talismans are finished they are placed back into the bowl. The Priestess explains that they will be kept with her until they are dispensed at the end of the Kalligenia portion of the Thesmophoria holidays. At that time, they will be given out. They may be used as they are and a small amount of grain planted, or their contents may be mixed with larger portions of seed grain for planting. They may be used to bless land for raising other foods, or to bless a city in general. Priestesses may carry them throughout the city, to the far corners, where they may be opened and their contents placed to bring prosperity and joy.

> The Priestess then instructs all to surround the table and raise their hands to the altar. She asks them to repeat the following lines:

> We bless these gifts.
> May the love of the King and Queen of the
>   Underworld
> Be united with that of the Great Mother of Life,
> To bring abundance,
> To bring joy and renewal,
> And to bring well-tended compassion.
> May these blessings live in power,
> And magic,
> Wherever these gifts are used,
> In the names of Demeter and Persephone.
> So be it!

Then she instructs all to visualize clockwise-swirling energies first of gold, then green, and then silver light, traveling over and throughout the talismans. When she feels it is done, she says:

So be it!

Priestess of Hecate: The Priestess raises her hands over the talismans. She repeats the following binding spell, then instructs all to repeat the lines, one by one:

Swirl the colors of gold and green,
Precious gifts in harmony.
Silver, glittering highest light
Keep your power clear and bright.
Hecate from Her cavern deep,
Bind the power 'round and keep
Enchantment sound, in purpose clear,
In fertile magic to grow here,
To bless the people and the land.
Remain under Hecate's (*He-ca-tays*) hand!
And so . . . it . . . shall . . . be!

X. Closing

Priestesses of Demeter and Persephone:
We honor the Great Mother and Her Holy Daughter,
As their cycle moves forward once again.
May the Two Goddesses
Bless us in the new season.
Hail Demeter and Persephone!

Priestesses Panagia/All:
Hail Demeter and Persephone!

Priestesses of Demeter and Persephone: Remove gloves. Set offerings of bread and fruit on the altar.

Priestesses Panagia/ All:
These are the Rites of Arkichronia!
This temple rite complete,
In grace and in joy,
May Her blessings proceed unto all!
To the feast!

Wash hands. Share the pomegranates or red apples.

THE THESMOPHORIA PROPER—OCTOBER 22ND

> ### Seasonal themes
> This holy day officially begins the new agricultural year. Planting of the grain may commence anytime after the Thesmophoria holy days, and before the Winter Solstice, depending on the rains. To begin the year, we celebrate Demeter's sacred laws, by whose blessings we live.
>
> ### Transcendent themes
> We pause in our lives to focus on the sacred values that a spiritual awareness imparts to the life experience. We consider the powers, influences, and blessings of the Holy Mother and Daughter. We honor the Great Mother, and our inherited divinity.

The third celebration of the Thesmophoria complex of holidays, Thesmophoria Proper, took place on Pyanopsion 11. For convenience, it may be celebrated on the Saturday one week following Arkichronia. The following two festivals (Nestia and Kalligenia) have been set up to be celebrated together, the day after this holiday. Not many of us have the luxury of celebrating the Thesmophoria festivals in their original five-day consecutive arrangement.

This holiday (as all of the Thesmophoria holidays) was pan-Hellenic and was celebrated throughout Greece, Asia Minor, and Sicily.[5] In addition to Eleusis, other cities such as Corinth, Cyrene, and Myteline had Demetrian temple sanctuaries. Many cities that did not have a sanctuary had a Thesmophoron, a sacred building in which Demetrian rites, and occasionally rites of other traditions, took place.

Thesmoi means "sacred laws" and *phoria* means "to carry." Demeter Thesmophoros means "Demeter of the Carried Sacred Laws." The Thesmoi are written on a double scroll (as were many texts of the time) and then placed in a protective cloth cover (see chapter 18, "thesmoi"). During the rite, they are carried around the

---

5   Brumfield, *The Attic Festivals of Demeter and their Relation to the Agricultural Year* (Salem, NH: Arno Press, 1981), p. 70.

circle, while sacred words are chanted. This is clearly reminiscent of the Jewish Torah being carried around the congregation while the cantor sings a holy song. The current synagogue ceremony was organized in the first century C.E. Considering the meaning of the name Thesmophoros (which dates before the first century), a similar use of a sacred scroll in Demeter's festival is likely and is re-created here.

The holiday of Thesmophoria Proper may have been concerned, in part, with honoring temple laws regarding customs and traditions for Demeter's festivals and mysteries. This compilation of laws may have been responsible for the fact that the religion of Demeter was spread throughout the Mediterranean. Divine or spiritual laws relating to the myth may have also played a part.

In the following interpretation, divine laws are honored and these are the primary focus of the festival. They arise from the religious beliefs within the mythology. The beliefs explored in chapter 4 influence much of the content of this rite. This festival honors the goddess' gifts, powers, and divinity. We are also reminded of our own divinity through hearing the sacred laws, the Song of Life and Death, and through participating in an anointing rite.

Ritual Outline

I.	Preritual
II.	Welcome
III.	Invocation of Hestia
IV.	Invocation of Demeter
V.	Group Song and Circle Dance
VI.	Procession of the Sacred Laws
VII.	Opening of the Thesmoi
VIII.	Offerings to Demeter and Candle Lighting
IX.	Closing

Clergy

Priestess of Demeter
Priestess of Hecate
Priestess of Hestia
Hierophant
Hierophantid of Demeter
Priestesses Panagia

The Main Altar for Demeter Thesmophoros

This altar must be against a wall. During the rite, the scrolls of the thesmoi will be displayed by unrolling them and standing them up against the wall. On the altar is a Demeter icon, the thesmoi, red taper candles to the right and left of the icon, and a votive candle in front of the icon. Vases of dried flowers are set on the altar along with the Hestia candle or lamp, several pomegranates (or red apples), a bowl of wheat or barley, a bowl of mixed seeds, and snake and/or pig effigies. There is a censer, and incense, matches, and a bottle of scented anointing oil. Unlit votive candles in holders (one for each cleric) are set on the altar. As participants enter, they will also set their unlit votive candles in holders on the altar. There are two smaller scrolls, copies of the thesmoi, for use by clergy during the rite (see chapter 18).

Stand for Hecate's Torch

Use a large container filled with sand or earth to serve as a stand for the torch (a terra-cotta pot or oak barrel are also possible choices). Or, you may use a 2-inch wide pillar candle instead.

Offering Table

This is an extra table next to the altar of Demeter. On it, have an extra dish of matches and the offerings of the clergy. As participants enter, they will add their offerings.

Preparation

Clergy and participants are asked to bring food for the feast, candles, and an offering for Demeter of fruit, breads, or bowls of grain. The dowels or sticks that hold the thesmoi scroll will be used to stand it up. They should be high enough so that they are visible when the icon of Demeter is in front of them.

Staging

This is the most stately of the rites, and clergy and participants may want to wear full Greek costume, or perhaps just the draping himation (see chapter 18). Fresh-flower crowns were traditionally not worn at the Thesmophoria, presumably because Demeter has yet to be reunited with the Maiden. The stand for Hecate's torch (or pillar candle) is to the side of the altar. Because of the use of the censer, you should have plenty of ventilation in the room. This rite may be done outdoors.

THE RITES OF THESMOPHORIA PROPER

I. Preritual

Priestesses Panagia: They instruct arriving participants to place their candles in holders on the Demeter altar but not in the center section near the thesmoi. Participants are also instructed to place their offerings for the goddess on the offering table next to Demeter's altar. Then participants are guided to stand in a semi-circle in front of the altar. The Priestess of Demeter lights the incense. The red taper candles are lit. The Priestess of Hecate lights the small torch (or pillar candle) to the right of the altar (see Chapter 18, "Torches").

Priestess of Demeter: The Priestess of Demeter anoints the edges of the icon of Demeter with scented oil, saying silently: Hail Panagia. Then, holding the censer, she blesses the icon of Demeter with fragrant smoke. She hands the censer to the Hierophant.

Hierophant: The Hierophant blesses the thesmoi with fragrant smoke. He then walks around the inside of the semi-circle, wafting incense over the participants as he goes.

Priestesses Panagia/All [Chant, establishing a rhythm, repeating until energy is raised]:
> Ela Dea,   *(Eh-la, De-ah)*   *(Come, Goddess)*
> Mother of Creation.
> On light wings we fly,
> On wings of devotion.

II. Welcome

Priestess of Hecate   [Picks up the small torch or candle, holds it aloft, and, facing the participants, says]:
> All welcome to the Rites of Thesmophoria.
> We have come to praise Demeter Thesmophoros
> And the Mysteries of Life and Death.
> Have all come to honor the Great Mother?

Priestesses Panagia/All:
> Yes!

Priestess of Hecate:
> Have all come with love and reverence?

Priestesses Panagia/All:
Yes!

Priestess of Hecate:
Have the offerings been brought?

Priestesses Panagia/All:
Yes!

Priestess of Hecate:
Then come, let us begin the Rites of Thesmophoria!

The Priestess replaces the torch (or pillar candle) on its stand.

III. Invocation of Hestia

Priestess of Hestia [At the altar]:
We call Hestia,
Goddess of hearth and temple fire,
Of the spiritual center of our world,
And of all sacred places.
Hestia, beloved Goddess of the spiritual flame,
Come, and enter this temple.
Make all that is here holy and sacred in Your name.
Bring to us the peace and sureness
Of that place which is home and hearth.
Bring Your purity and beauty to us
As we honor You,
Who are the center of the spiritual flame.
So be it.

Priestess of Hestia lights the Hestia lamp or candle. She raises it up and says:
Hail Hestia!

Priestesses Panagia/All:
Hail Hestia!

IV. Invocation of Demeter

Priestess of Demeter [At Demeter altar, facing the icon]:
Hail Demeter Thesmophoros.
All Wisdom is Thine.

Yours is the spirit inside the seed.
You cause roots to descend and leaves to unfurl.
You are the miracle of life and creation.
By Your power we live,
Remembering the miracle always.

Then, in our season,
Unto the Holy Daughter,
May we descend into Death with blessings and light.
And so we honor the Mother of Persephone,
The Great Creatress of Life.
Come Thesmophoros, and attend our gathering,
As we praise You on this holy day.

The Priestess lights the votive candle in front of the Demeter icon, turns to participants and lifts the candle.

Priestess of Demeter:
Hail Thesmophoros!

Priestesses Panagia/All:
Hail Thesmophoros!

V. Group Song and Circle Dance

Hierophant: Instructs all participants to join hands in a circle, then says or chants:
Herein Her grace and beauty lend,
To all who attend the gathering.
Lighten the heart and good will send,
To you Her blessings we bring.

Priestesses Panagia: All begin moving the circle in a clockwise direction, chanting repeatedly:
Enter grace, enter beauty,   *(En-ter grace, en-ter beau-ty,)*
Enter the heart into ecstasy. *(Enter the heart in-to ecs-ta-sy.)*

All continue circling and repeating the above short chant, until energy is raised.

Hierophantid of Demeter:
Holy Demeter,
We honor You for Your precious gifts,
For the seed and its everlasting nature,
As that which is culled from death begets life.

We honor You for the Mysteries of the luminous spirit,
For as we move even beyond Your brilliant form,
We find the eternity of the soul.
Great praises to the Holy Mother!

VI. Procession of the Sacred Laws

At the main altar, the Hierophant stands before the thesmoi. The Priestesses Panagia pick up the hand bells, rattles, or tambourines. The Hierophant picks up the thesmoi. All turn to the participants. The Hierophant raises the scroll up high.

Priestess of Hecate:
Listen to the Song of Life and Death
As the thesmoi are carried around the gathering.

Priestesses Panagia: Priestesses ring hand bells or shake rattles or tambourines three times and the clerics begin the "Song of Life and Death" (see below). The Hierophant begins the rite, carrying the thesmoi.

Hierophant: He carries the thesmoi, slowly walking clockwise around the outside of the gathering. The clergy chant or sing the "Song of Life and Death" as the Hierophant circles. The chant is sung at least twice, more if the gathering is a large one. If the gathering is small, the Hierophant may need to circle more than once. Then the thesmoi are returned to the altar and clergy rejoin the circle.

**The Hierophant and/or the Priestess of Demeter
and/or Priestesses Panagia** [Chanting or singing]**:**
The Song of Life and Death
Demeter Panagia,
Demeter Thesmophoros,
Mother of all Creation,
All born from Thy Holy body.
Born are we . . .
Who have our being in Your Creation.
Therefore . . .
Holy, Holy are we.
All, born from the Great Mother.
And when the cup of death is given
To Persephone we journey,
To Her embrace of light go we,
And then,
Unto Maiden creation again.

All hail the Two Goddesses,
Hail, hail, hail Thesmophoros,
Hail, hail, hail Thesmophoros!

Priestesses Panagia/All: When the procession of the thesmoi has ended and the scroll is placed on the altar, the Priestesses Panagia and all participants say:
May the rose blossom,
And the sheaves hang heavy,
Red the fair apple in season,
As the cypress does remain evergreen,
So the white lily rises again.

Priestess of Hestia: The Priestess of Hestia takes the scented oil from the altar and anoints the participant to her left in the center of the forehead, saying:
You are the shining soul
And the Song of Life.

She then passes the bottle of anointing oil to the one she has just anointed, who then anoints the one to her (or his) left. This continues around the circle until all are anointed.

VII. Opening of the Thesmoi

Priestess and Hierophantid of Demeter: They face the altar, relight the incense, and say quietly, "Hail Thesmophoros." Fragrant smoke is wafted over the thesmoi. They are uncovered and unrolled. The scroll is censed again.

Priestess and Hierophantid of Demeter: Each pick up a small one-page scroll of the thesmoi. They unroll them and face the participants in the circle. Together they say:
Now hear the Thesmoi of Holy Demeter.
May all nations be wise,
And honor the Great Mother.

Then together they chant the sacred laws of Demeter:

I.   Give praises to the Holy Mother—all that is born rises from within Her.
II.   All that sustains thee flows from Her body.
III.   The Wise and Holy Mother pleasures in peace and honest labor.

IV.   Tend to your life with gentle wisdom and to your days with
        love's compassion.
V.   Honor the Goddesses' rites and mysteries—to bring justice,
        peace, and the nation's fertility.
VI.   Know the cycle of the Blessed Seed—as the mystery of of the
        soul, revealed.
VII.   Honor the Pure and Holy Maiden—whose power is joy ever
        reborn.
VIII.   Praises to Royal Persephone—who at thy death will welcome
        thee.
IX.   Praises to the Holy Mother—whose song is the light of
        eternity.
X.   May you know of your immortal being, and drink of her cup
        everlasting.
        Hail, hail, hail Thesmophoros!
        Hail, hail, hail Thesmophoros!

VIII. Offerings to Demeter and Candle Lighting

Hierophantid of Demeter: The Priestess invites all to view the thesmoi,
leave their offerings, and then light their candle. They may ask Demeter for a personal blessing, or simply honor her, or both. Candles are lit and offerings are
given.

IX. Closing

Priestesses Panagia/All [Chanting or singing]:
        May the rose blossom,
        And the sheaves hang heavy,
        Red the fair apple in season.
        As the cypress does remain evergreen,
        So the white lily rises again.

Clerics/All:
        These are the Rites of Thesmophoria
            Proper!
        This temple rite complete,
        In grace and in joy,
        May Her blessings proceed unto all!
        To the feast!

THE FESTIVALS OF NESTIA AND KALLIGENIA–OCTOBER 23RD

Seasonal themes of Nestia

The Holy Daughter prepares to return to Demeter. Persephone's sadness and sacrifice, as she lays down her Underworld crown. Her departure from her beloved Plouton and the land of the dead is set in motion in order to serve the land of life.

Transcendent themes of Nestia

Sacrifice; its value and its sadness. Honoring right sacrifice as service and as noble action. Giving up a particular path, in order for good to arise in the future. Wisdom. Releasing the sadness of the past, and retaining the beauty of our best moments as we proceed forward with our lives.

Seasonal themes of Kalligenia

The ascent of the Maiden; Persephone returns as Kore. The fertile part of the cycle moves forward, in a joyful reunion of Mother and Daughter. The blessings of the Holy Mother and Daughter brings gifts to all. Planting may now commence.

Transcendent themes of Kalligenia

The beginning of any new or creative activity. A birth. The childlike energies of excitement and joy that feed a new beginning. Receiving encouragement and support. The union of joy and knowledge.

Nestia and Kalligenia are presented here as two rites celebrated on the same day. They took place on the Greek dates of Pyanopsion 12 and 13, and marked the end of the Thesmophoria complex of holidays. Nestia is known to have been a day of mourning, though the cause of this sadness is not known. In this interpretation, Nestia is concerned with Persephone's ascent from the Underworld. The cause of Her sadness being that She must leave Her life with Plouton.

Nestia was celebrated in Demeter's sanctuaries. Cities without a Demetrian temple used their Thesmophoron for the purpose. There were no animal sacrifices performed or any business conducted in the city on this day. In addition, it was a day of fasting.

In this rendition of Nestia, Persephone lays down her crown and drinks from the river of forgetfulness (the River Lethe). She crosses through the gateway of the Underworld to return to Earth. In sadness, she leaves behind her beloved Plouton, the souls of the dead, and the beauty of Elysium, though she knows she will return. In her royal nature are justice and compassion, and so she ascends to help bring back the verdant season to Earth. This is her gift to Demeter and to all humankind.

In Kalligenia ("fair born"), Demeter and Kore are reunited. The Mother receives the Holy Daughter at the gateway of the Underworld, where Kore crosses over into Demeter's waiting arms. Crowned with evergreen, the Maiden has returned to Earth. Now the seed grain can be planted in the body of the Earth, and the young green sprouts, the Korai, will rise.

Kalligenia included the blessing of young offspring; both human and animal. In this liturgy for Kalligenia, those in attendance are blessed, and the fertility talismans made at Arkichronia are given out. (If you have not celebrated Arkichronia, you may make the talismans ahead of time, see pp. 101–102.) They may be used as originally intended, as a blessing for farming or gardening. They may also be used in the near and far corners of your city to distribute the Goddess' blessings, their contents being cast upon Earth. Nestia-Kalligenia concludes with a great feast.

Ritual Outline

I.   Preritual
II.   Welcome
III.   Invocation to Hestia
IV.   Invocation to Mother and Maiden
V.   Call for the Maiden's Return
VI.   Song and Circle Dance
VII.   Ascent from Tartarus
VIII.   Transition to Kalligenia
IX.   Procession to the Main Altar
X.   Ceremony of the Lights
XI.   Blessings of Kalligenia
XII.   Closing

Clergy

Priestess of Hecate
Priestess of Demeter

Priestess of Hestia
Hierophant
Hierophantid of Kore-Persephone
Priestess of Athena
Priestesses Panagia

The Main Altar

On a table, set the framed icon or image of Demeter with several pomegranates or red apples around it. To the right and left of the icon place two tall red taper candles. The altar may also hold vases of dried grain and dried flowers, Hestia's lamp/candle, Demeter's votive candle, Kore's votive candle, a censer, incense, and a small representation of a snake.

You may add a wreath of grain, a bowl of water, a spurge, and the bowl of talismans from Arkichronia.

Side Offering Table

This is an additional small table near the main altar where participants will place their candles and offerings.

The Gateway to Tartarus

The gateway can be as simple is a black cord that marks the opening of the Ploutonian cave. Beyond the gateway is Persephone's chair. It may be draped with black fabric. On the chair are Persephone's vestments: her crown, her black diaphanous veil, her black himation, and her mask. (See chapter 18, "Persephone." Note that it is more difficult to speak lines while masked, and that the mask can be omitted.) Just on the inside of the gateway is a small table, a pillar of brick, or a pedestal. On it is a cup or chalice that contains the symbolic water of the River Lethe, the river of forgetfulness. Outside the gateway is set a basket of green leafy branches, at least one for each participant. There is also a green leafy crown for Kore (see chapter 18, "crowns").

Preparations

Participants bring a white taper candle and a holder for the Ceremony of Lights. For this very special feast day, bring your best dishes, your most fabulous recipes.

Staging

The main altar is against a wall, the offering table near it. On the other side of the room is the gateway to Tartarus. There needs to be sufficient space between the main altar and the gateway to allow procession. Clergy and participants may wear costumes: chiton and himation, or just the draping himation, as they choose (see chapter 18, "costume").

THE RITES OF NESTIA AND KALLIGENIA

I. Preritual

All participants place their white taper candles with holders on the side offering table and their feast foods in a designated place. Incense is lit, as are the two red taper candles. All gather into a circle.

II. Welcome

Priestess of Hecate:
> All welcome to the rites of Nestia and Kalligenia!
> These are the last celebrations of the Thesmophoria.
> Here sadness will be followed by great joy,
> As we witness the turning of the seasons.
>
> The Queen of Tartarus and Elysium resides below,
> While Holy Demeter dwells above, on Earth.
> This is the time for the vows of the Mysteries
> To be completed,
> The time for the Holy Daughter to ascend.
>
> We are here to celebrate the return of the Maiden
> And the blessings of the Great Mother.
> We praise the power of the Two Goddesses,
> As we await the Maiden's restoration.
> All Hail!

Priestesses Panagia/All:
> Hail!

III. Invocation of Hestia

Priestess of Hestia [Facing the lamp]:
> We call Hestia,
> Goddess of hearth and temple fire,
> Of the spiritual center of our world,
> And of all sacred places
> Hestia, beloved Goddess of the spiritual flame,
> Come and enter this temple.

Make all that is here holy and sacred in Your name.
Bring to us the peace and sureness
Of that place which is home and hearth.
Bring Your purity and beauty to us
As we honor You
Who are the center of the spiritual flame.
So be it.

The Priestess of Hestia lights the lamp or candle. She raises the lamp and says:
Hail Hestia!

Priestesses Panagia/All:
Hail Hestia!

IV. Invocation of Mother and Maiden

Priestess of Demeter [Retrieving the offerings for Demeter from the side altar]:
Holy Mother,
Powerful One who is besought by prayers,
Goddess of the Sacred Laws,
We call to You.

From the depths of Dark Melaina have come riches.
Fallow land prepares the fertile field,
As sorrow leads to compassion.
So we honor the Mother who has mourned long.

Holy One, You know the song
That resides behind the drama of life,
Supporting and creating all
Even in darkness,
For You, Panagia, are the Singer.
With great honor shall we witness the turning of the seasons.
Come Holy Demeter, and receive these offerings.

The Priestess sets the offerings on the altar, and lights Demeter's votive candle.

Hierophantid of Kore-Persephone [Retrieving the offerings for Kore from the side table]:
Fair Kore,
Deep within the heart of Death's Queen
Do You reside,

As Life resides always behind Death.
To the Realm of Plouton
You brought the soul of the Maiden.

Crowned and jeweled Governess of mystic light
Of wondrous fields flowering in beauty,
Great Queen of passion's embrace,
We call to You.
With honor shall we witness the turning of the seasons.
Come Holy Persephone; you who are also the blessed Maiden,
Come and receive these offerings.

The Priestess sets the offerings on altar, and lights the Kore candle.

V. Call for the Maiden's Return

Hierophant:
In this month of many rites,
The sacred field has been plowed and blessed
In the manner prescribed.
The powers of Baubo have blessed the Mother's heart,
And She is awake.
The seed grain has been sent up from its burial place,
The gift of noble Persephone,
And the herald of Her return.
In magic, this has been conjoined with the riches from deep
      below,
And the talismans have been made ready.
The Sacred Laws of Demeter
Have been honored and chanted aloud,
And the Holy Mother's table has been made full of offerings.
We fulfill our charge,
And now call out for the Maiden's return!

Hierophantid of Kore-Persephone: The Song and Circle Dance begins
(see below). At this point, the Hierophantid moves to the place that represents
the gateway to Tartarus. She throws the black himation over her shoulders and
puts on the mask of Persephone (optional), invoking the Goddess from within.
She then covers her head and body with a thin, black diaphanous veil. Onto her
head, over the veil, is set the crown. She seats herself on the throne, beyond the
gateway. She waits, remaining seated and silent, until the time of her ritual
ascent.

VI. Song and Circle Dance

Priestesses Panagia/All: The Priestesses instruct all to join hands in a circle and dance in a clockwise direction, repeatedly chanting this song during the circling:

In fallow darkness	*(In fal-low dark-ness)*
The season is changing,	*(The sea-son is chang-ing,)*
The Mother awake,	*(The Mo-ther a-wake,)*
And the Maiden arising.	*(And the Mai-den a-ris-ing.)*

VII. Ascent from Tartarus to Earth

Priestess of Athena: All remain in a circle, as the Priestess of Athena (facing Persephone) says:

Holy Persephone,
Now is the time of Your sacrifice
As you prepare to leave the Underworld.

I, Athena Parthenos, call to You,
She who is girt for battle,
Yet who is Maiden ever-fair.
I lend to You my courage and my wisdom,
So that You may now lay down the vestments of the Queen.
Come Lady, and drink from the River Lethe,
Cross the bridge into Maidenhood again,
For Demeter awaits Thee.

The Priestess of Athena then instructs all to repeat the following lines:

May the season turn.
May fallow become green growth.
Holy Persephone,
Lay down Your crown.
May the Maiden cross the bridge.
May seed take root
And fruit ripen again.
Persephone, ascend!

Priestess of Demeter: At the main altar, she invokes Demeter from within and places the crown of grain on her head. She turns toward the gateway to Tartarus and says:

Kore . . . it is time for your return.

The world hungers, and the seed
Must be cast into the heart of the Earth.
Come, my beautiful Daughter,
Arise from deep below,
For I who have birthed you
Now call you back from Death.

Arise Fair Maiden unto life again.
The flowering meadows yearn to be born,
The crocus and violets still sleep,
And the green fields
Await the power of your hand.
Return Beloved, to the land of the Sun.
With honor do I call upon Tartarus' Queen,
Resplendent and full of graces.
I call out through the dark gate,
So that sweet Kore may cross over.
With a heart full of hope
I journey to meet Thee.
Arise, arise my Kore!

Priestesses Panagia/All: The Priestesses Panagia and all the participants
proceed to the gateway of the Underworld, chanting repeatedly:
Will She return,
Laying down Her jeweled crown?
Will She return,
The Holy Daughter, the Maiden?

Priestess of Hecate: When the procession arrives at the gateway to
Tartarus, one more verse of the above is chanted. Then the Priestess of
Hecate says:
We are at the Gates of Tartarus.
Listen closely
And hear the lamentations of Queen Persephone
As She prepares to take the path
Between the worlds.

Hierophantid of Kore-Persephone: In her role as Persephone, she is
seated on the other side of the Tartarus gateway. Masked (optional), veiled, and
crowned, she says:
It is the work of my Mother
To feed and nourish the people of the world,

Not only with grain and all manner of foods,
But with hope, beauty, and compassion.

She has grieved long.
In Her grief the land wasted away
And hope was lost.
No fruit was born from the mighty Earth,
As beauty wandered below.

As I am the Queen of all that lies below,
So am I Kore, the seed and the soul of life.
Together with Holy Demeter,
We are Goddesses of Verdant Beauty,
Who bring glory to Earth.

But on this day of my Ascent, sadness covers my soul,
For the Underworld is filled with beauty.
There is joy in the blessed groves of Elysium, and justice in Tartarus.
Here grow glorious meadowlands of purple flowers,
Lit by soft iridescent light,
While the groves of the pomegranate rustle,
And the Netherworld breeze is as gentle as the one above.
Rivers run bright and clear;
Their sounds, like the laughter of young maidens . . .

Priestesses Panagia:
Between the tall cypress is the great house,
The palace where Persephone and Plouton dwell.
Her heart is joined with His for eternity.

Hierophantid of Kore-Persephone: She stands and moves behind her chair.
To the Lord of Death I have said farewell,
And understanding was born,
The knowledge that I must serve in two worlds,
For this is part of Life's Mystery.
In our last moments I drew Him close,
Drawing some of His essence into my heart.

But now, I must return.
And when I drink from the River Lethe,
The veil of forgetfulness will draw across my soul.
Yet somewhere within, His essence will remain . . .
I must return . . .

Reaching under her black diaphanous veil, the Hierophantid removes her mask and places it on the chair, so that the mask may be seen clearly. She removes her crown and sets it down. She walks slowly to the gateway to Tartarus, and stands next to the pillar that holds the cup of the symbolic water of Lethe. Slowly, she removes the black himation that is draped underneath the veil. The himation falls to the ground. In her role as Persephone, she says:

I am the way between Life and Death.

She takes the cup of water in both hands and brings it under the veil. She drinks, tilting her head back slightly. She places the cup back on the pillar. Her arms then lift the veil. Her face is revealed and turns upward. As the veil drops to the ground, Demeter steps forward to the gateway.

VIII. Transition to Kalligenia

Priestess of Demeter: Reaching over the entrance, the Priestess of Demeter takes the Hierophantid of Kore's hand and draws the Maiden to her side. Kore pauses, feeling the power of her transition. The two pause, and then embrace. The Hierophantid of Demeter crowns Kore with the green leafy wreath, gives her a kiss, and says:

Beloved Daughter,
Pure one, of all-holy blessings,
How precious you are . . .

[Kore looks around her, as if waking from sleep.]

Priestess of Demeter:

The blossoming fields have gone, My child,
But now they will return.

Hierophantid of Kore [Gains her strength, drawing it up from Earth with her breath. She says]:

The flowering meadows will come again,
In joy, shall beauty return to Earth.

Priestess of Demeter:

The green shoots of wheat and barley
Will rise once more, by our divine will.
Gently, shall I tend the life of the Maiden.
For all that grows will blossom in Her name,
And in honor and celebration
Of the Holy Mother and Daughter.

Priestess of Demeter and Hierophantid of Kore:
> Come, let us bless the land
> And the people also.

Priestesses Panagia/All:
> Hail Demeter! Hail Kore!

Priestess of Demeter and Hierophantid of Kore [Hand out green leafy branches to all saying]:
> The Maiden has returned.

IX. Procession to the Main Altar

Priestesses Panagia/All: Chanting or singing, and proceeding to the main altar, with the Priestess of Demeter and the Hierophantid of Kore at the head of the procession:
> Anados Kores, the Maiden rises,   *(An-ah-thosse Ko-res)*
> Rises in beauty
> She does delight us!
> The Holy Daughter has returned again;
> The Mother's heart is golden.
> The Holy Daughter has returned again;
> The Mother's heart is golden.

When all arrive at the main altar, the participants form a semi-circle facing the altar. The Priestess of Demeter and the Hierophantid of Kore reverently remove their wreaths, divesting themselves of deity. The two crowns are set on the altar.

Priestess and Hierophantid [Bow to the altar, and then turn to face the participants. They say]:
> The Wheel has turned!
> We welcome the season of Demeter and Kore.

Priestesses Panagia/All:
> We welcome the season of Demeter and Kore.

All participants place their green branches in the back of, or around, the base of the altar.

X. Ceremony of the Lights

Hierophant: The Hierophant asks participants to take up their unlit candles and form a semi-circle facing the altar.

Hierophantid of Kore: The Hierophantid lights her candle from the Kore candle on the altar. She lights the candle of the participant next to her and says:
>   The Maiden has returned.

Each participant then lights the candle of the one next to them, saying:
>   The Maiden has returned.

Hierophant: Instructs all to circle, raise their candles, and repeat the following lines:
>   The season of the Verdant Goddesses begins,
>   May Earth grow bountiful with their beauty.
>   Hail Demeter and Kore!

The Hierophant instructs all to set their candles on the altar (in holders).

XI. Blessings of Kalligenia

The Priestesses of Demeter, Kore and Hecate take their places at the main altar, to dispense the three blessings. In the receiving line, the Hierophantid of Kore is first and gives the Blessing of the Hands. Next, the Priestess of Demeter gives the Water Blessing. Finally, the Priestess of Hecate gives the Talisman Blessing.

Hierophant:
>   As Kore is the fair offspring of the Great Mother,
>   So are we all.
>   Come now to the altar,
>   And receive the blessings of the Two Goddesses.

Hierophantid of Kore: The Hierophantid asks the participant to state his or her name. Then she breathes energy up from the Earth, imaging it rising up through her feet and into her body. She sees it as sparkling silver light. She places her hands on top of the participant's head, blessing with the energy that she directs to flow through her hands. She says:
>   [Participant's name]
>   In the name of fair Kore,
>   I bless you with a heart that is full of light,
>   With love, and with well-being.
>   So shall it be.

Priestess of Demeter: Priestess asks the one receiving the blessing to place palms up in an open position. She invokes the energy as described above, seeing it as sparkling gold light. She says:
>   In the name of Demeter Panagia [with spurge, she sprinkles water on
>   head],

I bless you with health [on the heart],
With bright pleasure [on the right palm],
And with contented joy [on left palm],
So shall it be.

Priestess of Hecate: Taking in her hands one of the fertility talismans, the Priestess of Hecate invokes energy as described above, seeing it as sparkling green light. She infuses this imaged light into each talisman. She says:

In the names of Demeter and Kore,
May success be yours.
May your deepest desires grow and blossom,
With gentle affection, and in pleasant prosperity.
So shall it be.

She gives the talisman to the participant.[6]

XII. Closing

Priestesses Panagia/All:

These are the rites of Nestia and Kalligenia!
These temple rites complete,
In grace and in joy,
May her blessings proceed unto all!
To the feast!

---

[6]   Participants may use the talismans to bless their own gardens or other areas of land. Clergy use them at the planting that follows in November-December. They may also be set on an altar and then a candle lit for good fortune for any endeavor.

CHAPTER 10

The Winter Festival
Awakened Growth

From the dark Earth have come lavender crocus.
The white narcissus bloom.
The grain has risen
And the field is covered in emerald.

Winter brings continued rains. Mediterranean winters are mild, without the freezing cold of northern Europe. The Great Mother reveals Her powers as both wild meadows and agricultural fields become carpeted in green. The pure white narcissus bloom, a reflection of the point in the Demetrian yearly cycle. The Maiden, who returned at the end of the fall festivals, shows us her beauty. By January, the fall-planted grain is lush and green. The Earth Mother is vibrant, rich, and fertile. The *Haloa Festival* celebrates, among other things, the powers of Mother and Daughter, as beauty and green growth return to Earth. For those in northern regions, the Haloa Festival would be appropriate in mid-spring.

THE FESTIVAL OF HALOA—JANUARY 10TH

Seasonal themes

The new green growth of both wild nature and cultivated field. Appreciating the beauty that results from the relationship between Demeter and Kore. Magic to encourage continued success for this growth in cultivated fields. Blessings for orchards and vineyards, in preparation for their spring growth. The power of humor, used to maintain joy and fertility.

Transcendent themes

Celebrating the early successes of new beginnings. Continuing our right actions and prayers. Gratitude for new endeavors. An appreciation for the source of our tools, materials, energy, and inspiration. Continuing to work toward your goal, maintaining a healthful sense of humor.

Most evidence seems to indicate that the Haloa was a women's festival. In the following interpretation, the Haloa may be either a women's festival or open to all. Its original similarity to the Stenia festival is clear in its encouragement of fertility through sexual women's festival or open to all. Its original similarity to the Stenia festival is clear in its encouragement of fertility through sexual humor and bawdy actions. There are, however, some major differences. In order to provide a festival slightly different from the Stenia, I will emphasize differences rather than the similarities.

For this festival, food and wine were set out in a great display, perhaps as a banquet for the deities. There appears to have been a kind of freedom to speak out. Sacrifices were offered to Demeter, Kore, and Dionysus—nonanimal offerings of breads, cakes, and grains.

The Haloa festival was performed in Eleusis, however there are no records of performances in other city-states, as there were for the

---

[1]   Allaire Chandor Brumfield, *The Attic Festivals of Demeter and their Relation to the Agricultural Year* (Salem, NH: Arno Press, 1981), p. 130.

Thesmophoria holidays. The Haloa took place anywhere from mid-December to mid-January, on the last day of the month of Poseideon. This would therefore be the day before the New Moon. While this was the coldest part of the year, green was slowly returning to the land due to the fall and winter rains.

According to sanctuary accounts from 329–328 B.C.E.,[1] great bundles of wood were brought in for the festival, for use as both firewood and kindling. The all-night vigil *(pannychis)* of the Haloa may be similar in some ways to the all-night vigils with bonfires common throughout Europe in winter festivals, representing an invitation of heat and light into the coldest part of the year. Though an all-night vigil is not re-created here, the Haloa festival is nonetheless concerned with encouraging growth and life, not only for the cultivated fields, but for orchards and vineyards.

Ritual Outline

I.   Preritual
II.   Invocation to Hestia
III.   Myth of Haloa
IV.   Invocation to Demeter and Kore
V.   Song and Circle Dance
VI.   Greeting Eros
VII.   Honoring Dionysus
VIII.   Fire Chant and Dance
IX.   Fire Magic
X.   Anointing Magic
XI.   Libations to Mother and Maiden
XII.   Closing Song
XIII.   Closing

Clergy

Priestess of Hestia
Hierophantids of Kore and Demeter
Priestess of Hecate
Priestesses Panagias
Priestess of Demeter
Priest or Priestess of Eros
Priest or Priestess of Dionysus

The Main Altar

On the altar is an icon of Demeter. Around or over it is a small wreath of greenery and flowers that symbolizes Kore (see chapter 18, "flower wreaths"). To the right and left of the icon are tall white taper candles. On the altar are small green or flowering plants in a pot, the Hestia lamp/candle, a bowl or bowls of dried grain/seeds, a bowl of scented water, and a snake image (see chapter 18, "snakes"). There are opened bottles of wine and/or grape juice, a censer, and incense.

The Fire Altar

The fire altar is created on the floor in the center of the room. The following items are needed: a 3-foot, round or square, piece of 1-inch-thick wood, terra-cotta brick, a cast-iron or stainless-steel pot, sand, a small brass or stainless-steel pot, flammable alcohol (use 90 to 91 proof), and long matches. You should have enough alcohol to burn for 30 minutes (rehearse). See chapter 18, "fire altar," for instructions on assembling this altar.

Side Table

The side table is a place for participants to put their chalices or cups, and their feast food. The libation bowl that is used after the fire magic is also placed there.

Preparation

The Priestess of Hecate brings about a quarter of a cup each of dried pine needles, anise seed, dried rosemary, and powdered ginger, in separate bowls. In addition to food for the feast, participants bring offerings for Demeter and Kore such as breads or sweet cakes. The fire altar is set up, holding aside the flammable alcohol until needed.

Staging

The main altar is against a wall, while the fire altar is set in the center of the room. Greek costume (see chapter 18) or just festive clothing with the draping himation, are optional.

THE HALOA FESTIVAL

I. Preritual

Participants enter, bringing their food offerings for Demeter and Kore. These and their chalices or cups for libations are placed on the side table. The incense is lit.

Priestesses Panagia/All: The Priestess along with all participants, circle in the center of the room, around the fire altar. All begin a humming "MMM" chant.

Hierophantid of Demeter: She takes up the incense. Moving in a clock-wise direction, she censes the participants.

Priestesses Panagia/All: Establish a rhythm and chant three times or more.
> Hail bright Mother   *(Hail bright Mo-ther)*
> And fair Kore!   *(And fair Ko-ree!)*
> Holy Ones, come   *(Ho-ly Ones, come)*
> Unto me.   *(Un-to me.)*

II. Invocation of Hestia

Priestess of Hestia [At the main altar]**:**
> We call Hestia,
> Goddess of hearth and temple fire,
> Of the Spiritual Center of our world
> And of all sacred places.
> Hestia, beloved Goddess of the spiritual flame,
> Come, and enter this temple.
> Make all that is here holy and sacred in Your name.
> Bring to us the peace and sureness
> Of that place which is home and hearth.
> Bring Your purity and beauty to us
> As we honor You,
> Who are the center of the spiritual flame.
> So be it.

The Priestess of Hestia lights the lamp or candle. She raises it up and says:
> Hail Hestia!

Priestesses Panagia/All:
> Hail Hestia!

III. Myth of Haloa

Hierophantid of Kore:
> The Winter nights have been long and cold,
> And the dry bones of late Summer are gone.
> By the rains of Zeus,
> And the light of the Sun,
> The Mother's body is covered in green grasses.
>
> From the dark Earth
> Have come lavender crocus,

The white narcissus bloom.
The grain has risen and the field is covered in emerald.
The orchards of almond, apricot, and fig
Are barren of leaves,
But when spring flourishes, they will be covered
    in blossom.
Great praises to the Holy Maiden!

Hierophantid of Demeter:

The olive harvest has come and gone,
And Athena's fruit-bearing tree awaits the heat of
    late spring.
The vine, too, awaits the voice of spring,
As rich wine from autumn's last vintage ages.
The vine of Dionysus prepares its bare woody branches
To unfurl new green growth.
In this season, when we have waited long for fair days,
We know that spring will come
As deeply, the roots of all drink from Her ancient body.
Great praises to the Holy Mother!

IV. Invocation of Demeter and Kore

Priestess of Demeter:

We celebrate the cultivated field, vineyard, and orchard
By honoring Mother and Maiden,
They who are the power and beauty
Of the wild woodlands and the ancient mountains.
With praises, offerings,and fiery rites of fertility
We will celebrate their rites.

Beloved Demeter and fair Kore,
Blessed are we in Thy Mysteries,
For all that lives and grows and dies and is born again
Rests in the realm of Your creation.
Bright are Thy passions

To nurture and tend every living thing
In all the world.
With reverence do we call upon Holy Demeter
And Her Maiden Daughter
To come and receive our offerings.

All are invited to place their food offerings on the altar. Then the Priestess of Demeter lights the right and left taper candles, saying:

Hail Demeter,
Hail Kore.

V. Song and Circle Dance

Priestesses Panagia/All: Hands joined, circling and chanting/singing repeatedly.

Enter grace, enter beauty,   *(En-ter grace, en-ter beau-ty,)*
Enter the heart into ecstasy!   *(En-ter the heart in-to ecs-ta-cy!)*

VI. Honoring Dionysus

Priest or Priestesses of Dionysus: Instructs participants to retrieve their cups. All stand in a semi-circle, facing the altar. The cleric places his or her hands on the pitcher of wine/grape juice and says the following blessing:

Let us honor and thank the God of the vine,
The woodland reveler, who brings joy.
We thank Him for His generous gift
The fruit of the vine,
That brings pleasure and slakes the thirst.
I bless this wine (juice) in the name of Dionysus!
So be it.

Priestesses Panagia/All:
So be it.

Priest or Priestesses of Dionysus: Moves around the inside of the circle, pouring wine or juice into each cup saying:

Hail Dionysus!

Cups are raised and all drink together, with another Hail! After the last toast, all are seated around the fire altar, with cups of juice or wine.

VII. Greeting Eros

Priestess or Priest of Eros:

In the beginning did Earth and Sky
Savor blissful and ardent union.
Then came Rhea and Cronos, in the wild oak groves
     of Arcadia.
Then Hera and Zeus in Argolis,
Their night of wedded bliss lasting three hundred years.

Then came Demeter and Zeus on Mount Olympus,
Amidst a shower of gold and inebriated with divine nectar.
After the harvest did Persephone and Plouton lay in loving passion
Upon the Sacred Couch in Tartarus.
Demeter and Iasos rejoiced in the thrice-plowed field in Crete.
The Mother of Eros sported with . . . (only Eros knows them all).
Some say Demeter with Triptolemos, when he became a man,
Aphrodite and Hephaestos between the thunder,
Aphrodite and Ares, in Ares' bed at the Thracian palace. . .

Priestesses Panagia:

This story could go on forever.

Priest or Priestess of Eros:

Then the love of Aphrodite and Hermes arrived,
Only in Hermes' wishful thoughts.
Then, Aphrodite and Hermes.
Aphrodite delighted in Dionysus,
In Poseidon and Adonis, and in whomever She chose.
And so it continues.
For bright Eros, the child of Aphrodite,
Moves through Olympus, Earth, and Tartarus at will.
And sacred love and passion remain forever unconquered.
Hail Eros!

Priestesses Panagia/All:

Hail Eros!

All drink again.

Priest or Priestess of Eros:

And now, if any of you have any stories
Of Eros or Aphrodite,
Tell them, and tell them now!
But take care not to cause hurt or harm,
Else Nemisis will be at your door in the morning!

Any other stories of Eros and Aphrodite are told.

VIII. Fire Chant and Dance

Priestess of Demeter: She explains that a fire of Hestia will be created
and infused with the magic of Hecate, the purpose being to bless all fields and
cultivated lands with the warmth of fiery fertility. The Priestess instructs all to

stand, circled around the fire altar. She fills the liner in the cauldron with alcohol. Open windows for ventilation. The Priestess then says:

> Priestess of Hestia,
> Bring the lamp!

Priestess of Hestia: Taking flame from the lamp or candle with a long match and lighting the cauldron, saying:

> With the power of Hestia,
> Do I . . . [lights fire]
> Awaken this Creature of Fire!

She then returns the lamp to the main altar.

Priestess of Hecate: Brings her herbs for blessing the fire, reserving half for later use. She places her hands, palms facing the fire, in a position of blessing. She says:

> I call the great Hecate,
> Goddess of deep caverns and moonlit crossroad . . .
> O immortal Queen of power and magic,
> Come and enter bright Hestia's fire!

> By the Power of Earth . . . [throws pine into the fire]
> Shall what lies upon the rim of the world
> Move with our will.

> By the Power of Air . . . [throws anise into the fire]
> Shall our desires come to life,
> And move with our will.

> By the Power of the Moon . . . [throws rosemary into the fire]
> Shall magic enter into the dance,
> And move with our will.

> And by the Power of Fire . . . [throws ginger into the fire]
> As voices sing out and bodies dance,
> Shall words burn bright
> And move with our will.
> So be it!

Priestesses Panagia/All:

> So be it!

All participants repeat the following Chant or sing while circling around the fire:

Scarlet and gold	*(Scar-let and gold)*
Rising . . . higher and higher,	*(Ri-sing . . . higher and high-er,)*
Magic of Hecate,	*(Ma-gic of He-ca-tay,)*
Enter Hestia's fire!	*(En-ter Hestia's fi-er!)*

IX. Fire Magic

Hierophantid of Kore: After energy is raised, the Hierophantid of Kore brings out a bowl of grain. She explains to participants that each will state a blessing for all cultivated land, for the Korai, the sacred field, for orchards, vines, and all agricultural fields, so that the hungry will be fed, so that positive farming methods will be realized, or any other blessings for the world. The Hierophantid states the first blessing, throws grain into the fire and then passes the bowl to the one on her left. The bowl is passed around the circle and blessings are given.

Priestess of Hecate: She scatters more herbs in the cauldron, whether or not the fire is still lit. She instructs the participants to repeat the following lines:

By the Power of Hecate,
Whose magic weaves through the web of the world,
This magic is done.
It finds its mark.
Our visions flourish.
It lives, and blesses our lives.
So, it is woven.
So it is done.
So be it.

X. Anointing Magic

Priestess of Demeter: All are seated in a circle around the fire. The Priestess of Demeter takes up the bowl of scented water. She and the participant to her left turn to face each other. The Priestess asks the participant what (in one word) blessing he or she would like to have. The participant responds with one word. The Priestess of Demeter dips into the water and anoints the forehead of the participant, creating a blessing from Demeter or Kore for the participant. The participant then faces the person to her or his left and becomes the one to give the blessing. The process is repeated all around the circle.

XI. Libations to Mother and Maiden

Hierophantid of Demeter: Places a libation bowl down near the fire pit. There will be less splatter if she leans down toward the bowl when she makes her libation. You might want to arrange cloths for splatter protection. Wine or juice is again poured into everyone's cups. The Hierophantid explains, as participants pour into the libation bowl (leaving some for a last sip), they praise the Mother and Maiden. One by one, each performs a libation.[2] When done, all have a last sip.

XII. Closing Song
Priestesses Panagia/All:

> Blessed are we in Her Mystery.
> Hail mighty Demeter and sweet Kore.

XIII. Closing
Priestesses Panagia/All:

> These are the Rites of Haloa.
> Her temple rites complete,
> In grace and in joy,
> May her blessings proceed unto all!

Priestess of Hecate:

> Come, one more act before our feast,
> To place our magic upon the mighty Earth.
> All attend.

The contents of the libation bowl are poured into the fire or cauldron. The liquid is swished about, picking up the grain and any of the loose herbs from Hecate's magic. Then the cauldron of "herbed wine" is taken outside. All are instructed to follow. The Priestess of Hecate slowly pours this liquid onto the earth. She asks all to repeat the following lines:

> Magic of Hecate,
> Praises of Kore,
> Power of Hestia's flame . . .
> As in spirit done,
> Descend upon Earth,
> And work our will.
> So be it.

> Now . . . to the feast!

---

[2]   Allaire Chandor Brumfield, *The Attic Festivals of Demeter and their Relation to the Agricultural Year* (Salem, NH: Arno Press, 1981), p. 130.

Greek costume with flower wreath.
(Model Nerisha Bernand, photograph by Jery Stier, 1999.)

At the fire altar. Fire magic at the Festival of Haloa.
(Model Laura Janesdaughter, photograph by Tecia Layson, 1999.)

Altar to Demeter and Persephone.
(Arrangement by author, photograph by Jery Stier, 1999.)

Mask: The Maiden's Descent.
(Mask by author, photograph by Jery Stier, 1999.)

The Spring Festivals
Growth and Harvest

In the splendor of Earth's treasures,
Do our hearts rise to the infinite power
and loveliness of your creations,
And so, we shall praise you.

his season's festivals bring those luxurious months of pleasant weather, when the natural world flowers and the fruits of the earth ripen. The festivals of the Season of Growth and Harvest are: *The Festival of Chloaia,* a brilliant celebration of flowers and of the green Earth, and an honoring of the beauty of Mother and Maiden. *Thargelia* is the great harvest celebration, and *Kalamaia* is the threshing. For northern regions Chloaia could take place in late spring or even early summer. Thargelia and Kalamaia, would become fall harvest festivals.

THE FESTIVAL OF CHLOAIA—MARCH 1ST

> ### Seasonal themes
> A celebration of the Verdant Mother and Maiden Daughter, who have made the land beautiful, green, and flowering. The joyful relationship of Demeter and Kore. Festival of Flowers. Magic, wine tasting, dancing.
>
> ### Transcendent themes
> All that we have worked for now brings its first rewards. Celebrating the pleasures of success. Good relationship between mother and child. Enjoying what we have strived to achieve, remembering to honor and thank the divine source of life. Continued support through prayer.

The Festival of Chloaia celebrates both the greening of cultivated land and of wild nature. According to Brumfield, ". . . as an epithet, Chloe would denote Demeter's role as patroness of the green shoot, the growing crop."[1] Chloe, or Chloaia, means the "verdant," signifying the "green shoot, grass, or leaf of a plant, as distinct from its root, seed, or fruit."[2] This holiday took place in the Greek month of Anthesterion (February-March), a month whose name means "Month of Flowers." Although it takes place prior to the Spring Equinox, it was one of the Greek spring festivals, along with the Dionysia. Chloaia celebrated not only the greening of the fields, but also the grain's flowering. In the several seasons that I have planted grain, it has flowered in late February.

In the Santa Monica mountains, California poppies, lupines, and other wildflowers bloom in March and April. One can find the red Flanders poppy, *papaver rhoeas,* a European wild-meadow and grain-field poppy, in garden catalogs. I have planted these in November with the wheat, and they begin to bloom in early April, at about the time the grain matures. To decorate the altar at Chloaia, I have used lilies, hyacinth, and daffodils, all of which bloom in a Mediterranean

---

[1]   Allaire Chandor Brumfield, *The Attic Festivals of Demeter and their Relation to the Agricultural Year* (Salem, NH: Arno Press, 1981), p. 132.
[2]   Brumfield, *The Attic Festivals of Demeter,* p. 132.

climate in February and March. More northerly regions might consider April or May for this holiday. Any kind of flower or spring flowering bulb, cut or growing in containers, can be used for altar decoration.

Chloaia was the time for the official opening of the new wine. Dionysus thus has a role to play here. According to author and scholar Dr. Nanno Marinatos, the revels of Dionysus were celebrations filled with joy and abandon. Women walked into the mountains to dance in freedom and without restraint for the wild God of Nature.[3] Here, within the Festival of Chloaia, you will find a simple maenadic-style celebration for the God of the vine.

During the festival, Demeter and Kore are praised for the return of spring and thanks is given for the harvest to come. Participants give their blessing to the cultivated crops and encourage fertility through magic. There is much celebration, with singing, circle dancing, and a tasting of the new wines.

Ritual Outline

I.   Preritual
II.   Opening Procession and Offerings of Flowers
III.   Welcome
IV.   Invocation to Hestia
V.   Invocation to Demeter
VI.   In the Month of Flowers
VII.   Song and Circle Dance
VIII.   Candle-Lighting Magic for the Earth
IX.   Opening the New Wine and Honoring Dionysus
X.   Garlanding Rite for the Heart's Desire
XI.   Closing Prayer
XII.   Closing Words

Clergy

Priestess of Demeter
Hierophantid of Demeter
Hierophantid of Kore
Hierophant

---

[3]   Video interview of Dr. Nanno Marrinatos by Joel Westbrook, "Greece: A Moment of Excellence," prod. J. Westbrook, Jason Williams, Jenny Barraclough for Time-Life Video and Television, Alexandria, VA, 1995.

Priestess of Hecate
Priestess of Hestia
Priest of Dionysus
Priestesses Panagia

The Main Altar

The altar table is set against a wall, or to the side of the ritual area if out of doors. Set an icon or image of Demeter (or an image of Mother and Daughter) at the center, toward the back. To the right and left of the icon, set two tall taper candles. On the altar place a vase of fresh flowers, a green potted or flowering plant, a green leafy wreath and a wreath of flowers (symbols of Demeter and Kore). The altar also holds a candle for Demeter, a candle for Kore, a candle or lamp for Hestia, a bowl of water, and decorations with additional greenery, flowers, and colored ribbons. Add any other symbols of Demeter and Kore you wish: bowls of grain, snake and pig images, etc.

The Altar of Dionysus

Decorate this altar with an image of Dionysus: a framed icon, a mask, or other image of Dionysus (see chapter 18, "masks"). You may decorate the altar with ivy, pine, and purple taper candles. On the altar, place bottles of wine for tasting (juice, for those who do not drink wine), a wine-bottle opener, tasting cups, and crackers and other foods to clear the palate between each vintage tasted.

Preparations

Make the green and flowered wreaths for the main altar. All participants should make fresh flower garlands and bring a votive candle in a holder. All should bring flowers as offerings to Demeter and Kore. Greek costume is an option (see chapter 18, "wreaths," "garlands," and "costumes"). Prepare a potluck feast.

THE FESTIVAL OF CHLOAIA

I. Preritual

Participants place their votive candles in holders on the main altar. The two taper candles are lit. All line up for the procession to the main altar. Begin far enough away from the altar so that you will have a distance to process. Each participant wears a garland of flowers or greenery around the neck, as well as optional head wreaths. As an offering to Demeter and Kore, each participant carries flowers that will be set on the altar.

II. Opening Procession and Offerings of Flowers

Priestesses Panagia/All: Chant/sing the following (or use one stanza as a repeating chant), as the procession to the main altar is conducted. You may use drums, rattles, or cymbals to keep a rhythm.

> Welcome gentle spring, hyacinth blooming;
> Green the sweet meadows, flowers awaking.
> The Holy Daughter has retuned again;
> The Mother's heart is golden.
>
> Green meadows and fields, the grain
>   a-flowering;
> Wild is the greenwood, with blossoms shining.
> The Holy Daughter has retuned again;
> The Mother's heart is golden.
>
> White the springtime flower, the lilies growing;
> Soft in the green glen, violets arising.
> The Holy Daughter has retuned again;
> The Mother's heart is golden.

III. Welcome

All arrive at the main altar. They face the altar. The Priestess of Hecate stands next to the altar, facing the participants.

Priestess of Hecate:

> All welcome to the Festival of Chloaia!
> We have come to celebrate
> The Verdant Mother of Spring,
> And the Maiden Daughter.
> Through their power,
> The land has grown green again.
> The high mountains, the broad meadows,
> And the cultivated fields,
> All reveal the beauty of Demeter and Kore,
> And so we praise them.
>
> We are also here to taste the new vintage,
> And to honor Dionysus,

Whose wild nature has born the gifts of the vine.
But first we begin
By asking for the blessings of Hestia.

IV. Invocation to Hestia

Priestess of Hestia [At main altar]:

We call Hestia,
Goddess of hearth and temple fire,
Of the Spiritual Center of our world,
And of all sacred places.
Hestia, beloved Goddess of the spiritual flame,
Come, and enter this temple.
Make all that is here holy and sacred in Your name.
Bring to us the peace and sureness
Of that place which is home and hearth.
Bring Your purity and beauty to us
As we honor You,
Who are the center of the spiritual flame.
So be it.

The Priestess of Hestia lights the lamp or candle. She raises it high and says:

Hail Hestia!

Priestesses Panagia/All:

Hail Hestia!

V. Invocation of Demeter and Kore

Priestess of Demeter [At the main altar]:

Demeter Chloaia, Verdant One,
When the first green leaf of the hyacinth
Rises from the damp soil,
There is the sweet whisper of your return.
As, beneath the cool shadows of the clouds
You labor,
So that beauty may return to Earth.

And in the month of Anthesterion,
The hillsides and meadowlands appear
Dressed in emerald once again,
As the verdant Goddesses reign,

Jeweled in larkspur, lupine,
And blood-red poppies.

The spirits of the running stream,
The pine, and the cypress
All rejoice in the glory of the season,
For under the sea-blue skies,
Your song resounds across the land.

The lush green stands of wheat and barley
Bend and sway in the winds,
And it is You, Chloaia,
In Your Dance of Creation.

To You
We offer the gifts of the heart,
Of love, beauty, and reverence
O grant us the season's bright benedictions
As we honor the Great Mother of the land.
So be it.

The Priestess of Demeter lights the Demeter candle, saying:
Praises to Demeter Chloaia!

Priestesses Panagia/All:
Praises to Demeter Chloaia!

Hierophantid of Kore [At the main altar]:
Fair Kore, by Your power
Do the green grasses rise after the barren time,
The saffron crocus and the white narcissus rise,
And clouds of pink-and-white blossoms
Come to the once bare-branched orchard.
You awaken the curling vine of the reveling God,
Bless the air with the scent of sweet flowers,
And fill the Mother's heart with love.
O bright and joyous Maiden,
We honor You today with praises,
Come, bless us with Your joyful heart
As we honor the Maiden of spring.
So be it.

The Hierophantid of Kore lights the candle for Demeter saying:
> Praises to Kore!

Priestesses Panagia/All:
> Praises to Kore!

VI. In the Month of Flowers

Priestesses Panagia:
> In this month of flowering,
> Love may blossom.
> Not only the affections between Mother and Daughter,
> But unions of love and passion
> May also grow
> In this season of green fields and balmy days.

Hierophant:
> In this month were Dionysus and Ariadne wed,
> And so on Earth, it is the season of love.
> May you be wed today with your heart's desire,
> And may any sadness be healed.
> The Mother's blessings to you all!

VII. Song and Circle Dance

Hierophantid of Kore: Instructs all to circle and join hands, moving in a clockwise direction, as they sing/chant one or both of the following,

> Chloaia,   *(Chlo . . . ah-ee-ah,)*
> Verdant Empress of the Earth, *(Ver-dant Em-press of the Earth,)*
> Chloaia,   *(Chlo . . . ah-ee-ah,)*
> In beauty mine.   *(In beau-ty mine.)*

> Season of love,   *(Sea . . . son of love,)*
> Dionysus, Ariadne,   *(Dion-y-sos, Ari-ad-ne)*
> O season of love,   *(O sea . . . son of love,)*
> Of love divine.   *(Of love di-vine.)*

VIII. Candle-Lighting Magic for the Earth

Priestess of Demeter:
> In our magic today,

We seek to protect all crops in all places,
Just as the sacred field is protected
By Triptolemos, the servant of the Holy Mother.
We remember that, without food,
The people of Earth do not live.

All crops face peril,
And so we shall give our prayers
To all cultivated fields.
May successful harvests arrive
In their seasons and in all places around the world.

Priestess of Hecate [Standing at the main altar]:
Hecate, immortal Goddess
Of deep magic and twilight crossroads,
Of mystical caverns and moonlit rites,
By thy great power,
We ask that our prayers be sanctified.
With them, shall we protect the young Korai,
That they may come to fruition.
We shall envision the green and growing field,
As all of the vast fields belonging to the farmers around the
    world:
The rice fields of Asia,
The wheat fields of North America,
The potato fields of South America,
The barley fields of Africa and the Mediterranean,[4]
And more, all growing from the body of the Earth.

Today we pray, that these cultivated fields may be blessed
With glorious days of sun and rain,
With peace, in which to till and care for the land,
And with our visions of fruition
For the great harvests to come.

Priestesses Panagia:
Candle light grow,
O praise the green Earth,

---

[4]   Feel free to add to these lines, as you wish.

Her light to flow,
Power of rebirth.

The Priestess then explains that each participant is to come to the altar to light
a candle intended to bring good harvests, to bless the work of all who farm the
land, or to bless Earth in any other way. The above chant is begun again, as
each participant goes to the altar to light a candle. The chant acts as a supportive background, helping to create focus and a trancelike state.

Candle light grow,
O praise the green Earth,
Her light to flow,
Power of rebirth.

Priestess of Hecate: When all have lit candles, the participants are guided
to stand in a semi-circle before the altar. The Priestess of Hecate guides them to
raise their hands to the candle flames and repeat the following lines, building
energy as they go.

With the words of Hecate,
Shall Her power come to play,
By the power of three times three
As we will, so shall it be!

Bind the power of light, in time;
The power bound in league times nine,
By all the power of Earth and Sun,
As we will, it shall be done!
And so . . . it . . . shall . . . be!

All raise generous and raucous screams!

IX. Opening the New Wine and Honoring Dionysus
Priest of Dionysus [At the altar of Dionysus]:

Dionysus, beloved God,
You are the vine that refreshes and brings healing,
That comforts and brings joy.
We give praises unto you,

O Lord of Woodland Revels,
You are the young fawn under dappled light,
And the sacred bull of high Summer.

O ivy-wreathed and flute-playing God of the green mountains,
Sweet and pleasing,
Come and bring rapture to the heart.

Here is Your generous gift,
The wine from last year's vintage,
Grown and pressed and matured into the blessed drink.
For this we thank You,
And raise the cup in Your honor.
All hail Dionysus!

Priestesses Panagia/All:
Hail Dionysus!

Priest of Dionysus: He now invites participants to come to Dionysus' altar and begin the rounds of tasting the new wine (grape juices may be used if desired). Before the first tasting, there is a toast to Dionysus. During the tasting of the samples of vintage, participants may spontaneously toast to other deities, or to other life blessings. The rite becomes informal, as each vintage is named, described, and tasted. Between vintages, crackers, cheese, etc., are offered. When the tasting is done, participants are again gathered into a circle.

Priestesses Panagia/All: All join hands, circle, or spiral in and out, singing and chanting. If the song or chant is not memorized by someone in the circle, then one or more may stand out as a chorus to sing or chant with percussion (perhaps tambourine). The following may be repeated as needed:
Mighty bull of Summer,
Sweet fawn in Spring,
O Lord of Woodland Revels bring,
The sacred vine, the aged wine,
And wild maenads, dancing free.
For Dionysus, Dionysus, passion's King,
For Dionysus, Dionysus, passion's King.

Deep within the dappled green,
Of the ancient wood,
Revels the horned and lusty God.
Heat is rising, in the dancing;
The river of desire flowing.
For Dionysus, Dionysus, passion's King,
For Dionysus, Dionysus, passion's King.

Hear the flute-playing God of the green,
In beauty his sweet song,
Steals into your heart at last,
And you rise with him on the shining wind,
Into the heart of beauty, O you are cast
With Dionysus, Dionysus, passion's King.
With Dionysus, Dionysus, passion's King.

X. Garlanding Rite for the Heart's Desire

Hierophantid of Demeter: nstructs the celebrants to remove the garland
from around their necks, close their eyes, and listen while the following prayer
is recited:

In this month of the marriage of Dionysus and Ariadne,
The heart is prepared for delight
And you may be wed with your heart's desire.
You shall be blessed with this garland of flowers,
A gift from the Mother and Maiden.
With the blessings of Dionysus and Ariadne,
May their magic
Bless your heart with love, affection, and joy,
And fill thy soul with the contentment
Of a dream found.
And so it shall be.

Hierophantid of Kore: Participants (including all clerics) are seated in a
circle, on chairs or on the floor. The Hierophantid of Kore explains the rite. She
turns to the person to her left and asks for his or her garland. Then she says:

What is your heart's desire?

Participants respond by stating the blessing wished for. The Hierophantid then
places the garland over the participant's head, saying:

In the name of Dionysus and Ariadne you are blessed with . . .

She rephrases the heart's desire in an affirmative way. A kiss may also be given,
if it is appropriate and desired in the group. (Decide this when doing your ritual
planning.) Also, if the group is larger than twelve participants, divide up into
smaller groups, or start at two places in the circle. When finished, all stand.

XI. Closing Prayer

Priestess of Demeter and Hierophant [Guide the closing chant]:

> Blessed are we in their Mystery;
> Hail mighty Demeter, and sweet Kore.

Then, together they say:

> With praises and thanksgiving
> For the Holy Mother and Daughter,
> With candles lit, and magic done,
> With rich wine
> And garlands of blessing,
> We have celebrated this holy day.
> May the joy and pleasure of Spring bless us all!

XII. Closing Words

Priestesses Panagia/All:

> These are the Rites of Chloaia.
> Her temple rites complete,
> In grace and in joy,
> May Her blessings proceed unto all!
> To the feast!

THE FESTIVAL OF THARGELIA—MAY 15TH

Seasonal themes

Gathering in the grain; the harvest celebration. Bountiful Demeter as Harvest Queen. The grain and the Maiden have matured. Hecate separates Kore from Demeter with the sickle.

Transcendent themes

Gathering in what you have sown. Reaping the rewards. The complete fruition of a dream. An abundance of blessings. Giving thanks.

Thargelia marks the beginning of the harvest season. It was not celebrated at the temple at Eleusis with the public pomp with which some of the other seasonal festivals were. This does not mean that the harvest of the grain from the temple's Rharian Field was not a special and much revered time. Perhaps the lack of the combined attendance of Eleusinian and Athenian clergy in Eleusis for these rites may be attributed to the fact that magical encouragement is most needed earlier, when the seed is first sown and when the crops are young and vulnerable. In addition, the harvest is primarily concerned with the work of gathering in the grain.

This first harvest may have been a private affair for Eleusis, the grain of the Rharian Field being sacrosanct. Thargelia was celebrated by individual farmers and took place at varied times, as harvest times differed in the island between coastal and inland city-states. Demeter's harvest name is Evalosia, "the good harvest." She also enjoyed titles for threshing, grinding, and baking.

There are records of state celebrations taking place in Delos, Boetia, and Athens. In the Athenian celebration of Thargelia, Apollo came to take part. His portion of the Athenian ritual was something called the *pharmakos* rite, about which little is known. Perhaps this concerned rites for the seed used in the making of the sacred drink for the mysteries.

The name of the festival, Thargelia, is taken from the month in which it occurred. The entire month of Thargelia, from approximately May 15th to June 15th, was harvesttime, the barley maturing prior to the wheat. The harvest could extend into early summer (in the northern regions, this ritual might take place anytime from August to September). Another name for the festival was *Thalysia* ("to ripen"). The thalysia were first fruits. First-fruit offerings were presented to the Goddess as a baked offering loaf, or as a mixture called *pansperma* ("many seeds," see Appendix 1). Pansperma was an offering of boiled grains and seeds. Today in Greece, there is a similar mixture eaten at funerals by mourners at the time of burial. You will find the use of pansperma in the Skira festival in June, where it is eaten after the Maiden's descent into Tartarus.

In the following interpretation of the festival, the grain is cut and bound into sheaves. If you have not grown your own grain, you may be able to purchase sheaves from a craft store or a local farming community. To replace the moments in the rite when the grain is separated from the earth by cutting, you may ceremonially cut a bottom portion of the stalks. If you have not grown, or are unable to obtain, sheaves of wheat (barley is more difficult to thresh), you will need to pass over Thargelia and wait for the Skira festival to continue your celebrations. This may be a good time to find a seed catalog or farming supply company from which you may order seed for future rituals (such as for the rite of Arkichronia, in Thesmophoria) and for a future planting. See chapter 19 for information on procuring and planting grain.

During Thargelia, the Goddess is thanked and honored with offerings. If the weather is hot, the sheaves are set up in the field to dry before the threshing. It is best to harvest the grain after it has thoroughly matured. It will be yellow, the heads hanging over just a little. If there is threat of moisture (in the case of my coastal field, this may include morning fog), the sheaves may be stored in a garage or storage area.

Ritual Outline

I.   Preritual
II.   Welcome
III.   Invocation to Demeter
IV.   Offerings
V.   Harvest
VI.   Giving Thanks
VII.   Closing

Clergy

Priestess of Demeter
Hierophant
Priestess of Hecate
Hierophantid of Demeter
Priestesses Panagia

Demeter's Altar

The altar may be on a small table, or the ritual items can be set directly on the ground. Included is an icon or image of Demeter, two vases with water on either side of the icon (to receive flowers during the rite), a dish of mixed grain or seeds, a sickle (whose handle is tied with colored ribbons), censer and incense, an uncut loaf of bread, wine and a chalice, pig images (see chapter 18, "Pigs"), and 1-foot lengths of yellow or gold ribbons (one for each participant), in a basket or bowl.

Preparations

If you are performing Thargelia without a planted field, bring sheaves of wheat whose ends can be cut to emulate harvesting. If you have not grown red poppies, bring red roses or other red flowers to replace the poppies. These will be placed on the altar during the rite. Participants should bring sharp scissors, offerings of grain, seeds, dried fruit, nuts, or beans in small bowls, and food for an outdoor picnic. Twine and a wheelbarrow, and a box or cloth to receive the bound sheaves should be set to one side of the field.

THE FESTIVAL OF THARGELIA

I. Preritual

All circle in the field, or around the planted area. A box or wheelbarrow is on one side of the field. Participants have sharp scissors or sickles. On the side of the field is the altar with an icon or image of Demeter, a sickle, a censer and incense, one gold ribbon for each participant, two vases of water (to receive the flowers), and pig images.

Priestesses Panagia/All: Chanting.
> Hail Evalosia, great Thargelian Queen,
> Thy work is done O blessed One.
> Golden, Thy rich bounty.
> The ripened seed, Thy ecstasy;
> Hail to the Harvest Queen!

II. Welcome

Hierophant:
> Welcome to the Rites of Thargelia!
> The grain has ripened,
> And the promise of Demeter and Kore has come to fruition.
> The seasons all have blessed the sacred seed,
> And so we give thanks.

Priestess of Hecate:
> With the blade of Hecate
> The Maiden will be separated from the Mother,
> And the season will change again
> So that the cycle of life may continue.

Hierophantid of Demeter:
> We rejoice at our good fortune,
> Thankful for Earth's bounty and for the beauty
> Of all Her creations.
> May we continue to enjoy the simple pleasures of life:
> Caring for those we love,
> Participating in good and honest labor,
> Expressing caring and compassion,
> Honoring the Divine Mother,
> And enjoying the satisfactions of a full cupboard.
> For all this, we give praises.

III. Invocation of Demeter

Priestess of Demeter:
> Great Mother, Thargelian Harvest Queen,
> You have fulfilled Your holy powers of Creation.
> The wisdom that You have placed inside the seed
> Has attained its sacred design,
> And the planted field has flourished in Your name.
> All fruits that ripen, those of field, tree, or vine
> That leaf out and bear fruit, are Your children.
> O Glorious Goddess,
> Enthroned in Your great fields of wheat and barley,
> Crowned with grain and ruddy cheeked,
> You revel in the joy of harvesttime.

Hierophant: Guiding all to repeat the following lines.
> Luminescent and golden Mother of all,
> Drinking of divine nectar
> You partake in the ecstasy of Your creations
> And flood the world with joy.
> Come Lady,
> And receive these offerings from those who love you.

IV. Offerings

The Priestesses Panagia cut some of the poppies in the field, or they have brought red flowers. They place them in empty vases to the right and left of the Demeter icon, saying:

> For the Holy Mother.

Then participants are invited to bring their offerings (nuts, seeds, grain beans, or dried fruit) in small bowls to the altar. They offer them to the Goddess, saying:

> For the Holy Mother.

V. Harvest

Priestesses Panagia/All: All join hands, and face the grain field. The following is spoken or chanted:

> Swing the reaper,
> 'Cross the blessed field,
> The scythe and sickle,
> How they dance and sway.
>
> Here stands the golden grain,
> Where the green once stood,
> Praise to the Holy Mother
> Upon our harvest day.
>
> O the Goddess of the night,
> Brings her blade unto the day,
> Knowing her purpose true,
> We shall welcome Hecate.

Priestess of Hecate:

> Let the Harvest begin!

She then instructs all to pick up their cutting tools and begin the harvest.

Participants: On the first cut, say the following:

> By the powers of Hecate!

Each participant takes hold of some of the wheat toward the base of the stalks and cuts it several inches above the ground. These small bunches are cleaned of leaves, bound into sheaves with twine, and are then set into the box or wheelbarrow or onto the cloth. At the end of the harvest work, they will be stacked or tied into a shock(s), and set in front of the altar. The Priestess of Hecate places a sheaf on the altar, in front of the Demeter icon.

Hierophantid of Demeter: Instructs all to circle around the field, or semi-circle around a portion of the field. The harvested grain is in the center. (In northern regions replace the third to the last line with "Perish in the cold of winter's hand.") The Hierophantid says:

We give thanks for the rains of Zeus,
And for the Mother's fertile power.
In the season past, did the Maiden
Rise with verdant and flowering beauty.
Now, the green stands of grain
No longer grace the sacred field.
The grasses and vines of mountain and meadow
Shall in the days to come
Perish in the heat of the summer sun.
It is then that the Maiden will be called to Death's Domain,
For this is a part of the eternal cycle.

Priestess of Hecate: The Priestess goes to the altar, places her hands in blessing over the bread, and says:
We break bread with the Goddess,
Sharing in this holy offering.
May this that we take into our bodies
Infuse us with strength, joy and well being,
In the name of Demeter Evalosia.
So be it.

All are invited to come up to the altar. A piece of bread is given to each participant with the words: "May you never hunger." A gold or yellow ribbon is tied gently around the wrist of each participant, with the words, "With the blessings of Evalosia." All circle in or around the field and eat. Then a cup of wine is shared with the words, "May you never thirst."[5]

VI. Giving Thanks

Priestess of Demeter [Taking the sickle]:
Now we give thanks,
For not only the abundance that is born
From the great Earth,
But for the many blessings that have graced our lives.
We pause to consider what we have been given.
As the sickle is passed around the circle,
State the good things in your life
For which you are thankful,
And then pass the sickle on.

---

[5] I first heard "May you never hunger," and "May you never thirst" at a Wiccan ritual of Moon Berch Grove in Los Angeles, in 1980.

The Priestess goes first, as the example. When all have taken a turn, the sickle is set back down on the altar.

Priestess of Hecate:
>Holy One,
>All the world is filled with Your treasures.
>Not the gold and silver of the dusky cavern,
>But the myriad forms of teeming life that thrive under
>   the Sun.
>And when we bring in all that we need to live,
>We partake of You, Evalosia.

Hierophant:
>The harvest is a grand thing,
>For we have worked and labored hard
>To bring the field to fruition.
>And all that we do,
>That is planting, weeding, and tending,
>Leads to the joy of harvest day.

Priestess of Demeter:
>All honor to the Mother of the Good Harvest,
>Full of splendor and crowned with grain.
>The riches of life, streaming from the palms of Thy hands
>Bring us joy and sweet pleasure.
>Great praise and thanksgiving do we give to Thee,
>As we say: Hail Demeter Evalosia!

Priestesses Panagia/All:
>Hail Demeter Evalosia!

VII. Closing

Priestesses Panagia/All [Circling with hands held, chanting]**:**
>Filled with gifts, the chalice of plenty
>Overflows with good fortune.
>How blessed are we, who love and honor
>The Mother, and the Holy Daughter.
>May we drink from the Queen's cup.

Priestesses Panagia/All:
These are the rites of Thargelia.
Her temple rite complete
In grace and in joy,
May Her blessings proceed unto all!
To the feast!

THE FESTIVAL OF KALAMAIA—JUNE 7TH

> ### Seasonal themes
> The threshing. Honoring the Grain Mother and Triptolemos, teacher of agriculture. Freeing the seed from the chaff. Separating out portions of seed for various uses; deciding which of the seed will be used for replanting, for food, and for ritual purposes.
>
> ### Transcendent themes
> Seeing what is good within past experience, and choosing to release those influences which you no longer want, from your spirit. Deciding where your resources will go. Setting part aside— some for use now, some for the future, and a portion for the sacred, or spiritual purposes. Honoring the source of your bounty, and those who taught you the skills by which you profit.

The Festival of Kalamaia marks the beginning of the threshing season that, in some cases, lasted well into the summer. It may have been that some of the grain was separated out at this time, for replanting, for ritual purposes, and for food use. There are records of celebrations at Eleusis and also in Piraeus. These took place in the month of Skirophorion (June-July).

In a schematic reconstruction of the Eleusinian sacred calendar by Dow and Healey, "Kalamaia" is listed as occurring before the harvest.[6] Dow and Healey may have been led to erroneously list the threshing as

---

[6] Sterling Dow and Robert F. Healey, *A Sacred Calendar of Eleusis* (Cambridge: Harvard University Press, 1965), p. 44. Copyright © 1965 by The President and Fellows of Harvard College. Reprinted by permission of Harvard University Press.

prior to the harvest by the fact that the tablet that contained their original source information covered primarily the festivals of Proerosia, Thesmophoria, and Skira. These festivals were the focus of their text. In order to present the reader with a larger view of the Eleusinian year, the authors found it "necessary to tabulate the festivals likely to have had entries"[7] by basing their list on H. G. Pringsheim's *Archeologische Beitrage zur Geschichte des Eleusinischen Kults*.[8] Perhaps Pringsheim's work was the source of their error.

In *The Attic Festivals of Demeter and their Relation to the Agricultural Year,* Brumfield suggests that the Kalamaia was most likely a threshing festival, naturally occurring after the harvest, and that the word *kalame* was used, not only to refer to the stalk, "but also to the husks which covered the seed, and to the chaff, straw and refuse in general."[9] Straw was valuable, and saved for a variety of purposes. It was used for baskets, hats, mats, bedding material for the poor, and floor coverings for barns. Greco-Roman writers also suggested a compost made from a combination of poultry, horse, and sheep dung mixed with straw.

The threshing floor, sacred to Triptolemos, was cleansed before the threshing commenced. As Demeter's grain missionary, Triptolemos was a part of both the beginning (the preplowing rites) and the end (the threshing) of the growth cycle. It has been said that most farmers had an altar to him, particularly those who cared for the temple's sacred Rharian Field.

If you have not grown your own grain (see chapter 19), there are a couple of ways you may obtain it. Sheaves of wheat may be available in local craft stores, where they are sold for dried floral arrangements. A florist shop may also be able to obtain some for you. You may also want to check with the local farming community.

In the following portrayal of the rite, the sheaves with the best seed are chosen and set aside to use for the next season's planting and then all is threshed. I remember the first time that I saw freshly threshed grain (it was red winter wheat). As the threshing went on, each of us would place a portion of seed into a large wooden bowl. When we were done, some of us could not resist scooping it up and letting it flow through our hands. It seemed to me like running your fingers through small amber and garnet jewels.

---

[7]   Dow and Healey, *A Sacred Calendar of Eleusis,* p. 44.

[8]   Dow and Healey, *A Sacred Calendar of Eleusis,* p. 42.

[9]   Brumfield, *The Attic Festivals of Demeter,* p. 151.

Ritual Outline

I.   Preritual
II.   Procession to the Main Altar and Offerings
III.   Invocation to Demeter
IV.   Inner Threshing
V.   Blessings of Triptolemos
VI.   Blessing the Threshing Place
VII.   Threshing of the Grain
VIII. Closing Prayer
IX.   Closing Words

Clergy

Priestess of Demeter
Hierophant
Priestesses Panagia
Priestess of Hecate
Hierophantid of Demeter
a child or youngest member of the group
Priest of Triptolemos

The Main Altar

The altar holds a votive candle for Demeter, a sickle whose handle is tied with colored ribbons, two taper candles to the right and left of the Demeter icon, a vase or vases of dried grasses and flowers, snake and pig images (see chapter 18, "snakes" and "pigs"). And baskets of fruit, bowls of nuts and/or seeds.

Participants Bring

Offerings of fruit, flowers, breads or sweet cakes, a small bowl for threshing, and food for the feast after the ritual.

Side Table

A table on which participants will set their offerings, bowls, and feast foods.

Preparations

Have ready scissors, tied bundles of grain, hand bells for the Priestess of Hecate and the Hierophantid of Demeter, censer and incense, two bowls to hold the threshed grain, and twine and colored ribbon to tie the sheaves of grain that will be kept for decorative purposes. Have large, plastic zip-seal baggies into which you can put the threshed grain after the day's festivities are over. After the threshing, put the grain into the freezer for two weeks to kill any possible pests.

Staging

The location for this rite is out of doors. Place a large basket or cloth below and to the front of the main altar. Have the threshing area (at which is the censer and incense and two bowls to hold threshed grain) sufficiently far from the main altar so that there will be a certain distance to walk in procession. Since the censer will be picked up and carried during a part of the rite, it needs to be a swinging censer or a censer that is placed in a secondary bowl, lined with two inches of sand.

THE FESTIVAL OF KALAMAIA

I. Preritual

When participants arrive, they place their offerings and feast foods on the side table.

II. Procession to the Main Altar and Offerings

All line up to process to the main altar, by way of the threshing area. A child or the youngest member of the group leads the procession and carries a tied bundle of grain (as an offering for Demeter). Participants carry bundles of grain to be threshed and offerings of fruit, flowers, breads, or sweet cakes. They process to the threshing area, chanting:

For Evalosia,	*(For Ev-a-lo-see-ah,)*
These sacred offerings,	*(These sa-cred off-rings)*
To honor the Mother	*(To hon-or the Mo-ther)*
Of all growing things.	*(Of all grow-ing things.)*
Praises. Praises. Praises.	*(Prai-ses. Prai-ses. Prai-ses.)*

The grain to be threshed is laid down in the threshing area. The chant is continued as all walk in procession to the main altar. Upon arrival at the altar, the Priestess of Hecate and the Hierophantid of Demeter ring hand bells three times.

Child or Youngest: Places the bundle of grain onto the altar and says:
   Praise to the Holy Mother!

Priestesses Panagia/All:
   Praise to the Holy Mother!

Participants place their offerings on the altar, saying:
   For Demeter Evalosia.

Their bundles of grain are placed on the cloth (or into the large basket) below and to the front of the altar.

III. Invocation of Demeter

Hierophantid of Demeter:

>Now shall we invoke Demeter Evalosia,
>Who reigns as Queen of the golden harvest.

Hierophantid and Priestess of Demeter:

>Lady of all good harvests,
>Our stores are filled again
>With Your generous bounty,
>O You who are the blessings of Earth,
>Who sustain both body and spirit.
>Hail!

The Hierophantid lights the incense.

Priestess of Demeter:

>Beloved Demeter, You spin out Your magic
>From the Mysteries of the Seed,
>Bringing us the miracle of life and growth . . .
>The riches of the vine,
>The orchard and the cultivated field.
>Are all born of Your power.
>And so we honor the Great Mother of the land.

Priestesses Panagia:

>O Mother of life,
>We were born from the infinite seeds of Creation,
>And live through the powers of Earth.

Priestess of Demeter:

>Our spirits rise with Your beauty,
>For You are everywhere:
>In every broad meadow and mountainside,
>In every lovely field and flower,
>And in every living and growing thing.

Today at the threshing we honor You,
Bringing You offerings and praising Your name.
We thank You for all that You give,
And ask that You
Come and bless this threshing with ease and joy,
Hail Demeter Evalosia!
Hail!

The Priestess of Demeter lights the center votive candle in front of Demeter's icon.

Priestesses Panagia/All:
Hail Demeter Evalosia!

IV. Inner Threshing

Priestess of Hecate: The Priestess picks up the sickle with the colored ribbons from the altar. She asks the participants to form a semi-circle, open toward the altar. Facing the participants, she says:
By Hecate's blade,
The grain was separated from the Earth
So that the threshing could begin.
It is fitting at Kalamaia,
When seed shall be separated from chaff,
For us to note anything
Which we no longer want in our lives
And wish to be separated from.

We will pass the sickle around,
Praying aloud, or silently
For whatever it is that might be beneficial for you
To be separated from, that it be done so now.

Begin with the words . . . By her blade . . .
When you are done, breathe upon the blade.
End with the words . . . Hail Hecate.
Then go to the altar and pass the sickle blade
Over Demeter's flame.

With both hands, the Priestess holds the sickle and says:
By Her blade . . .

She then prays aloud or silently. When she is done, she breathes upon the blade and says:

Hail Hecate.

Priestesses Panagia/All:

Hail Hecate!

Priestess of Hecate: Goes to the altar and passes the sickle blade over Demeter's candle flame. She then returns to the circle and passes the sickle to the one next to her. The process continues until all are done. The sickle is placed on the altar.

V. Blessings of Triptolemos

All process to the place of threshing, in front of the censer for Triptolemos.

Priest of Triptolemos:

Now shall we honor Triptolemos,
Who at Proerosia,
Was invoked to the thrice-plowed field.

Sacred son of Eleusis,
Emissary of the Great Mother,
From Holy Demeter did You receive and then impart
The arts of agriculture,
Which lay the foundations for civilization.
And so we honor You.
Hail Triptolemos!

The Priest of Triptolemos lights the incense.

Hierophant:

Wise One,
It is with food stores set aside
That we enjoy the luxury of time
In which to glorify the Muses,
Follow the paths of justice,
And honor the Great Mother
With festivals and celebrations.
These are the blessings that You, Triptolemos,
In concord with Her,
Have given to all of humanity.

Hierophant and Priest of Triptolemos:
> Treasured God of plowing and sowing,
> We thank and honor You
> As we bless this threshing place
> In Your name,
> So be it.

The Priest of Triptolemos raises the censer, letting the smoke rise up, saying:
> Hail Triptolemos!

Priestesses Panagias/All:
> Hail Triptolemos!

VI. Blessing the Threshing Place

Hierophant: Picks up the smoking censer. He carries it around the threshing area. All follow him in procession, repeatedly chanting:

May good enter this place	*(May good en-ter this place)*
With gentle ease and	*(With gen-tle ease and*
blessed grace,	*bless-ed grace,)*
Where chaff is freed	*(Where chaff is freed)*
From the blessed seed	*(From the bless-ed seed)*
And the cloak of the grain	*(And the cloak of the grain)*
Shall Aeolus chase.[10]	*(Shall Ae-o-lus chase.)*

VII. Threshing of the Grain

After the threshing area is censed, the best heads of grain are separated in a pile. These will be the first to be threshed, the seed then saved for next season's planting. These will be threshed and placed in a bowl. The rest of the grain will be threshed and used for the fertility talismans of Arkichronia and for cooking and/or baking. This seed will be placed in another bowl. Both of these bowls will later be brought to the main altar. Some of the remaining unthreshed sheaves will be saved to make ceremonial wreaths and to decorate altars. Clean these sheaves by removing any of the small leaves and leaving just the bare stalk. Bind these sheaves together and tie them in small decorative bundles with twine. Cut the bottom ends straight across. Then decorate them with colored ribbon. The rest of the grain will be threshed (see chapter 19).

---

[10]   Aeolus is the Greek God of winds and breezes.

Some of the straw and chaff needs to be saved to be burned at the rites of the coming Skira festival. If you wish, some of it may be saved for weaving, or for garden mulch. You will end with sheaves for altar decoration, a tied bundle or bundles of straw, and two bowls of threshed seed.

When done, the bowls of threshed grain are picked up and carried to the main altar in procession, as are the decorative altar sheaves. The sheaves are placed in front of Demeter's icon and the bowls of grain to the sides.[11]

VIII. Closing Prayer

Priestesses Panagia/All [The Priestesses instruct all to form a semi-circle around the main altar]:

> Filled with gifts, the chalice of plenty
> Overflows with good fortune.
> How blessed are we, who love and honor
> The Mother and the Holy Daughter.
> May we drink from the Queen's cup.

IX. Closing Words

Priestesses Panagia/All:

> These are the rites of Kalamaia.
> These temple rites complete,
> In grace and in joy,
> May Her blessings proceed unto all!
> To the feast!

---

[11] When the festival is over, the two bowls of grain are emptied in separate zip-seal baggies. They are then placed in the freezer for a period of two weeks to kill any unwanted pests or their eggs. After two weeks, the bags are placed in the urn that will be used for the Skira festival.

C H A P T E R   1 2

The Summer Festival
The Fallow Time

Will she descend?
Here lamps have grown dim, and Tartarus' meadows die.
For lack of her light, the perished shall perish.

"Mediterranean summer days are hot, and sometimes completely without rain. The grain has already been harvested. In July and August, 90 to 100+ degree weather can continue for days on end. Waves of heat take the remaining moisture from the land. The countryside withers and for the ancient Greek farmer, most agricultural fields lie fallow and await the fall rains. The *Skira Festival* is one of the year's major holidays, as it contains the drama of the Maiden's descent. In northern regions it would be appropriate for the Skira to take place in late fall not long after the harvest.

THE SKIRA FESTIVAL—JUNE 28TH

Seasonal themes

Honoring the Harvest Mother. The call of Plouton. The descent of the Maiden and the storage of the seed grain. Transition from the fertile part of the year to the barren part of the year.

Transcendent themes

Giving thanks to the source of life for your success. Taking note of what you have learned, and gained. Storing resources in a place of protection. Transition from life to death. Facing fear, and/or the unknown. Courage, independence, a transformation.

The Skira festival, also known as the Skirophoria, took place on the old Greek-calendar date of Skirophorion 12. The Gregorian-calendar date would be sometime between late June and early July. As in the Thesmophoria and Haloa festivals, husbands were expected to pay their wives' expenses for the Skira. Prefestival ceremonies included an honoring of heroes in a procession in which objects were carried. Unfortunately, it is unclear exactly what these objects were. Also included in the festival were offerings to Demeter, Kore, Athena, and Poseidon. It is known that, during the rite, something was placed into the ground. Brumfield suggests that grain from the previous harvest and materials with which to store the grain may have been carried in the procession and then set into the ground.

At this point in the seasonal cycle, the heat and lack of rain have dried out not only the fields, but the meadows and hillsides as well. The fallow period is beginning. Those in northern regions might choose a date for the beginning of the fallow period when the cold weather sets in, at the end of October or the beginning of November.

By the time of this festival, offerings of the first harvested and threshed grain (the *aparchai*) have already arrived and been stored in temple granaries. The aparchai were sent from all of the Greek city-states to Eleusis, in hopes that the blessings of the two Goddesses would be bestowed upon all. The Temple of Eleusis could both sell and store these grain offerings. Storage pits and structures for the first-fruit offerings were located in several areas of the sanctuary.

Grain from the temple's Rharian Field was used not only as food, but for preparing sacred offerings, such as sacrificial cakes, as well.

Emblematic of that place where Triptolemos taught the arts of agriculture to the people of Eleusis, the Rharian Field embodied the whole myth of Demeter and the Holy Daughter. Grain from this field must have been stored in a very special granary, separate from that of the aparchai. Perhaps during the Skira festival, when the harvest had been completed and the fallow period begun, the grain from the Rharian Field was stored with great ceremony.

The Skira festival, or Skirophoria, was one of the most important holidays of the Eleusinian calendar. The storage of the seed grain signals the descent of the Holy Daughter. The lush green of late winter and early spring have faded, and the heat of dry summer is beginning. In the following interpretation of the Skira festival, the Maiden descends into the Underworld. Her purpose is to join the god Plouton in love, and to bring light and beauty into a place of darkness. She takes with her the seed grain for the fall planting (and for the making of the Arkichronian fertility talismans). The grain is carried in an urn. During the rite, the urn of seed is mythically stored in the regenerative depths, to be cared for and nourished by the passions of the God and Goddess of the Underworld.

Ritual Outline

I.	Preritual
II.	Welcome
III.	Invocation to Hestia
IV.	Honoring Demeter Evalosia
V.	Dance on the Plains of Nysa
VI.	Procession to the Gates of Tartarus
VII.	Voice of the Dark Lord
VIII.	Fires of Nysa
IX.	Maiden's Descent
X.	Hecate's Magic,
XI.	Storage of the Seed Grain
XII.	Rite of the Pansperma
XIII.	Closing Song
XIV.	Closing Words

Clergy

Hierophantid of Demeter
Hierophant
Priestess of Hestia
Priestess of Demeter

Priestesses Panagia
Priestess of Kore-Persephone
Priest of Plouton
Priestess of Hecate
Priestess of Athena

Main Altar

The altar holds also an icon of Demeter with a candle on either side of it, and a votive candle in front. There is also a wreath of dried grain (see chapter 18, "crowns") with yellow, gold, and red ribbons through it, Hestia's lamp or candle, and an incense burner and incense, along with dried flowers and seed pods. There is an urn of seed and a vase within which two packages of grain have been set. The two packages of grain will be used later in the year, one for the planting and the other for the Rites of Arkichronia. I suggest that zip-seal baggies be used for the packages. You may also wish to have effigies of snakes and pigs on the altar (see chapter 18, "snake and pig effigies").

Participant Offerings and the Offering Table

Participant offerings of baked goods and/or bowls of seeds, beans, or nuts as well as all other items to be used during the ritual, are set on this table. Participants bring feast foods, a small cup and a spoon, and red flower petals. The Hierophantid of Demeter brings an uncut loaf of bread. The Priestess of Demeter brings the Pansperma (see Appendix 1) and a serving spoon. The table also holds bowls of dried herbs: whole bay leaves, pennyroyal and/or dried wormwood, and mint leaves. There is a pencil and a small square of paper for each participant that will be used in the magic portion of the festival.

For the storage of the seed grain you will need a 12-inch circle of cloth, a cord or ribbon for tying the cloth over the top of the urn, approximately one yard of black fabric to set the whole urn into, twine, scissors, and several yards of red and purple ribbons to tie the black cloth, creating a bag that will encase the whole urn.

Gateway to Tartarus

The gateway to Tartarus may be symbolized by two pedestals, two small tables, or two stacks of brick that Persephone will pass through. Set a candle on each pedestal of the gateway. Set a 2-foot-square layer of brick, cement, or terracotta tiles on the floor in front of it.

Fire Altar

If the ritual is outdoors, set the following on the brick, cement squares, or tile in front of the gateway; a small cone made out of pieces of dried straw, the pieces leaning up against each other, with a layer of straw surrounding the cone, and small dry twigs or pieces of dry wood. Surround these items with a "box shape" of stacked, small dry branches or pieces of wood. The altar should be small, fitting into the center of the brick floor in front of the gateway. Before the ritual, drip bits of candlewax here and there over the wood and straw, particularly on the cone in the center. Practice creating a fire from this ahead of time. Have small dry pieces of wood and straw to one side of the fire altar to be added if needed. If the ritual is indoors, use a fire altar cauldron as explained in chapter 18. Have an empty bowl and a bowl of dried red flower petals ready on the other side of the fire altar.

Persephone's and Plouton's Vestments

The maiden wears a white himation and a dried red-flower crown. As Persephone, her vestments are a black himation and a crown. Plouton's vestments are also a black himation and crown (see chapter 18, "Persephone's Vestments" and "Plouton's Vestments"). Persephone's himation, a broach or pin to secure it when draped, and her crown are set next to the gateway to Tartarus.

Storage Area for the Grain

If the festival is done outdoors, the grain storage area, will be in a pit or other storage area such as a shed. If indoors, it can be under the altar, or in any special hidden, out-of-the-way spot that you designate for the purpose. The urn of seed will be placed symbolically into the Underworld. If the festival is performed outdoors, dig your storage pit and line it with stone or brick, or coat it with dry chalk. The top of the pit should be covered by a slab of stone or a large terracotta tile. You may also create an above-ground storage area.

Staging

The areas needed are: the main altar, the offering table, the gateway to Tartarus, and the storage area for the grain. The storage area for the grain should be just beyond the gateway to Tartarus. It may be under another altar that represents the cavern of Eleusis. Adjacent to the storage area is a small table or pillar upon which is a chalice of water and Persephone's crown. Greek costume (see chapter 18) is optional, but the Priestess of Kore-Persephone should wear a white himation that she will remove before passing through the gateway to Tartarus. She begins the ritual, wearing the crown of dried red flowers that will also be removed during the rite.

THE SKIRA FESTIVAL

I. Preritual

Participants place their offerings for Demeter, and their cup and spoon, on the side table. Dried red flower petals are set into the empty bowl at the fire altar. Feast foods are placed on a side table. All form a semi-circle around the main altar.

Priestess of Demeter [Lights the taper candles, saying]:
    Hail Demeter! Hail Kore!

She censes the icon of Demeter and the urn of seed.

II. Welcome

Hierophantid of Demeter:
    All welcome to the Skira Festival!
    The grain has been harvested and threshed,
    And we praise the Great Mother, Demeter Evalosia.
    The poppies have flowered blood-red,
    And the time of green fields has passed.

    The crocuses and lilies have gone,
    And the golden seed is gathered in.
    Now is the time for the Holy Daughter's transition.

Hierophant:
    The fertile season passes, and the barren season soon begins.
    Will the Maiden descend into the Underworld,
    And let fall the lily veil?
    Will She cast away the poppy crown,
    And cross the black bridge to destiny?
    These are the questions of the Rites of Skirophoria.
    But first, we shall invoke Hestia . . .

III. Invocation of Hestia

Priestess of Hestia [At the main altar]:
    We call Hestia,
    Goddess of hearth and temple fire,

Of the Spiritual Center of our world,
And of all sacred places.
Hestia, Beloved Goddess of the spiritual flame,
Come, and enter this temple.
Make all that is here holy and sacred in Your name.
Bring to us the peace and sureness
Of that place which is home and hearth.
Bring Your purity and beauty to us
As we honor You
Who are the center of the spiritual flame.
So be it.

The Priestess of Hestia lights the lamp or candle. She raises it up and says
Hail Hestia!

Priestesses Panagia/All:
Hail Hestia!

IV. Honoring Demeter Evalosia

All participants are asked to retrieve their offerings from the offering table and stand for the invocation.

Priestess of Demeter [At the main altar]:
Holy One,
All the world is filled with your treasures.
Not the gold and silver of the dusky cavern,
But the myriad forms of teeming life that thrive under the Sun.
And when we bring in all that we need to live,
We partake of You, Demeter Evalosia.

All honor to the Mother of the Good Harvest,
Full of splendor and crowned with grain,
The beauty of the forest and the broad meadow,
The great mountains and shimmering silver lakes,
The rose, the lily, and the wild starlike anemone
Have all been bestowed by Thy gracious powers.
The riches of life, streaming from the palms of Thy hands,
Bring us joy and sweet pleasure.
Great praise and thanksgiving do we give to Thee,
As we bring to You our offerings.
All hail Demeter Evalosia!

Priestesses Panagias:
> Hail Demeter Evalosia!

The Priestess of Demeter lights the center votive candle. The Hierophantid of Demeter places the first offering, an uncut loaf of bread, onto the altar, saying:
> For Evalosia.

The Priestess of Demeter places the offering of the Pansperma on the altar, saying the same words. Then all leave their offerings for the Harvest Mother, saying:
> For Evalosia.

V. Dance on the Plains of Nysa

Hierophantid of Demeter: The Priestess explains that before the holy Daughter's descent, she and the Daughters of Oceanus danced on the plains of Nysa. We will dance as they did, imagining that we are beside the sea. The Priestess instructs all to join hands and circle, and move in a clockwise direction as the following is chanted, sung, or spoken (it may be repeated). If the words are not memorized, one or more may stand out as a chorus. (Now, behind the gateway to Tartarus, the Priest of Plouton dons his vestments.)

Priestesses Panagias/All:
> O ancient Mother of the Sea,
> Singing, we bring sweet blossoms.
> Dea Daira, Mother of beauty
> To this simple circle, come Lady!
>
> In splendor, rising like the silvery moon,
> Dark hair flowing in the blue indigo wave,
> Rises the Sea Mother, garlanded in white pearl,
> Redolent in power, from Her ancient cave.
>
> Maidens are dancing upon the shore,
> Barefoot with their garments streaming,
> To honor the Goddess of the vast untamed Sea,
> Of the deep waters and of dolphins singing.

VI. Procession to Gates of Tartarus

The circle stops and the Priestess of Hecate says:
> Upon the Plains of Nysa,
> Did the Maidens rest after the dance.

They rested, and Kore dreamed that she heard
A song of great yearning and sadness
Rising from deep below the earth.
A song that issued from the very Gates of Tartarus.
Come, let us journey there
And listen . . .

All proceed to the gateway of Tartarus. The following items are taken from the offering table and carried in procession to the gateway: the urn of seed, the storage materials for the grain (the dried herbs), the fabrics and ribbons to encase the urn, and the paper and pencils for the magic.

VII. Voice of the Dark Lord

Upon arriving at the gateway, the Hierophant says:
Listen to the words of the Dark Lord.
It is Tartarus' King who sings to the Holy Daughter
As she rests beside the everlasting sea.
He calls Her to the lands below, and awaits the hand of Fate.
Hear now, the words of the Lord Plouton.

Priest of Plouton: In black himation, and crowned.
Blind with grief and longing,
I have been called the Unseen One
For whom Tartarus' throne has become a prison.
I cannot live above, and yet my heart is given to the Holy
    Daughter.
But will She descend?
Here, lamps have grown dim, and Tartarus' meadows die.
For lack of Her light, the perished shall perish.

She is full of beauty and light . . .
I have kept Her in my heart,
Praying that my time of waiting will soon be over.
In a dream, spellcast by Hecate,
The Maiden has heard my song
As she rested on Nysa's Plain.

In Her dream She has seen me . . .
And now wakes to Eros' flame.
I will go to the Grotto of the Black Stallions

And harness the waiting steeds.
Up into the light of the world
We shall go,
To meet the Maiden at the Dark Gate.

The Priest of Plouton leaves the area, but will return when the celebrants are engaged in the Maiden's descent.

VIII. Fires of Nysa

Priestess of Hecate: At the fire altar, before the gateway, the entrance to the Underworld, the Priestess of Hecate lights the fire. She raises her hands before the flame and says:
Fires of change, burn away the past.
For as surely as the wheel turns,
The Queen of the Underworld will take up Her cloak and crown.
Spring has gone, but in its time, will come again.
O flames of change, bless this holy transformation,
And create the black bridge to destiny!

The Priestess places small pieces of wood, dried chaff, and wheat stalks on the flame.

Priestesses Panagia: [Sung or spoken]:
O Holy Daughter, the time has come,
Time to cross over; gone is the Maiden.
The fire burns; darkness awaits Thee yet.
The heart yearns for destiny magnificent.

O leave the land of light, the Dark Lord is singing.
The souls of the dead, for You they are waiting.
Cross over the embers red; the smoking black Earth
Will take You; descend into the Land of Death.

Praise the fair Daughter, so sacred and holy,
For the Crown of Death awaits Persephone only.
And when the shadowy steeds arise and come for Thee,
Go then, and embrace the Unseen, for there Your heart shall be.

Priestess of Kore-Persephone [Facing the fire]:
What lies beyond the flame?
If I had the strength of the Virgin Warrior,

Then would I choose, to walk across the field
Of ember and flame, and embrace the Lord of the Dark.
If the Virgin Warrior's strength was mine.

Priestess of Athena [Approaching Kore from behind]:

Bright Kore . . . now is the time of your sacrifice.
You have called for aid and I, Athena Parthenos, am here.
She who is girt for battle, yet who is Maiden ever fair,
Shall lend to You Her courage.

Chaste Maiden, cross over and take up the vestments of the
     Queen.
Come, lay down the flowered crown
And receive the royal robes of Persephone.
Cross the bridge from Maidenhood to Queenship
And enter the chariot of the Dark Lord, for He awaits thee.

Priestess of Kore-Persephone:

How shall I leave the land that gave me birth?
My departure will be death to the One who bore me.
But youthful spring has passed, and the fires of Eros flow
     through me.
So does Aphrodite seem both light and dark,
For today I must choose between love and love.

I desire . . . to follow my destiny and move with the Fates.
And so, I shall let go of Nysa's flowered crown, and of the
     lily veil.
Farewell to the Daughters of Oceanus and to the unending sky.
Farewell to Great and Beloved Evalosia;
All Honor and praises unto her.
I will keep the beauty of Earth forever in My heart.
I will remember.

Now, Plouton and the souls of the dead await me,
Fear will be cast aside, and I will be their
     Queen!

IX. Maiden's Descent

Small pieces of dry fuel (not liquid fuel!) are added to the fire if necessary.

Priestess of Kore-Persephone: She stares into the fire. She unpins her white veil and lets it fall behind her, saying:
>Farewell to the Maiden.

Priestesses Panagia/All:
>Farewell to the Maiden.

Priestess of Kore-Persephone [Removing her dried poppy-red flower crown and casting it into the flame]:
>The power of the Queen shall rise.

Priestesses Panagia/All [Casting dried poppy petals and/or other red flower petals into the flame]:
>The power of the Queen shall rise.

Priestess of Hecate [Draping the black himation onto the holy daughter, and pinning it at the shoulder]:
>May Persephone flourish in the Lands Below.

Priestesses Panagia/All:
>May Persephone flourish in the Lands Below.

Hierophantid of Demeter [Handing the urn of seed to the Holy Daughter]:
>May Persephone keep the seed safe,
>Until the time for planting comes again.

Priestess of Persephone:
>The seed grain is now in my keeping.
>I will not fail you,
>But will keep it sound and whole.
>Until the time for planting comes again,
>I will preserve the fertile power
>With which it has been endowed by the Great Creatress.

Carefully, Persephone steps over the flame and/or charred remains, passes through the gateway, and walks across the pathway into Tartarus.

Plouton [Takes Her hand and says]:
>Of all Goddesses, You . . . are the most beautiful.
>Of all Queens, You . . . are the most noble.
>Of all who are loved, You . . . are the most yearned for.
>And so I welcome you to the Palace of Tartarus.

They embrace and kiss.

Persephone:
>Of all Gods, You . . . are the most beautiful.
>Of all Kings, You . . . are the most noble.
>Of all who are loved, You . . . are the most yearned for,
>And so, I shall begin a new life in the deep of the Underworld.

He points her way to the chalice of water. She hands him the urn of seed.

Persephone [Takes the chalice of water from the spring of memory, of Mnemosyne, from the adjacent pedestal or table. She holds the chalice up, saying]:
>Waters from the Spring of Memory . . .

Then she drinks. Holding the cup with both hands, she closes her eyes, and remembers all of the cycles that have gone before and her many seasons as queen. She sets the chalice down.

Plouton [Setting the urn down and placing the crown upon her head]:
>The Queen is with us!
>All hail Persephone!

All:
>Hail Persephone!

Persephone and Plouton take the urn to the storage site. They set it down on a large piece of purple fabric, around which all can circle. All participants circle, hands held.

Priestess of Hecate and Hierophantid of Demeter [Sprinkling wormwood and pennyroyal or mint into the urn and chanting]:
>Seed of Demeter, in power Be!
>Descend in darkness, blessed are thee!

X. Hecate's Magic

Priestess of Hecate: The paper and pencils are retrieved and passed out. The Priest of Plouton and the Priestess of Persephone write wishes for the well-being of the seed on the paper. Together, they hold the urn of grain. It is explained to participants that they should write a wish, something they would like to be made manifest over the next few months. All hold their paper(s) in their hands during the following invocation.

Priestess of Hecate:

> Hecate,
> The seed is in the hands of the God and Goddess of the
>   Underworld.
> It is a time of magic and so we call to You.
> Wise and all-knowing Mistress of crossroads, and deep caverns,
> Of the potent cauldron,
> And of the Moon in the dark night,
> Lady, come to our circle.
> Bless this seed and also our deepest desires.
> Bless these with Your power and protection,
> For the greatest good.
> Let our wishes be made manifest and enter into the river of life.
> Infuse them with Your power
> O Queen of fortune and magic!

All Participants: A circle is formed by all participants with hands held, the rolled or folded papers still in hand. They circle clockwise and chant or sing until energy is raised:

> Hail Hecate Mother of change,
> By Thy power magic gained,
> Hail to love and passion's fire,
> Fertile magic of desire!

The Priestess of Hecate breaks off the circle and leads the group in a spiral dance around the urn. She weaves the spiral to the left and then spirals to the right. All the while, the chant continues. The original shape of the circle is re-formed around the urn. Each participant places her or his written wish onto the cloth around the urn, as the chant continues.

XI. Storage of the seed Grain

Priest of Plouton and Priestess of Persephone seal the top of the urn by covering the contents with dried bay leaves and tying a piece of fabric over the top. The large piece of black cloth is pulled up over the urn and tied tightly with twine. The whole thing is then decoratively tied at the top with red and purple ribbons. The Priest and Priestess stand holding the urn. They guide the participants to hold their palms up toward the urn, and repeat the following lines:

By the powers of Hecate; the wise One,
By the powers of Persephone and Plouton;
And their bond of Sacred Love,
By the powers of Earth and of the silver Moon;
The magic is alive and this spell is done.
It is woven and set,
And good fortune flows
As bright as the flame of Hestia.
So be it.
So be it!
So be it!

The clerics for Persephone and Plouton now store the grain in the designated place. Over the urn is sprinkled wormwood and pennyroyal. If underground, extra chalk is added. The god and goddess remove their vestments with reverence, divesting themselves of deity. The vestments are carefully folded and set down adjacent to the storage area. They then return to the group.

XII. Rite of Pansperma (many seeds)

Priestess of Demeter: The Priestess asks all to retrieve their spoons and cups and then come to the main altar. She goes to the main altar to serve the pansperma to the participants (see Appendix 1). The Priestess places small portions of the mixture into each participant's cup asking them not to eat yet. She says:

A gift from the Mother and Daughter.

Priestess of Hecate: When all have received portions of the pansperma, they are directed to proceed to the gateway to Tartarus. There, the Priestess of Hecate holds her cup over the (now unlit) fire altar and says:

These are the seeds of life.
We eat them at the beginning of the Season of Persephone.
Now does life feed death, just as death feeds life.
So it is, and ever shall be.
Hail Demeter! Hail Persephone!

Now participants eat. When done, all take their empty cups and spoons and place them on the offering table. A circle is made.

XIII. Closing Song
Priestesses Panagia/All [Spoken, chanted, or sung]:
>By the Sacred Lovers, shall the lands below
>Renew their splendor, and with love's passion grow.
>Immortal Persephone, Great Queen of Death,
>Now shall all Tartarus blossom again in rebirth!

XIV. Closing Words
Priestesses Panagia/All:
>These are the rites of Skirophoria.
>These temple rites complete,
>In grace and in joy,
>May her blessings proceed unto all!
>To the feast!

PART IV

The Mysteries

CHAPTER 13

Introduction to the Mysteries

Brandish the flaming torches . . . Iacchus!
Oh Iacchus! Bright luminary of our nocturnal Mysteries.
The meadows sparkle with a thousand fires;
The aged shake off the weight of cares and years . . .
blessed deity, lead the dances of youth
upon this dewy carpet of flowers.[1]

A mystery implies secrecy. Initiates thus took a vow of silence about the rites of the Greater Mysteries. Those who reported any of the events from the rites were dealt with severely, and transgressions against the vow of silence were tried in a court of law. Punishment could include ritual cursing by Eleusinian clergy, death, or banishment and the loss of personal property.

One might ask how, with any sense of respect for this history of secrecy, I can present a liturgy for Demeter's mysteries? The answer is that the rites are an integral part of the yearly holidays, and, without them, this work would have been incomplete. As in the case of the seasonal festivals, many of the facts are not available. Major elements of the mysteries still remain hidden, and so we must make do with the bits of evidence we have. The mythology and theology provide

---

[1] *Aristophanes: The Eleven Comedies*, n. trans. (New York: Horace Liveright, 1930), p. 210. (The publisher notes: "originally published by the Athenian Society, London, 1912.")

the groundwork. The muse provides the rest. One can only have good intentions and pray mightily.

Some authors have gone to great lengths to state what the Greater Mysteries were not. Kerényi even titled a portion of a chapter, "No Drama was Presented at Eleusis."[2] There is actually no hard evidence to prove whether or not there was a dramatic presentation of the myth during the Greater Mysteries. My experience in ritual tells me that any religion's major holiday is concerned with one dramatic presentation of at least a portion of the religion's myth.

The quotes that we have from initiates (see chapter 1) about their experiences at the Greater Mysteries were vague on substance, but clear on essence. There was an experience of great illumination, of a holy light. Another common experience was the loss of the fear of death. Generally, the idea imparted is that, after we leave the physical world, we will experience wonder and divine beauty.

THE LESSER MYSTERIES

The Lesser Mysteries took place in the early spring, during the Greek month of Anthesterion. They are known to have occurred in a village called Agrai, on the banks of the Ilissos River not far from Athens. There was once a small temple there. It has been suggested that these rites may have developed somewhat independently from those at Eleusis (Athens was only 14 miles from Eleusis).

By the fourth century B.C.E., the Agrai rites had become a prerequisite for participating in the Greater Mysteries at Eleusis. Every fourth year, the Lesser Mysteries took place twice. Some say they were performed in the Telesterion's outer courtyards. This second celebration of the rites occurred just after the Eleusinian games (the Eleusinia) in August, and just prior to the Greater Mysteries in September. Why the Lesser Mysteries were celebrated twice every fourth year is unknown. Perhaps those who had traveled to see the games of the Eleusinia remained in order to participate in both the Lesser and Greater Mysteries.

The Lesser Mysteries honored Demeter and Kore-Persephone, though some lexicographers include Dionysus and Zeus Meilichios

---

2   Carl Kerényi, *Eleusis: Archetypal Image of Mother and Daughter* (Princeton, NJ: Princeton University Press, 1991), p. 6.

(the Kindly) as well. Kore's descent and ascent may have been explained at this time, as well as her dual role above and below. There may have been explanations of the myth and the theology. Some call the Lesser Mysteries the Mysteries of Persephone. Although we know that there were sacrifices and a purification ceremony, most of the ritual remains secret.

There is an urn in the National Museum of Rome (the Lovatelli urn), that shows the purification of Herakles at what may be a celebration of the Lesser Mysteries. In the first scene, Herakles presents a pig to an altar priest. In the second scene, he sits on a stool, his head covered by a cloak. A priestess holds a winnowing fan over his head. In the third scene, Demeter sits enthroned and crowned with grain. Beside the throne is a snake. Herakles, who appears younger than in the first scene, extends his hand toward Demeter's snake, while Kore stands in the background. This may be representative of parts of the Lesser Mysteries: the initiate's offering, a cleansing, renewal, and the befriending of the goddess' snake.

The Lesser Mysteries, as I present them, are a preparation for the Greater Mysteries. This includes a personal dedication to Demeter and an understanding of her qualities. The meanings of all of the yearly festivals and mysteries are presented. There is also a purification ceremony, after which the initiate becomes *Demetrioi* (De-mee-troy), the Beloved of the Goddess. The initiates are consecrated and crowned.

THE GREATER MYSTERIES

The celebrations of the Greater Mysteries took place at approximately the end of September or early October. The week of precelebrations began in Athens and culminated in Eleusis, with the rites of the Greater Mysteries themselves. Prospective initiates came from all over the Hellenic and, later, the Roman world. Messengers were sent out to all of the Greek city-states to announce the coming of the Greater Mysteries, and to proclaim a fifty-five day truce (requiring that all conflicts cease and arms be laid down). The truce commenced before the mysteries began and ended after they had concluded. In addition to this holy truce, the messengers (who were from the families of Eumolpidae and Kerykes), requested from each city-state the offering of a tithe for the Temple of Eleusis. In Roman times, these messengers were sent as far as Egypt. Like all messengers from Eleusis, their expenses were paid by the sanctuary treasury. The various city-states then sent special delegations and gifts to Eleusis, in gratitude for the blessings of the goddess.

Boedromion 14:   On the 14th of Boedromion (somewhere between the end of September and early October), the priestesses of Eleusinian Demeter removed the hiera (the holy objects) from the Anaktoron. The top of the cista mystica that contained the sacred objects was secured by red ribbons. All of the primary Eleusinian clergy accompanied the hiera to Athens in an elaborate procession. In Roman times, they were accompanied to Athens by a military escort called the Ephebes.

A short distance outside of Athens, the procession was met by the populace and guided by Athena's clergy into the city. They proceeded directly to the Eleusinion, situated below the northwest corner of the Acropolis. The hiera were placed within. Then a priest of Eleusis was sent to the Parthenon to announce formally to the High Priestess of Athena that the cista mystica had arrived and that the Greater Mysteries would soon commence.

Boedromion 15:   This was considered the first day of the celebrations. The date of Boedromion 15 was called *Aghyrmos*, the Day of Gathering. The people met at the Stoa in Athens' Agora, the town center. The Hierokeryx (sacred herald) made the sacred proclamation. A part of the proclamation invited all those who had "clean hands and intelligible speech" (perhaps indicating that speaking Greek was a requirement), and who had not been found guilty of "pollution" (homicide, treason, or conspiracy). In addition, the proclamation invited those who believed themselves to be free of evil, and who had lived a just and good life, to attend Demeter's mysteries. All others were asked to abstain.[3]

Boedromion 16:   Day two, Boedromion 16, was called *Elasis* (Day of Carriages), and also *Helade Mystai* (To the Sea, Initiates). Traveling throughout the city, the heralds called out to the mystai to go and immerse themselves in the sea. The mystai, in the company of their mystagogos (sponsors who had previously been initiated), walked or rode in carriages to the sea. Chariots or carts carried the initiates to Athens' shores to be purified in the waters of the sea. Each initiate

---

[3]   George Mylonas, *Eleusis and the Eleusinian Mysteries* (Princeton, NJ: Princeton University Press, 1961), p. 247.

was immersed, as was the piglet that was most probably the offering sacrificed the following day.

Boedromion 17:   Day three, Boedromion 17, was called *Hiereia Deuro,* the Day of Sacrifices. On this day, the Archon of Athens offered sacrifices to the two Goddesses for both the city and also the country as a whole. These ceremonies were conducted at the Eleusinion. This was a formal state occasion, and representatives from each city-state offered sacrifices and prayers. Following this, the initiates, with their sponsors, gave their sacrifices.

Boedromion 18:   Day four, Boedromion 18, was called *Epidauria,* the Day of Asklepios. According to myth, the healing God Asklepios was late in arriving from Epidauros to his own initiation into Demeter's mysteries. In honor of his late arrival, this day was used for those who were late in coming to Athens for the celebrations. Being late was always a possibility for those traveling from afar, over land and sea. On this day, latecomers could offer their sacrifices and bathe in the sea. For other initiates, this was a day of rest and preparation.

Boedromion 19:   The fifth day, Boedromion 19, was called *Pompe,* the Day of Procession. On this day, all traveled in procession from Athens to Eleusis, a fourteen-mile journey. At the head of the elaborate procession was a statue of the God Iacchos, appearing as a young Dionysus crowned with myrtle. He was set into a special carriage and carried a torch that would be lit later. The clergy of Eleusis were arrayed in their finest vestments, while the initiates wore dark clothing, perhaps in imitation of the wandering Demeter. They carried packs of additional food and clothing with them, as well as the money needed to pay the various fees once they arrived at the Eleusinian sanctuary.

In the light of early morning, the procession lined up as tradition dictated: first the Dadouchos, carrying a torch, then the priests, heralds, various priestesses, the priestesses in charge of the cista mystica (in a carriage), officials of state, foreign dignitaries, initiates and their sponsors, and, finally, the pack animals. At the exit gateway of the city, the carriage of Iacchos joined at the front of the procession. His torch was lit and, with joyful cries of "Iacchos!" the procession set out to Eleusis down the Sacred Way.

The procession led out of the city and northward into the countryside. It led around the foothills of Mount Parnassus, passing many monuments and the sanctuary of Apollo. Then the Sacred Way

turned downward to the sea. Arriving at the seaside shrine of
Aphrodite, the initiates left small offerings in the rock niches of the
shrine. This would be one of several rest stops. Then the road forked
and they turned inland.

Continuing along the Sacred Way, the procession soon turned
back to the sea. Finally, they came to a bridge over the Rheitoi River.
They had now arrived at the border of Eleusis. Mylonas suggests that,
here, they may have rested during a rite called the *Krokosis,* a tying of
a saffron ribbon to the right wrist and left ankle. Close to the sanctuary was the last bridge, this one over the Eleusinian Kephisos River.
On this bridge, the inhabitants of Eleusis greeted them with the
Bridge Jests, comedic insults and licentious words and actions somewhat reminiscent of the humor of the Stenia festival.

Soon the procession arrived at the sanctuary of Demeter. Here
they were welcomed and, I am sure, happily assigned lodgings so that
they could rest from their long and exciting day. But first there were
the offerings to be made at the entrance to the Underworld, the
Ploutonian temple cave. Here, the Child from the Hearth of Athens
set down the pelanos and myrtle boughs, and asked the Goddess to
grant her blessings to the initiates during the mysteries, and to all of
Greece.

Boedromion 20–21:   During these two days, there were special
purification ceremonies for the initiates and offerings were given.
Sacred tables may have been set for all of the Eleusinian deities. I
believe that all kinds of food was set out for each deity as an offering
feast. Dow and Healey discuss sacred table offerings[4] that appear to
have been nonanimal offerings, including honey, wine, and grain.
The special offering of the pelanos (made from the wheat and barley
of the temple's Rharian Field) was also a part of the offerings.

The various rites of the Greater Mysteries took place on both
Boedromion 20 and 21. It may have been that on Boedromion 20,
the *dromena* (sacred drama) was presented in order to provide the
background for the mystery rites of initiation. Sanctuary landmarks
could have been used as stage settings for the *dromena,* including the
sacred well where Demeter rested in her wanderings, or the cavern to
the Underworld, or Demeter's temple, the Telesterion.

---

[4]   Sterling Dow and Robert F. Healey, *A Sacred Claendar of Eleusis* (Combridge, MA:
Harvard University Press, 1965), pp. 23–31.

Boedromion 21 may have included the partial fast and abstinence of wine spoken of in several sources. Diet restrictions would have been appropriate if the *kykeon* (sacred drink possessing an hallucinogen), was imbibed on this night. It is also suggested that their was a simulated journey to the Underworld. *Legomena, Deiknymena, Epopteia,* and *Telete,* were also a part of the mysteries and are explained below. During these rites, clergy were barred from wearing jewelry, cosmetics, or clothing of mixed colors or ornamented with embroidery.

The rites of *Legomena* included invocations as well as mythic theological explanations. The drinking of the *Kykeon,* and its possible hallucinogens, may have been an important part of the ceremony from this point on. *Deiknymena* was a showing or a rite of the hiera. The cista mystica was opened and the sacred objects displayed. While I have made definite choices in my liturgy for the Greater Mysteries, it is not precisely known of what the hiera consisted. We may make some inferences from the objects on the outside of the cista mystica: grain, poppy pods, myrtle, and poppy rosettes.

Clement of Alexandria, a staunch Christian from the second century C.E., stated, in his *Exhortation to the Greeks,* that the sacred objects were "sesame cakes, pyramid and spherical cakes, cakes with many navels, also balls of salt and a serpent . . . pomegranates, fig branches, fennel stalks, ivy leaves, round cakes and poppies . . . marjoram, a lamp, a sword and a woman's comb."[5] Since he calls the ancient Greek temples "godless sanctuaries," we can assume that he never saw Demeter's rites at Eleusis and was urging his readers toward Christian monotheism. We may thus consider his writings to be somewhat suspect. In addition, he seems to mix information about the mysteries of Cybele and those of Dionysus with the mysteries of Demeter. Clement's information came from the Alexandrian version of Demeter's rites. Held in an area of Alexandria called "the District of Eleusis," the rites carried no vow of secrecy.

The so-called passwords of the initiates given by Clement are quoted in several later sources and so must be mentioned here. He gives this version of certain passwords: "I fasted, I drank the draught, I took (the hiera) from the chest, having done my task, I placed (them) in the basket, and from the basket into the chest."[6] These

---

5   Titus Flavius Clemens, *Clement of Alexandria: The Exhortation to the Greeks,* G. W. Butterworth, trans. (London: William Heinemann; New York: G. P. Putnam's Sons, 1919), p. 45.
6   *Clement of Alexandria,* p. 43.

words appear to be a rite involving the hiera and the cista mystica. In my interpretation of the Greater Mysteries, it is the Hierophant, rather than the initiates, who performs the rite with the hiera. In the liturgy that I present, sacred words are spoken, not as a formula, but as explanations of the meanings of the sacred objects.

After the Kykeon came the *Epopteia* in which the essence of the mysteries was brought forward. This was the highest stage of initiation. Initiates' eyes were opened to the beatific vision and its experience of holy light. Finally, the *Telete,* the last experience of secret initiation took place. Perhaps it was after this that the initiates were crowned with the ribbon and myrtle wreaths. At some point, each initiate's name was inscribed on a wooden tablet.

Boedromion 22:   Day seven, Boedromion 22, was the initiates' last day at Eleusis. On this day, there were prayers and rites for the dead, followed by ceremonies for the fertility of the land in the new planting season. In particular, there was a rite called the Pourings of Plenty, the *Plymochoai.* In the Ploutonian cave, two vases of wine were set up next to an opening in the cavern floor (the *Chthonian Chasma*). One was set up on the east side and one on the west side. Sacred words were spoken as the two vases were overturned and their contents poured into the opening. Included were the two words *Hye!* (flow) and *Kye!* (conceive). I have used an adaptation of this at the end of the Proerosia, the preplowing rites.

The white chitons worn by the initiates during the mysteries, were saved for special uses. Once taken home, they were made into clothing for young children, the idea being that these sanctified garments would protect the children from illness.

The rites presented in chapter 15 for the Greater Mysteries provide a mythic glimpse of life after death. This is intertwined with the myth of the Great Creatress and her Holy Daughter. I freely admit that the ritual is lacking in the sacred drink. I am, however, not prepared to suggest a hallucinogen that has not been refined by generations of spiritual use, and is not presented by an experienced ministrant. We can, however, use chanting, music, myth, and devotional rites in order to create the higher state.

The Lesser Mysteries

I crown you in the name of all Holy Demeter.
Her blessings are sealed upon you,
for joy in life, for wisdom, and for compassion.
May joy rise up from your heart,
O beloved initiate of the Great Mother.

For those who sought the experience of the Greater Mysteries, the rites of the Lesser Mysteries were the first step toward that goal. The Lesser Mysteries took place after the Festival of Chloaia, sometime between our mid-February and mid-March. For the following reconstruction of the rites, a date in April (after Chloaia) has been chosen. There is a practical reason for this; it creates a longer interval between Chloaia and the Lesser Mysteries. Greater energy and attention can then be given to the latter by clergy and prospective initiates.

The Lesser Mysteries are an opportunity to dedicate yourself to Demeter and prepare for the Greater Mysteries. During the following rite, various parts of the mythic and seasonal cycle are brought together so that the initiates may see them as a whole. This introduces all of the festivals and mysteries in chronological order. It also demonstrates that, in a sense, there is no beginning or ending point in the cycle of life.

Please note that, in some parts of the rites, there are periods of time where the initiates need to wait their turn, such as in the purification, the consecration, or the crowning. During these times, you may want to have soft, meditative recorded music in the background, or you may want to increase the number of clergy performing those parts of the ritual with the initiates.

Ritual Outline

I.	Preritual
II.	Welcome
III.	Song: The Holy Names of Demeter
IV.	invocation to Hestia
V.	Invocations to Demeter and Kore
VI.	Circle Song and Offerings
VII.	Lighting the Wheel
VIII.	Purification Ceremony
IX.	Rite of Consecration,
X.	Crowning
XI.	Closing Song
XII.	The Closing Words

Clergy

Priestess of Hecate
Priestess of Hestia
Priestess of Demeter
Hierophantid of Kore
Hierophant
Hydranos Priestess
Priestesses Panagia

Clergy Preparations

In Part 4 of the celebration, "Lighting the Wheel," a candle is lit for each of the seasonal festivals and mysteries, in chronological order. Their mythic and seasonal themes are presented. In preparation for this ritual, in which clergy are assigned parts, you should decide who will light the respective festival candles. The holidays are: Proerosia, Stenia, Arkichronia, Thesmophoria Proper, Nestia, Kalligenia, Haloa, Chloaia, the Lesser Mysteries, Thargelia, Kalamaia, Skira, and the Greater Mysteries. It may be helpful for clergy to have read about each of the corresponding rituals in previous chapters prior to this ritual. In this way, they will have gained an understanding of the holiday, and be able to present more easily its seasonal and mythic meaning as the corresponding candle is lit during the rite.

Initiate Preparations

I.   The initiate should have read the myth (chapter 3) and the chapters on Demeter and Persephone (chapters 5 and 6). They should know the meaning of each of Demeter's names.
II.   The initiate brings offerings of flowers for both Demeter and Kore.
III. The initiate creates or brings $1^1/_4$ yards of 3-inch wide strips of cloth in three colors (green, red, and yellow). The cloths are laid together lengthwise and sewn together in one spot, about 10 inches from one end. During the rite, the cloths will be twisted and tied into a crown. Green represents the green of spring, the verdant Mother and spring Maiden. Red symbolizes poppies and pomegranates, and the fertile Mothers of both Earth and Elysium. Yellow denotes Demeter of the harvest, and the sickle-bearing saffron-cloaked Hecate.
IV.   The initiate brings a small bowl and flower offerings.
V.   The initiate should consider, prior to the rites, all things within that may need to be released and purified. It is suggested that the initiate write these things down and bring them as a list.
VI.   The initiate should eat lightly during the day of the ritual, but not so lightly as to be hungry when the rites begin.
VII. Greek costume is optional. It may be best however, for all to be in costume, or for all not to be (see chapter 18, "Greek costume").

The Main Altar

On a table set against a wall, place an icon or image of Demeter in the center toward the back. To the right and left of the icon, place two white taper candles. You may add a vase, or vases, of fresh flowers. Leave an area in front of the icon clear for the offerings of flowers that will be set there during the ritual. Arranged on the altar are the Hestia lamp or candle, the Kore votive candle, the Demeter votive candle, a bowl of dried cedar or cypress leaves, a bowl of dried mint, a bowl of dried rosemary, and scented oil for the anointing.

The altar holds a lustration bowl of water mixed with a small amount of salt for use by the Hydranos Priestess. This is on one corner of the altar, along with a stick or wand with which the contents of the bowl will be stirred between initiates' anointings. There is also sheaf of grain and/or a bowl of barley. In addition you may add snake and pig effigies (see chapter 18, "snake and pig effigies").

The Side Table

This is a table set not far from the main altar. It will hold the initiates' bowls, cloth "crowns," list of things needing purification, and flower offerings, until they are ready to be used in the ritual.

The Censer Altar

The censer altar may be set up in the center of the room. It can be a round or square table covered with fabric, or a square of cloth laid out on the floor. You need a censer large enough to hold three censer coals. You can use a ceramic bowl that has a 2-inch layer of sand in the bottom. Place three coals on the sand. (These should be the round, self-lighting incense coals.) Have long matches available for lighting the coals and a pair of tongs to hold the coals up while you light them. (I suggest holding them over a candle flame for a few moments). Place the censer in the center of the altar area and elevate it by setting it on two or three bricks. Have plenty of ventilation in the room. You may want to arrange things so that the censer altar is next to a window. Also, for use in the purifications, there is an unlit taper candle in a holder and a large empty metal or ceramic bowl below or near the censer altar.

As an alternative, you may have a second censer altar set up outside for the purifications. An outdoor censer allows the smoke that will result from the inititates individual rites to dissipate outdoors. If you use an outdoor censer altar, take care that the initiates remain silent and do not come out of sacred mental space as you make the transitions from indoors to out, and back again.

You may want to place river rocks (available at landscaping stores) or other stones on the table, circling the censer. Place evergreens such as pine, cypress, juniper, cedar, or rosemary around the edges of the stones. Arrange fresh flowers here and there over the greenery.

Around the indoor censer altar, set thirteen votive candles or tealights, in holders (these are short, squat candles). Tie a green ribbon around one candle. This will represent the Rites of Proerosia, and will be the starting point for the candle-lighting portion of the rite that explains the Demetrian Wheel of the Year. Place a bowl of sandalwood, myrrh, or whatever other powdered or resin incense you like on the altar. Have plenty of matches.

General Preparations

Clean, ventilate, and cense the temple area. Set the altars well ahead of time. Add fresh flowers to the censer altar(s) just before the ritual. Have soft relaxing instrumental or other sacred music ready to play while the initiates wait to get started. Have a small light meal available for everyone after the rite. Clergy may consider wearing Greek costume (see chapter 18, "Greek costume").

THE RITES OF THE LESSER MYSTERIES

I. Preritual

About 15 minutes before the rites start, begin to play the soft instrumental/ sacred music. You may want to have the lights a little low. Create plenty of ventilation in the room. The prospective initiates (mystai) enter the temple in silence. In silence, a priestess directs them to place their offerings of flowers, their bowl, and their cloth crown on the side table. The initiates are asked to review the things they wish to release, and then put the list away.

When all have arrived, light the coals in the censer. Turn off the recorded music. Light the taper candles. Instruct all to stand in a circle. Join hands and chant in Greek or English:

Demeter kai Kore,	*(De-me-ter kye Ko-ree,)*	(Demeter and Kore,)
Hierea Mystica,	*('eye-ray-ah Mys-tee-ca,)*	(Holy Mystery)
Demeter kai Kore,	*(De-me-ter kye Ko-ree,)*	(Demeter and Kore,)
Ela, ela, ela!	*(Eh-la, eh-la, eh-la!)*	(Come, come, come!)

II. Welcome

Priestess of Hecate:

Welcome to the Rites
Of the Lesser Mysteries of Demeter and Kore.
These, and the Greater Mysteries,
Draw us into the power of the Great Mother
As we journey within the realm of Her Creation.

Today you will be purified in Her temple,
Consecrated to Her,
And crowned as a sign of your dedication.
As you reach out to Her, She will reach out to you
And a reverent bond will be created
Between you and the Great Mother Goddess.

We call all those who seek this bond, the mystai (*mi-stye'*).
When this bond is formed,
It reaches into the depths of the heart
To nourish the soul with love.
This is initiation.

All Clergy:

By the powers of the infinite
Do we live within the sacred patterns of Creation
And the song of the humming Cosmos.
All blessings of goodness, strength, and joy unto us all.
And so it is.

III. Song: The Holy Names of Demeter

Priestesses Panagia and all clergy [Singing or chanting]:
> O bless-ed mystai,
> By the laws of Her temple have you prepared.
> O bless-ed mystai,
> Into Her Mysteries have you dared.
>
> Demeter, Demeter Panagia . . . Hail!
> Demeter, Demeter Chloaia . . . Hail!
> Demeter, Demeter Antaia . . . Hail!
> Demeter, Demeter Thesmophoros . . . Hail!
> Demeter, Demeter Chthonia . . . Hail!
> Demeter, Demeter Melaina . . . Hail!
> Demeter, Demeter Evalosia . . . Hail!
>
> O bless-ed mystai,
> By the laws of Her temple have you prepared.
> O bless-ed mystai,
> Into Her Mysteries have you dared.

IV. Invocation of Hestia

Priestess of Hestia [At the altar]:
> We call Hestia,
> Goddess of hearth and temple fire,
> Of the spiritual center of our world,
> And of all sacred places.
> Hestia, beloved Goddess of the spiritual flame,
> Come, and enter this temple.
> Make all that is here holy and sacred in Your name.
> Bring to us the peace and sureness
> Of that place which is home and hearth.
> Bring Your purity and beauty to us
> As we honor You,
> Who are the center of the spiritual flame.
> So be it.

The Priestess of Hestia lights the lamp or candle. She raises it up high and says:
> Hail Hestia!

Priestesses Panagia/All:
> Hail Hestia!

V. Invocations of Demeter and Kore

The Priestess of Demeter and the Hierophantid of Kore [At the altar]:
> Beloved Demeter and fair Kore,
> Blessed are we in Thy Mysteries.
> For all that lives and grows and dies and is born again
> Rests in the realm of Your creation.
> Bright are Thy passions
> To nurture and tend every living thing
> In all the world.
> With reverence do we call upon Demeter and Kore
> To bring Their blessings unto these rites.
> And so it shall be.

The Hierophant/Hierophantid places a small amount of sandalwood or myrrh on coals on the censer altar. When the smoke rises he or she lifts the smoking censer high and says:
> May Demeter and Kore bless these rites!

The altar is censed.

Priestess of Demeter [At the altar]:
> Beloved Mother,
> You are the hand of the eternal,
> Whose powers and forces compose the Dance of Life.
>
> Verdant and lush Goddess,
> Great Empress of rich and ripening fruit,
> Crone of the black and the fallow;
> Your every countenance is full of magic.
>
> Deep, dark soil and its alluvial riches
> Are the blessed remnants of Death,
> As the green and fruit-bearing seasons of Life
> Follow unseeming decay.
> From the ashes of Death
> Do You, Chthonia, forge new Life,
> So that Being never ceases, but only changes form.

You are the magic of creation,
Never ending and always changing.
And with this power You entered below,
Bringing the gifts for which You are renown.

You have born all,
From Earth's spiraling seasons and many gifts,
To the precious and Holy Daughter.
Come Beloved One, O Demeter of the Mysteries.
Teach us to see the divine patterns of the seasons
As elements of the living, changing, and eternal soul.
So be it.

Priestesses Panagia:
So be it.

Priestess of Demeter [Lights Demeter's candle, and says]:
Hail Demeter! Dea Mystica!

Priestesses Panagia repeat the hail.

Hierophantid of Kore [At the altar]:
Fair Kore,
Full of grace and light and beauty,
O my soul and my heart,
In purity were You born of the Great Mother.

All that glistens as new life,
The babe, fresh from the womb,
The green grasses that rise after the barren time,
The saffron crocus and the white narcissus,
And every bud that breaks into bloom
To create a glorious Spring,
All, all are Thee!

It is You, lovely Maiden,
Who, living within the realm of time,
Make the long journey.
And within the season of the Crone on Earth
Do You dwell in the deep Below,
Where, as Persephone You reign over Elysium,
In union with your Great Beloved.

O You who are as my very soul,
May I learn Thy wisdom,
From the divine patterns of the seasons,
And from You who are the elements
Of the living, changing, and eternal soul.
So be it.

Priestesses Panagia:
So be it.

Hierophantid of Kore [Lights the Maiden's candle, saying]:
Hail Kore-Persephone! Dea Mystica!

Priestesses Panagia and all repeat the hail.

VI. Circle Song and Offerings

The Hierophantid of Kore instructs the initiates to retrieve their flowers from the side table. The chant/song below is done several times. Then the Hierophantid explains that all will place their flower offerings on the altar, with the words: "For Demeter and Kore." The chant/song below can continue as supportive background.

Priestesses Panagia: [Chanting or singing during the offering]:
Blessed are we in Her Mystery, *(Bless-ed are we, in Her Mys-ter-y,)*
Hail mighty Demeter   *(Hail, migh-ty De-me-ter)*
And sweet Kore.   *(And sweet Ko-ree.)*

VII. Lighting the Wheel

Two Priestesses Panagia [Picking up the Demeter and Kore candles, and facing the participants]:
Within the cycle of life, all things turn and return,
Moving and flowing in creation, ending, and creation
   again.
Each holy day is a part of the sacred circle,
Each season comes, and goes, and returns again,
As time spirals onward.
Know that there is no beginning and no end,
Just as alpha and omega meet at each point
Of the ever-flowing circle of the seasons.
Listen initiates, to the names of the holy days . . .

The candles are set down. The Priestess of Demeter begins the candle-lighting ceremony with the candle for the Rites of Proerosia. She lights the candle, states the name of the festival, and the festival's meaning. She ends by saying,
    And the season turns.

Then, going in a clockwise direction, the next clergy member moves to the next candle, and states the next rite and its meaning, ending by saying,
    And the season turns.

Priestess of Demeter [Lighting the candle with the green ribbon]:
    This signifies the Rites of Proerosia . . .
    In Proerosia, we prepare the barren field for planting.
    We honor the forces in play:
    The Earth Mother, Zeus of the Rains,
    And Triptolemos, emissary of Demeter.
    And we ask for their blessings.
    With holy rites we plow the sacred field
    To prepare it for its new beginning.
    And the season turns . . .

The next clergy member lights the next candle, stating the name of the next chronological festival, and its meaning, clergy ending with, "And the season turns . . ." The candle-lighting continues until all candles are lit. The following is a list of the points of the wheel and their meanings. Please review the rites in question. Clergy may elaborate as desired.

Rites of Proerosia: Preplowing rites. Blessings and magic to prepare the sacred field.

Stenia Festival: Bawdy humor, sacred sexuality. Through Baubo, barren Demeter becomes the fertile Mother.

Rites of Arkichronia: Creation of fertility talismans. Combining Earth and Underworld powers. Fertile gifts from the Land of Death are brought up from the megara.

Thesmophoria Proper: A celebration of Demeter's sacred laws, and of the powers of the two goddesses. Remembering our divinity.

Rites of Nestia: The Sadness. Queen Persephone leaves her beloved Plouton and the Underworld.

Rites of Kalligenia: The Rejoicing. Rebirth. The ascent of the Maiden to the Land of Life. Reunion of Demeter and Kore. The season of planting may begin.

Festival of Haloa: Celebration of new green growth in both cultivated field and wild nature.

Festival of Chloaia: Festival of flowers, of verdant Demeter and
Kore, and of the green Earth. A celebration of Dionysus and of the
new wine.

The Lesser Mysteries: Ceremony of the whole festival cycle.
Purification. Consecration to Demeter.

Thargelia: The Harvest. Demeter, the Harvest Queen. Both the
seed and the Maiden have matured. Demeter and Kore are separated
by Hecate's blade.

Kalamaia: The Threshing; freeing the seed grain from the chaff.
Honoring Triptolemos.

Skira Festival: The Maiden's descent to the Land of Death, and Her
transformation to Persephone. In love, Plouton and Persephone
unite. The grain is stored. The fallow period begins, and in the following months Demeter becomes Crone.

The Greater Mysteries: The sacred drama; the reconciliation of
Demeter, Plouton and Persephone. The Rite of the Cista Mystica, the
Thanatos Rite, the Crowning.

Priestess of Demeter [When all 13 candles have been lit]:
> Then comes Proerosia again,
> And the season turns.
> Here are the holy days of the Two Goddesses,
> The pattern of Life, Death, and Rebirth.
> Here is the great cycle of life.

A clergy member throws sandalwood or myrrh on the coals in center of censer
altar.

VIII. Purification Ceremony

Make certain there is plenty of ventilation in the room. This is essential. Open
windows if necessary. Or perform this part of the rite outdoors at an additional
censer altar. The initiates are instructed to get their bowls and lists of things
needing purification from the side table. They are guided to circle around the
censer altar (indoors or outdoors). The Priestesses Panagia then go around the
inside of the circle, placing small amounts of cypress or cedar, rosemary, and
mint into each initiate's bowl, saying:
> To purify thy heart and mind.

Priestess of Demeter:
> Initiates,
> We will begin the purification ceremonies.
> You have been given cypress (or cedar) for banishing,
> Rosemary for purification,
> And mint for cleansing and healing.
> Be prepared to let go those influences of the past,
> That you have chosen to release.
> You will use the herbs,
> Placing small amounts onto the burning coals,
> To carry that which you no longer want
> Away from your soul.

Priestess of Hecate [Instructs each initiate to place a hand over their bowl of herbs and repeat the words of the following blessing]:
> Hecate,
> Immortal Goddess of crossroads, caverns, and moonlit rites,
> Come and bless these herbs,
> That they may serve us here.
> Queen of magic,
> Lend Your powers unto this rite.
> May all that needs to be released.
> Be removed from its enclosure
> And set upon the purifying coals
> With Your blessings.
> So be it.

Hierophantid of Kore [Calling upon the Holy Daughter]:
> We call upon the Daughter of Holy Demeter,
> Upon She who is both Maiden and yet Underworld
>   Queen.
>
> Beloved Kore,
> With courage have You ventured into the unknown
> And come back again.
> For You who are Maiden of sunlit meadows
> Are also Persephone, Queen of the lands below.
> Reigning with Plouton upon both the dark throne
> And in the bright flowering groves,
> You have come to know the powers of Your deeper soul.

Priestess Panagia:

> There, with compassion do You dispense Themis' law;
> Mending, healing, and bringing justice to all.
> To all of good heart; to initiates
> And to those who have sought the truth,
> You reveal the beauty of the immortal soul.
> Upon Earth do You bring riches unto the land,
> Where, hand in hand with Demeter,
> The land blossoms and all things grow.
>
> Tonight we call upon Your powers,
> That You may bless the initiates.
> Come, fair Persephone,
> And assist us in these rites of purification.
>
> As we place those things we wish to release
> Onto the burning coals,
> Be with us, O Noble One, purifying all,
> Bringing to us a new life of clarity and freedom
> As we send our praises unto the Holy Daughter.
> And so it is.

Priestess Panagia: The initiates are seated. Soft meditative music may be played in the background, set on continuous play. Every initiate is asked to review the list of things he or she wishes to release. A taper candle is lit from the Kore candle and set on, or below, the censer altar. A Priestess Panagia places a stool or chair next to the censer altar (the one to be used for the purifications). The Priestess invites each initiate one by one to come to the censer altar with his or her bowl of herbs for the purification. The bowl and the written list are given to the Priestess. For each initiate, the Priestess does the following: The initiate is asked to be seated and to close his or her eyes. The Priestess draws up the power from Earth with the breath. She then places her right palm lightly on the initiate's forehead and says:

> Fair Persephone,
> Come, be with this pure-hearted initiate.

The initiate is asked to extend both palms upturned together. In them, the Priestess pours the initiate's herbs. The initiate is instructed to bring forward from the mind, heart, and body the things he or she wishes to release. The initiate is instructed to image-gather these unwanted energies during the inhalation of the breath and release them slowly with the exhalation of the breath, and to direct these energies out of the body and into the herbs. When done with the process, the initiate opens his or her eyes. At this signal of completion, the Priestess instructs the initiate to place the herbs onto the coals. Priestess says:

> Noble Queen,
> Here, burn away the past.

At this, she assists the initiate in lighting the paper list with the flame of the taper candle. It is allowed to burn as fully as possible over the bowl, before being placed in the bowl. Then the initiate is asked to let go all thought, relax the shoulders, hang the head forward in complete release. If required, the Priestess may ask again for the deep breath and release. (If done indoors, other clerics monitor the room, and open more windows if needed.)

Hydranos Priestess: The Hydranos Priestess escorts each initiate who has finished the censer-fire purification, to the lustration area. There, the Priestess cleanses the initiate with a mixture of salt and water. First, she cleanses the center of the palms of the hands, using the water in a circular motion. Then she places small amounts of water onto the initiate's head, forehead, shoulders, heart, and back. As she does this, the Priestess says:

> Cleansed with the waters of the sea.

When she has finished, she says to the initiate:

> Be at peace.

She then leads him or her to a seat. She takes the next one from the Priestess at the censer altar. Between initiates, she stirs the contents of the lustration bowl. Soft, meditative music continues to play in the background. When all are done, the music is turned off. The censor is placed outside, if it is not outside already.

IX. Rite of Consecration

Hierophant or the Hierophantid of Demeter [The mystai are asked to stand and close their eyes]:

> Now begins the Rite of Consecration.
> Initiates, please repeat the lines of the following prayer
> In this Dedication to the Great Mother:
>
> Holy Mother,
> Beloved Goddess,
> Radiant in beauty,
> Rich in power and in passion,
> You, who created the Mysteries of the Seed

And the magic of Earth,
Who turns the seasons and creates the cycles of nature,
I am Thine.

Beloved Goddess,
Fill me with Thy Eternal beauty and Thy ecstasy,
And I shall be awake
And know the miracle that is life.

I shall honor You
Who are the Mother of life,
Offering respect for Your great mountains, seas, and lands,
And for the air,
That wraps itself around the body of the Goddess
As a cloak of unseen ethers.

Panagia,
Be with me this day and into the night,
And in all the days and nights to come,
Until Thy Holy Daughter
Receives me in fair Elysium.

Shine Thy blessings upon my life,
Granting me health, prosperity, and peace.
I give all honor and praises unto You.
As I say
Hail, to the Great Mother!
So be it.

Priestesses Panagia: The initiates are asked to open their eyes. The forehead of each is anointed with scented oil by the Priestess Panagia, as the following words are spoken:

She is with you,
For you are Demetrioi (*De-mee-troy*),
Initiate, and beloved of the Great Mother.

X. Crowning

Priestess of Demeter: The Priestess of Demeter stands at the main altar with the Hierophant or Hierophantid of Demeter beside her. She instructs the initiates to retrieve their colored cloths from the side table and to stand in a semi-circle around the main altar. The priestess says:

Initiates.
You have in your hands the colored cloths.
Listen to the meanings of the colors.

Hierophantid/Hierophant:
Red for poppies and pomegranates,
For the fertile Mother, and for Queen Persephone . . .
Green for Demeter Chloaia, for Kore the Maiden,
For glorious spring, and for the powers of rebirth . . .
Yellow for the Harvest Mother,
And for the magic of saffron-cloaked Hecate and Her harvest
    sickle.
In these colors, we honor Demeter, Persephone, and Hecate,
The crown of Demeter's Temple.

Priestess of Demeter: The initiate is asked to hold the sewn end, while
the Priestess of Demeter twists the three cloths together. The Priestess says:
The Three, as One.

She then ties it toward the end, leaving some of the end loose. She asks the ini-
tiate to close his or her eyes. She ties the twisted cloth crown onto the initiate's
head saying:
I crown you in the name of All Holy Demeter.
Her blessings are sealed upon you,
For joy in life, for wisdom, and for compassion.
May Her joy rise up from your heart,
O beloved initiate of the Great Mother . . .
Go in peace.

The initiate is asked to open his or her eyes. The clergy bow their heads to the
initiate, bowing to the great divinity that resides within the spirit of the initiate.
That initiate is seated. When all are crowned, initiates are gathered together in a
circle.

XI. The Closing Words
All Clergy:
Initiates,
You have been purified,
Anointed, and crowned,
And in these Rites of Consecration

You have become a part
Of the Temple of the Goddess Demeter.
May peace reside in your heart.
May the wisdom of the Great Mother be with you
As you follow the changing seasons.

And in the world that shall follow this,
Will the Holy Daughter welcome you
To a land of beauty and light,
As the pure heart reunites with the infinite spirit.

These are the rites of the Lesser Mysteries.
Initiates of Demeter,
The Greater Mysteries are now open to you.
Her temple rites complete,
In grace and in joy,
May her blessings proceed unto all!

A light repast is provided.

CHAPTER 15

The Greater Mysteries

Just as persons who are being initiated into the Mysteries
throng together at the outset amid tumult and shouting . . .
so too at the beginning of philosophy: about its
portals also you will see great tumult and talking and boldness . . .
but he who succeeds in getting inside . . .
adopts another bearing of silence. [1]

The Greater Mysteries took place on the nights of Boedromion 20 and 21, in the early fall. The Greek months began on a New Moon, so these dates were in the waning portion of the lunar cycle. For this reconstruction of the Greater Mysteries, a date near the Autumn Equinox has been chosen.

The mysteries occur at the end of the fallow period, before the fall rains. This is a pivotal time, between the barren and fertile periods of the yearly cycle. While Demeter's loss of her Daughter has brought the fallow time to Earth, the Holy Daughter has brought her blessings in the land of death. With a desire for reconciliation, Demeter eventually seeks her Daughter and descends into Tartarus. As a result of Demeter's journey into the Underworld, the powers of

---

1   Plutarch, *Plutarch's Moralia*, vol. I, Loeb Classical Library, Frank Cole Babbitt, trans. (London: William Heinemann; New York: G. P. Putnam's Sons, 1927), p. 435.

life and death meet and, ultimately, come into balance. Demeter and Plouton come into accord, with Persephone as the uniting bond.

Several rites of which we know, have been included in this rendition of the Greater Mysteries. These are the preparatory ritual bathing (although not in the sea, unless you are so inclined), the prayers and offerings to Aphrodite, and the rites of the cista mystica (mystery basket) with the hiera (holy objects). I have included the *Dromena,* or sacred drama (about which there is some debate), and have added the Thanatos Rite, a journey to death.

The essential symbols of the sacred drama are represented by the hiera (holy objects). The hiera are used by the Hierophant in the Rite of the Cista Mystica. The exact identity of the hiera is unknown, however, for this re-creation, I have chosen objects such as a sheaf of wheat, a snake, and myrtle wreaths. While the hiera are items from nature, they are steeped in meaning, not only because of their natural qualities, but because of their placement within the sacred drama. There is actually no record of whether there was one, or many, cista mysticas or exactly how the hiera were used in the rites.

I believe that there was one permanent set of hiera residing in the Anaktoron (the central chamber of Demeter's temple), and that the objects were made of precious materials. An example of the kind of objects they may have been is pictured in *The Road to Eleusis,* by authors Hofmann, Ruck, and Wasson: a sheaf of wheat that has been dipped in gold.[2] Other examples of the Greco-Roman goldsmith's art are two wreaths that have been exhibited at the J. Paul Getty Museum in Malibu, California. In one case, the leaves are made of very thin beaten gold, with flowers of glass beads. The other is a very realistic representation of a laurel wreath, in gold.

The cista and its precious hiera were important enough to be taken in procession to Athens before the Greater Mysteries. There they would reside for several days before being returned to Eleusis for use in the mysteries. They were housed in Athens in a building called the Eleusinion, below the Acropolis.

One Hierophant is known for having saved the hiera. During an attack by the Sarmations on the Eleusinian sanctuary, he removed the hiera from the temple and took them to Athens for safekeeping. The hiera were the Hierophant's responsibility; it is from them that

---

[2]   Albert Hofmann, A. P. Ruck, and R. Gordon Wasson, *The Road to Eleusis* (New York: Harcourt Brace Jovanovich, 1978).

he gets his title. Perhaps during the final attack on the sanctuary, in the late fourth century C.E., the Hierophant again removed the hiera from the Anaktoron, but was never able to return them because the sanctuary was destroyed and never rebuilt. The question is then: where are they?

During the Mycenaean and Mid-Helladic periods, areas of the acropolis of Eleusis were used for chamber tombs, pot burials, and cremation urns. A shrine to Plouton, the God of the Underworld, was built above the acropolis cave some time between the Archaic Period and Peisistratean Times (700–550 B.C.E.). By the fourth century B.C.E., a small temple of Plouton was built into the larger of the two cave chambers, replacing a cave edifice. Including the front portico, the temple was quite small, in total only 3.77 meters by 6.64 meters. Inside this cave chamber that housed the temple, archaeologist George Mylonas found a pit. It measured about 1 meter (3.28 feet) in diameter. I believe that this pit had an important mythic connection to Persephone and Plouton, since the cave was considered a gateway to the Underworld. (The temple site is open to the public, but the pit has since been filled in.)

Though not previously identified as such, I believe that this pit was the underlying space for a structure that led mythically to the Underworld. As described in chapter 13, the pit was probably used for a fertility rite called the Pourings of Plenty. This was performed on the day after the Greater Mysteries. But I suggest that the pit, as part of a structure within the Ploutonian temple cave, had another important function.

In the sacred drama of the Greater Mysteries presented in this chapter, wedding gifts are given to Persephone and Plouton from several of the immortals. As you will see, these are placed into the cista mystica (the mystery basket). With the addition of the pomegranate from Persephone, these become the hiera (the holy objects). While I believe that one permanent set of hiera were made of precious materials, I think that there was a second set of hiera, of completely natural materials (pomegranate, cakes, grain, pine, etc.). I believe that, after the sacred drama, the cista mystica containing the natural hiera was taken from Demeter's temple and carried into the cavern. There, I believe, these gifts (the natural hiera) were given to the God and Goddess of the Underworld by placing them into the pit.

I include an additional and all-important use of the hiera during the Festival of Thesmophoria (that follows the Greater Mysteries).

It is known from several sources that, during the Festival of Thesmophoria, women drew up the contents of a pit they called the megara (chamber), in order to make fertility talismans. I have included this rite during the Arkichronia portion of the Thesmophoria holidays (see chapter 9). Sources have described the contents of the megara as the remnants of previous offerings, though, as far as I am aware, they have not been connected to the Greater Mysteries. The contents have been described as pigs, cakes, pine branches, and other offerings. I believe that these were the remains of the natural hiera from the Greater Mysteries, plus the most common animal offering given to Demeter and Persephone, the pig. I believe that this megara, and the pit of the Ploutonian temple cave, may have been one and the same.

The Greater Mysteries presented here, are composed of many rites that build on each other. The parts are connected, just as the seasonal festivals connect one part of the year, and one part of the myth, to another. As this is a long ritual, allow plenty of time for your preparations. Become somewhat familiar with the ritual outline. You may choose to begin your preparations far ahead of time. If there are only a few of you, each will need to take several roles.

During the mysteries, the initiate honors the primary Eleusinian deities, celebrates the powers of the Great Creatress and her Holy Daughter, observes the sacred drama, and witnesses the powers of life and death coming into accord. The hiera are shown to be important symbols—concepts that can bless and shape our lives. The initiate also experiences a journey to death, the Thanatos Rite. In the Thanatos Rite, you, as the initiate, are prepared for your own future experience when life and death will meet. It is in this rite, as a priestess chants over your body, that you may perceive your own hallowed nature: that *you* are a part of the pure light of the Everlasting.

Ritual Outline

I.   Preritual
II.   Rite of Lustration
III.   Welcome
IV.   Altar Song
V.   Invocation of Hestia
VI.   Dance of Creation
VII.   Invocation of Aphrodite
VIII.   Honoring Plouton
IX.   Invocation of Hecate

X.   Invocation of Demeter
XI.   Invocation of Dionysus
XII.   Invocation of Persephone
XIII.   Song of Tartarus
XIV.   Dromena: Prologue and Descent
XV.   Dromena Part I: Demeter Mourns
XVI.   Dromena Part II: Sacred Marriage
XVII.   Dromena Part III: Reconciliation
XVIII.   Dromena: Epilogue
XIX.   Rite of the Cista Mystica
XX.   Thanatos Rite
XXI.   Crowning
XXII.   Closing Prayer
XXIII.   Closing Song
XXIV.   Closing Words

Clergy
Priestess of Hecate
Priestesses Panagia
Priestess of Hestia
Priestess of Aphrodite
Priestess of Plouton
Priest of Dionysus
Priestess of Demeter
Hierophant
Hierophantids of Demeter and Persephone
Priestess of Gaea
Priest of Plouton
Priestess of Rhea

Initiate Preparations
The initiate has previously experienced the Lesser Mysteries of Demeter and
Kore (see chapter 14). The initiate has learned the Rite of Lustration (see chapter 7). The initiate wears white to the ritual, either comfortable white clothing or
a chiton and himation (see chapter 18). It is suggested that all be dressed in the
same manner. If white himations are not being worn, then the initiate brings
a himation (a length of white fabric approximately 2 yards long) upon which
the initiate will lie during the Thanatos Rite. The initiate takes a bath in
Epsom or sea salts prior to the ritual, envisioning that he or she is being
cleansed in the sea.

   The following offerings are brought: seashells and/or roses for Aphrodite
(small votive statues of doves were traditional), bread or bowls of grain/seeds
or dried fruit for Demeter, and flowers for Persephone. Also rose petals are
brought for the sacred couple. The initiate eats lightly during the day prior to
the ritual. The initiate is aware that the temple will be entered in silence.

The Main Altar

The main altar is set against a wall. It has an icon of Demeter (see chapter 18), with two taper candles, one to the right and one to the left of the icon. There is another candle in front of the icon. There is a vase of flowers both to the right and left of the icon. On the altar is a censer, incense, and a bowl of water for the lustrations. There is an oil lamp or candle for Hestia, and a white taper candle with a wax guard for the Dance of Creation. There is a spare candleholder to receive the candle from the Dance of Creation. There is wine (decanted) or grape juice, small cups for individual drinks, and one myrtle or green leafy crown for each initiate (see chapter 18, "Crowns").

The Shrine of Aphrodite

The Shrine of Aphrodite is set on a table that is against a wall. It may be covered with a blue cloth. On it you may have an image or icon of the Goddess, (see chapter 18, "Icons") or simply a large chalice of water with trailing blue ribbons. There is a candle that will be lit for the Goddess. Flowers, seashells, and images of doves may be added as decoration.

The Anaktoron

Create the Anaktoron in the following way. Clear the center of the room that will be used as the temple. Mark the dimensions of the Anaktoron on the floor as a rectangular shape. Its shape should be approximately 1 by 4 feet. Lay out its boundaries with stones, ribbon, or cord. Inside the Anaktoron, place the empty cista (basket) with a lid. (You may want to tie the lid down with red ribbon.) Place purple fabric and a red ribbon inside of the basket. During the rite, the sacred objects will be put inside this fabric and then tied with the ribbon. At each corner of the Anaktoron, place a votive candle in a holder.

General Preparations

Clergy who will invoke the deities bring the following offerings. The Priestess of Aphrodite brings roses; the Priestess of Plouton brings myrtle; the Priestess of Hecate brings incense (I suggest frankincense and a censer coal, but self-lighting incense will suffice); the Priestess of Demeter brings bread (for the pelanos offering loaf, see Appendix 1); the Hierophantid of Demeter brings flowers and a small bowl or basket of fruit; the Priest of Dionysus brings an offering of figs and the wine; and the Hierophantid of Persephone brings flowers.

If you wish to wear Greek costume, see instructions for the making of chitons and himations in chapter 18. Prepare what will be the gifts of the immortals (the heira) for the sacred drama: two myrtle wreaths, a clay or plasticene snake serpent, saffron-and-rose anointing oil (see chapter 18), two red roses, two pine branches, two sheaves of grain, and a pomegranate (or red apple, if a pomegranate is not available).

Place the black cloth that will be used to cover each initiate during the Thanatos Rite, and the black strip of fabric that will go over the eyes, under the main altar. Place there also the pillow or pillows for the initiate's head. Place a basket of rose petals under the altar, and the pomegranate (or apple) listed above. The Priestesses Panagia each have a rattle or tambourine.

Staging

Set up the altars and the Anaktoron well in advance. If you use meditation music, set up your tape player for continuous play, if possible, and designate who will be in charge of the music. Have seating for the initiates at the outer edges of the room, with the Anaktoron in the center. Have a light meal ready in an adjacent room, to consume following the rites.

To Perform the Mysteries in Two Parts

Because this is a long ritual you might find this option more convenient. In the afternoon, perform the sacred drama. This includes Section XIV, Dromena; Prologue and Descent, through Section XVIII, Epilogue to the Dromena, then break for a light dinner. Change into your ritual garments and then proceed with the remainder of the rites.

The Rites of the Greater Mysteries
I. Preritual

The temple area has been cleaned and censed. The main altar has been censed, as has Demeter's icon. Before the censer is set down, it is lifted in homage to the goddess. There is appropriate ventilation in the room. Care has been taken so that there will be no interruptions during the rite, such as the telephone. About 5 minutes before the rites begin, the two taper candles to the right and left of Demeter's icon are lit, and the Hierophantid of Demeter says:

Hail Demeter!
Hail Persephone!

II. Rite of Lustration

The prospective initiates enter in silence, to the sounds of soft meditative music. They are directed to place their various offerings down near their seats. They are next directed by the Hydranos Priestess to perform the Rite of Lustration individually and then be seated.

Each initiate performs the words and actions of the Lustration Rite, upon entering the temple area.

Eye of spirit where wisdom enters,
May her good enter from the right hand
May her good enter from the left hand
For she dwells within
And without,
In beauty
And honor,
Hail!

When all are done, the music is turned off.

III. Welcome

Priestess of Hecate:
All welcome to the Greater Mysteries of Demeter and Persephone.
Tonight we will witness the Sacred Drama,
Observe the Rites of the Cista Mystica,
And be guided through the Thanatos, the Journey to Death.

Hierophant:
Many will be invoked, and to them offerings will be presented:
To Aphrodite and Dionysus, to Hecate and Plouton,
And to Holy Demeter and Royal Persephone.
In the story of Demeter and Her Maiden Daughter
Does the Great Mother rejoice in the creation of life,
Reveling in the verdant season of flowering
And in the rich harvest.

Priestess of Demeter:
When the Holy Daughter descends into the Underworld,
The Earth becomes barren and the Mother mourns.
But it is from dark mourning
That joy and deep understanding are born.
Then, the Great Mother flourishes once again,
As in the spiraling seasons of life,
May we in joy also flourish.
So be it.

IV. Altar Song

Priestesses Panagia/All [Spoken, chanted, or sung]**:**
Here is Her wisdom,

For She is within;
Here is the Mystery
Where all life begins.
Hail, Hail, Hail.

V. Invocation of Hestia

Priestess of Hestia [At the main altar]:
We call Hestia,
Goddess of hearth and temple fire,
Of the spiritual center of our world,
And of all sacred places.
Hestia, beloved Goddess of the spiritual flame,
Come, and enter this temple.
Make all that is here holy and sacred in Your name.
Bring to us the peace and sureness

Of that place which is home and hearth.
Bring Your purity and beauty to us
As we honor You,
Who are the center of the spiritual flame.
So be it.

Priestess of Hestia [Lights the candle or lamp. She raises it up high and says]:
Hail Hestia!

Priestesses Panagia/All:
Hail Hestia!

VI. Dance of Creation

Priestess Panagia: Lights a taper candle (with a wax guard) from the Hestia flame. She invites the participants into a circle to prepare for a dance. Participants are instructed to join hands. The Priestess holds the candle up in her right hand, with the hand of a participant in her left. (Some clergy may sit out, to sing or chant the lines below, or remain in the dance, having memorized the song.) The Priestess Panagia begins to move, weaving and flowing the dance line throughout the room. The Priestess may want to spiral in and then spiral out, then end by resuming the circle in which you began.

Priestesses Panagia:
Dark Mother of deepest Mystery
You gave birth to the soul's pure light.

Great Mother of forest and sea,
You gave birth to the world so bright.

[The dance stops and the Priestess holds her candle in both hands. She says]:
Praises to the Mother of Creation.

Then she passes the candle to the one to her left, who repeats the same words, and so on down the line. When done, the candle is set into a holder on the main altar.

VII. Invocation of Aphrodite

Priestess of Aphrodite [Instructs all to retrieve their offerings for Aphrodite. She sets roses onto Aphrodite's shrine and says]:
Aphrodite, bright Lady of the Sea,
With love and honor
Have we prepared Your offerings.

Glorious Goddess, risen from the blue Aegean waves,
Jeweled in white moonstone, shell, and pearl,
You are rich in beauty and sweet loving.
With hair unbound and garments streaming,
You dance upon the shore, before the bright
        dolphins,
Gulls flying and white doves singing.

O Aphrodite of the loving heart,
Whose powers none can halt,
Hear our prayers.
Come, and receive our offerings.
May these gifts,
That will be sent into the waters of Earth
When the Sun rises again,
Carry to You our truest dreams and
        needs.
Grant to us our heart's desires,
O fair Lady of beauty and sweet loving.

The Priestess lights the candle and invites all to come to the altar of Aphrodite, to place seashells and flowers as offerings. Then each may pray to Her for a blessing. The following day, the offerings will be taken to a nearby shore and given to Her by being placed into the water.

VIII. Honoring Plouton

Priest or Priestess of Plouton: With the offering of myrtle in hand, the Priest or Priestess of Plouton approaches the space created as the Anaktoron. The clergy visualizes the Anaktoron as the cavern entrance of Eleusis and mentally moves through the gateway to Tartarus, calling down to the Underworld:

O Lord of the Dead and Beloved of fair Persephone,
We call to You.
On this holy night, open for us the Gates of the Underworld
When we light the corners of the Anaktoron.
May this sacred space awaken as a holy entrance.

Guide, with Persephone,
The initiates to an understanding of the journey of life and
    death,
And after a long and favored life, grant us a gentle death
As we come to fair Persephone with a glad heart.
So be it.

The myrtle is set down in the Anaktoron, and the four candles inside the Anaktoron are lit.

IX. Invocation of Hecate

Priestess of Hecate [At the main altar]:

Mighty Hecate,
Mistress of dark crossroads and moonlit rites,
Depart from Your ancient cavern and attend to the initiates
On this holy night.

In the moments between transforming flame and gentle
    darkness,
Bless us in the Thanatos Rite.
May we awaken to an understanding of our divinity,
And may that realm that lies beyond words
Be revealed to all.
Hecate, by the power of thy immortal hand,
Shall we be awake in the mystery!
Hail Queen of Magic!

The Priestess lights the incense on the main altar. Then she carries the smoking censer to the Anaktoron. She censes its perimeters. At each corner she says:

By Thy immortal hand!

She places the censer back on the main altar.

X. Invocation of Demeter

Priestess of Demeter [At the main altar, holding the pelanos offering loaf]:

    Panagia . . . Antaia . . . Thesmophoros . . .
    Goddess of many names,
    You rose from the precious Earth,
    Fair wisdom in Your hand,
    The gifts of Your bounty even then taking shape,
    Imparting to Eleusis and all the world,
    The honorable way to live,
    To bring sustenance from the Earth
    With appreciation and thanksgiving.
    And through Your Mysteries, that are those of the soul,
    You reveal our own divinity,
    Which is the greatest beloved.

    All Holy Demeter,
    Pure luminous Mother of Creation,
    You turn barren lands into fields rich with wheat and
        barley.
    You entice orchards to grow lush and green,
    And to bear their weight of sweet fruit.
    In Your name, meadowlands are covered with brilliant
        flowers,
    As, in its time, the patient ewe gives milk for the lamb.

    And in the month of Anthesterion
    The hillsides and meadowlands appear
    Dressed in emerald once again.
    As You Chloaia, and Thy Maiden Daughter reign,
    Jeweled in larkspur, lupine, and blood-red poppies.

Hierophantid of Demeter [At the main altar, holding flowers and a bowl or basket of fruit]:

    Holy One,
    All the world is filled with Your treasures;
    For You have born all myriad forms of life
    That thrive under the Sun.
    And when we bring in all that we need to live,
    We partake of You,

O Mother of Good Harvests.
The ripened grain, the sweet apricot and the
    pungent herb
Are but a portion of Your great bounty.
For we praise Your riches as we find them;
From the wild woodland berry,
To the sweet orchard apple.

Priestess and Hierophantid of Demeter:
All honor to the Holy Mother,
Full of splendor and crowned with grain.
The riches of life, streaming from the palms of Thy
    hands
Bring us joy and sweet pleasure.
Great praises and thanksgiving do we offer Thee
O Great Creatress.
Come, and bring us Your blessings,
As we invoke You to attend these sacred rites.
Infuse them with Your ancient and holy power
O Mother of all,
As we offer You our love, on this Night of
    Mysteries.
All hail Demeter!

Priestesses Panagia/All:
Hail Demeter!

The Priestesses set down their offerings saying:
Hail Demeter!

Priestess of Demeter: Lights the votive candle in front of the icon. The initiates are invited to bring their offerings of bread, grains and/or fruit to Demeter at the main altar saying:
Hail Demeter!

As each initiate sets his or her offering down, the Priestess of Demeter tears a small piece of the pelanos loaf, and gives it to the initiate saying:
A gift from the Holy Mother,
We will eat together.

When all have been given a portion of bread she says:
All eat in Her honor.

XI. Invocation of Dionysus

Priest of Dionysus   [Sets down an offering of figs and bread for the God at the main altar, saying]:
>   Hail Dionysus!

He takes up the decanted wine and says:
>   Dionysus, beloved God and Lord of woodland revels,
>   You are the young fawn under dappled light
>   And the sacred bull of high summer.
>   O ivy-wreathed and flute-playing God of the green mountains,
>   Sweet and pleasing,
>   Come and bring rapture to the hearts of the initiates!
>
>   You are the vine that refreshes and brings healing,
>   That comforts and brings joy.
>   Here is Your generous gift,
>   Grown and pressed and matured into the blessed drink.
>   For this we thank You, as we drink in Your honor.
>   All hail Dionysus!

Priestesses Panagia/All:
>   Hail Dionysus!

Priest of Dionysus: Pours small cups of wine or juice (a few sips) for each initiate. He passes the cups out saying:
>   A gift from the God of the vine.

When all have received wine he says:
>   All drink in His honor.

XII. Invocation of Persephone

Hierophantid of Persephone: Facing the Anaktoron, scatters flowers around the interior perimeter (reserving a small portion), and then mentally moves through the gateway to the Underworld. She chants:
>   Peaceful and bright reigns She,
>   Over the bless-ed dead.
>   Deep in the groves of Elysium
>   Grows the pomegranate red,
>   Grows the fruit of death so red . . .
>   May we drink, from the Queen's cup.

She invokes Persephone:

> Hail Queen of Tartarus and Elysium!
> Generous Lady who has brought light to the realms below,
> Beauty You have brought to Elysium,
> And perfect justice to the realm of Tartarus.
> You are the Beloved of Death, who brings joy
> To the King of the Underworld.
> In rich robes, jeweled and crowned,
> Wise, and full of loving-kindness,
> You reside in Tartarus' palace,
> Enthroned with the Lord Plouton,
> Dispensing in compassion Themis' law.
>
> And in Elysium,
> Wreathed and garlanded in fragrant blossoms,
> You welcome the dead under the spreading pomegranate tree
> Where You prepare them for another way of being;
> One in which divinity is awake in the heart.
> O fair Persephone, Mistress of beauty and light,
> Come, and bless us Your pure-hearted initiates.

Priestesses Panagia/All:

> Hail Persephone!

The initiates are invited to bring their offerings of flowers to Persephone at the Anaktoron. When all have finished, the Hierophantid scatters the last of the flower petals inside the Anaktoron, saying:

> May the Queen of Tartarus and Elysium bless these rites.

XIII. Song of Tartarus

Hierophant and Priestesses Panagia   [Singing or chanting, while initiates remain standing]:

> O Lord of Tartarus, Host of the Dead,
> For us You shall take . . .
> Tears of past weeping,
> And leave us bright gems in their stead.
> O leave us bright gems in their stead . . .
>
> Through ever dark portals
> Flow the souls of the dead,
> Unknowing . . . of joy or jubilation,

Until the Great Queen is met.
Until Persephone is met . . .
May we drink from the Queen's cup.

XIV. Dromena: Prologue and Descent

Hierophant:

Initiates, please be seated for the Sacred Drama.
Listen as the Dromena is revealed;
We begin the story of life, death, and rebirth,
Of Demeter and Her Holy Daughter . . .

Hierophantid of Persephone:

All was green upon the land.
Kore, the lovely Daughter of Holy Demeter
Played on the woodland hilltops of pine and cypress.

She searched with the Daughters of Oceanus,
And they made wreaths of violets, saffron crocus, and
    white narcissus.
Lush were these crowns of fragile beauty,
And when set upon the heads of the divine virgins,
They became the enchantment of nature's great power.

The maidens walked toward the sea,
Laughing and dancing, and singing sacred songs.
They reveled in the beauty of Earth and Sea,
Then, wreathed and garlanded, they rested from their play.

Hierophantid of Demeter:

Far from the Holy Daughter labored Mother Demeter.
Tending the fields of wheat and barley
And all that grew upon the great Earth.
In joy, She watched the red poppies begin to bloom
Among the stands of grain now turning to gold.
Here was Her gift, precious food for the people of the world.
Soon it would be harvesttime, and Demeter's song flowed
    across the land.

Priestesses Panagia:

Time moved forward, and so came the harvest.

The scythe was raised and swung, again and again,
And the cut sheaves bound together.
The green of the season had passed,
And Demeter reigned in Her glorious ecstasies as the Great
    Harvest Mother.
The meadows on the plains of Nysa turned yellow with age,
The green grasses were gone,
And the blood-red poppies gave out their last brilliant burst
    of life.

Priestess of Hestia:

The season was changing.
It was then that the sleeping maidens,
Kore and the Daughters of Oceanus,
Were approached by saffron-cloaked Hecate.
With the power of Her immortal hand,
A spell was laid upon the maidens.
Whispering into the ear of Kore,
Hecate caused visions of the lands below to enter
    Her dreams.
She charged Kore to see what was transpiring in the dark
    of the Underworld,
And this is what Demeter's Daughter saw . . .

Hierophant:

A great King was below, sighing and weeping in loneliness.
On a throne of carved black marble He sat,
Bent over as one who is forlorn and lost.
Beside Him was an empty throne upon which lay a jeweled
    silver crown.
Lord Plouton then began to sing
A song of such yearning and sadness
That all of the souls below began to mourn with Him.
Their sounds rose up to the very Gates of Tartarus.
Plouton sang until His beautiful and haunting sounds
Found the ear of fair Kore.

Hierophantid of Persephone:

Far above, in the Maiden's dream,
Kore's heart was flooded with love and compassion
For He who has been called the Unseen One.
Her heart had awakened not only to love, but to passion.

She wished only to bring Her light and Her beauty to the lands
    below;
To bring the essence of the Sun,
And the beauty of the green Earth,
To the Lord Plouton, and to the souls of the dead also.

Priestess of Hestia:

He had seen Her, the Lord of Tartarus.
From His palace whose lamps had grown dim,
He went to the grotto of the black stallions.
There, outside of Elysium,
He harnessed the steeds to their waiting chariot.
The dry meadows of Nysa turned to flame,
And beyond the red and golden flame, the Earth burst asunder.
Great mounds of Earth spewed out
As the black stallions entered the world that had not born
    them.
Beyond the field of ember and flame,
The God of the Underworld drew up his chariot and waited.

Hecate raised Kore from the ground, and the Maiden knew
    fear.
The Holy Daughter removed Her flowered crown,
And with courage, She cast it into the remaining flame,
Her gaze upon the face of Her Beloved.
Uncrowned, She walked across the field of ember and flame
To embrace the Lord of the Dark.
Her veil, embroidered with lilies, was left behind.

Priestesses Panagia:

Around the shoulders of the Maiden,
Invisible ones drew a black himation,
Bordered with luminous silver threads
And set with precious gems.

Then, into the waiting chariot She fled, into the arms of
    Tartarus.
The brilliance of passion filled Her heart
As Plouton drove the black steeds around the Earth
And then down into the lands below.
With the God of Death, She descended.

Then, having arrived below,
She drank from the shining silver spring of Memory,
And Persephone awoke to the knowledge of Her Queenship.
The silver crown appeared upon Her head,
And the voices of the dead rang out in jubilation.
In joy, the Queen was received
And a great celebration began.

Hierophant:
Then, to the plains of Nysa She came,
She who is the Mother of the land,
From whom all that is good and bountiful comes forward.
Holy Demeter came in search of fair Kore.
There, on the broad plains beside the sea,
The scar of charred and black remains was to be seen.
The poppies and lupines had gone.
Only the delicate veil embroidered with lilies could She find,
Cast in haste upon the ground.
Holding the veil to Her heart, the Goddess let out a mournful cry.

To the edge of Nysa She went,
Calling out to the vast sea before Her,
But the sea was silent.
For nine days She searched the mountain hilltops and the wood-
     land meadows.
She did not eat of ambrosia nor drink of divine nectar.
On the ninth day, She found Euboleus, child of Baubo and
     Dysaules.
Euboleus told the Sorrowing Mother
That Kore had descended in the chariot of Tartarus.

Hierophantid of Demeter:
The Divine Mother of all that grows upon the Earth,
Tore Her golden diadem from Her head and rent Her flowing
     garments.
She took the form of the black-robed Crone, of Melaina.
In grief, She wandered across the Earth, and the land wasted away.
The rains came. The farmers cast their seed upon the ground
Again and again, but to no avail.
To Eleusis came the Goddess, hidden in Her garments of the
     Crone.

She sat at the well to rest.
It was there that She met Baubo, wife of the farmer Dysaules,
Mother of Euboleus, Triptolemos, and Eumolpos.
In kindness, Baubo asked the grieving Crone to come with her,
And so to the home of Baubo and Dysaules,
The Crone went and was made welcome.

Priestess of Hestia:

In the home of the Eleusinian family,
Demeter Melaina sat in silence, eyes cast down.
But Baubo made the Mother laugh,
As She lifted up Her garments in a dance.
And in that moment, when the joy of laughter reigned,
Was the Goddess' true and holy nature revealed.

The Crone's dark garments were cast aside
And the glorious Goddess rose in a brilliant and resplendent
      light.
Her golden hair hung in heavy long plaits,
Her flowing garments embroidered
With red poppies and sheaves of wheat.
Upon Her head the golden diadem was set
And from Her very presence emanated a sweet and gentle
      fragrance.

But even in Her great beauty did She still mourn.
Baubo went to the people of Eleusis,
And told them of the sorrows of the Great Mother.
In awe and reverence,
Honoring the bounty that they once had, and fearing famine,
The people of Eleusis built a temple for the Mourning Goddess.
There Demeter came to reside.

Now initiates, listen to the words of the immortals,
First hear the words of Holy Demeter,
As She mourns in Her fragrant temple.

XV. Dromena Part I: Demeter Mourns

Priestess of Demeter [as Demeter]:

I am the Erinys, avenging and sad.
The people cry out to me
But I have no will to make the land blossom.

Let it whither!
For She who was born from my womb is no longer at my side.
She dwells in that place of darkness, and I mourn.
Together, we brought such beauty to Earth.
She was the child of life, brighter than the morning star.
But once She heard the song of the Dark Lord,
I could no longer keep Her as my child.

She who was once blossoming and full of beauty
Has now descended into Death.
And so . . . now all must prepare for famine . . .
For I will not move my immortal hand
To bring back the verdant days of Earth,
Until the Maiden has been restored to me!
May Tartarus be wise and listen to the words of the
    Erinys.

Priestesses Panagia [As the souls of the Dead]:

Plouton roams His palace, moaning and crying out,
Searching for a way to end His grief.
For, although fair Persephone dwells with Him,
She is no longer at peace. Her heart has been rent in two.

In the first flush of Their love
Did the Sacred Couple lie upon the couch of Aphrodite,
Entwining Their jeweled arms
In the fiery embrace of love and passion.
For days upon days did the Queen of the Underworld
Rejoice in the arms of Her Beloved,

Until one day, came the sound of Her Mother's weeping.
And from that day Her heart was rent in two,
One half for the Mother and one half for Her Beloved.
From that day, She would neither eat, nor drink,
Nor lie upon the Sacred Couch,
Nor take Her place in fair Elysium or shadowy
    Tartarus.
And so, the Lord Plouton mourns,
Not knowing how to heal the heart of His Beloved.
Listen, as Tartarus speaks . . .

Priest of Plouton [as Plouton]:

> Before She came, I was blind, not knowing joy or light.
> Stern Guardian of the Underworld and Host to the Dead,
> This was my lot and my duty.
> It was Hecate who told me of the fair Maiden,
>
> Possessing a bright and loving nature,
> And a wisdom that is pure and holy.
> And so I began to sing to Her.
>
> The Maiden heard my song and love grew.
> We journeyed into the deeper Realms,
> And lay for seeming eternity in the joys of love and passion.
> Through our passions
> Were flowering fields born in the Land of Tartarus,
> Like those of Earth; no different.
> An incandescent light arose even in Tartarus,
> While the groves of the pomegranate were born in fair Elysium.
> Everywhere, light and beauty awoke,
> As I and the souls of the dead were blessed by Her presence.
>
> But now, She begins to waste away.
> She only hears the sounds of Her Mother's weeping
> And will receive no love or food or solace.
> And so I cry out to the Great Mother of the Land.
> Holy Demeter, Beloved of all mortals, hear my voice!
> And I cry out to Hecate and to Aphrodite,
> O come to the aid of the Dark Lord!

XVI. Dromena Part II: The Sacred Marriage

Priestesses Panagia [As the souls of the dead, chanting or singing]:

> Now comes the wisdom of Hecate,
> Who sees the love that lies below.
> And so brings She, the magic of Aphrodite.
> To the depths of Tartarus Her power flows.
>
> Into Tartarus journeys Aphrodite,
> Bringing myrtle crowns and the red rose.
> Into Tartarus goes the Great Hecate,
> To preside over the wedding vows.

Hierophant:

Hecate and Aphrodite move through the Gates of the
    Underworld
And follow the paths of the dead.
They bring with them both Dionysus and Gaea,
Descending, they come finally to Tartarus' palace.
Finding Persephone alone,
They bid Her to rise and have courage.
Together, they move through the halls of the
    gemmed palace,
Until they arrive at the Tartarus' throne.
Then Aphrodite speaks . . .

Priestess of Aphrodite [as Aphrodite]:

Lord Plouton, step down from Your throne.
We have journeyed far to heal sorrow,
So that lamentation will be replaced with joy.
Plouton, step down and prepare to receive my gifts
And the gifts of Gaea, Dionysus, and Hecate.

Persephone and Plouton stand side by side and face the immortals. Each one of
the immortals carries a gift for the sacred couple. Aphrodite carries myrtle
crowns and red roses, Dionysus, pine boughs, Gaea, an image of a snake, and
Hecate, the saffron-and-rose anointing oil. Aphrodite places the myrtle crowns
on the heads of the sacred couple. She hands them each a red rose and says:

I bless You both in Your union of Sacred Love.
I sanctify this union, for it is right and proper
And in accordance with divine will.

Persephone, let Your beauty rise again.
Grow in power, love, and courage
Great Queen of Tartarus and Elysium,
Bring light and life to those souls
Who have stumbled in darkness.

Priest of Dionysus [as Dionysus]:

The God of the vine gladly confers his gifts upon You both.
May wildness, fertility, and joy bless Your sacred union.
May the beauty of the high mountains and of the evergreen pine
Sustain Your love in all times and in all seasons.

He hands the sacred couple each a pine branch, saying:
> Blessings upon You both.

Priestess of Gaea [as Gaea]:

> I, Grandmother Gaea,
> Give You what may seem a strange and eerie gift,
> But I assure You that there is wisdom in it.
> The sacred serpent sheds its skin and is reborn over and over
> > again.
> In this act of renewal is life and continuity.
> The snake knows the undulating rhythms of life,
> For all things change and change again, in order to be
> > renewed.
> This primeval emissary knows the deep and ancient past
> And can reveal wisdom for the future.
> Listen to and honor my gift.

She opens the lidded basket that she has brought and brings out a snake. She shows the snake to the sacred couple, who respectfully place their hands upon it. Then Gaea places it again into the lidded basket. She places the basket at the couple's feet and says:
> Now receive the gifts of Hecate.

Priestess of Hecate [as Hecate]:

> Persephone and Plouton, with the powers that I have been
> > allotted,
> I confer upon You my blessings:
> May You, Persephone,
> Continue to grow as Queen,
> In power, wisdom, and beauty,
> Keeping the light always emanating from Your heart.
> May You, Plouton,
> Always remain open to that light,
> As it becomes a part of You,
> Who are King of these Lands.

Now Hecate anoints their foreheads with the saffron-and-rose scented oil, saying the following words to Persephone and then again to Plouton:

> I bless this Sacred Union;
> It is perfect and complete,

And in accordance with divine will.
May its magic bring joy to You and Your Beloved,
And to the souls of the dead also.

Persephone and Plouton embrace.

XVII. Dromena Part III: The Reconciliation

Hierophant:

And now, from above, a miracle occurs.
A great light descends into the Underworld.
It is Holy Demeter.
She has let fall the darkness of Melaina and the face of the Erinys.
For She has seen from above
The tender love that the Lord Plouton has for Her Daughter.
The Mother's golden light fills the palace of Tartarus
With rays that seem of the Sun.

Persephone is filled with joy, as Mother and Daughter embrace once again. Demeter gives Persephone a kiss.

Priest of Plouton [as Plouton]:

Welcome, Great Mother of the land. Praises!
You have heard my prayers, and have come to our aid!

Priestess of Demeter [as Demeter, speaking to Plouton]:

Greetings, to Tartarus! Fear not, all will be well.
Lord of this mighty realm,
Once I thought that You had conspired with Zeus
To rob me of that which is most dear.
But now I have seen that this is not so.
Although I grieve for my loss,
I have come to understand the love that You have for my
     Daughter,
And the love that She has for You.
I have missed Her, but I know the ways of Aphrodite.

Priestess of Demeter [as Demeter speaking to Persephone]:

Beloved Daughter, love has blessed You.
And who am I to question Aphrodite?
I know that nothing can stop the magic of Her powers.

Even I must bow to Her, as I have done,
In the fields of Crete with fair Iasos.
So, be at peace again, for I love thee as I ever have.
You are still my child,
But You are also a great Queen, to whom I bow.

Priestess of Persephone [as Persephone]:

Then Mother,
Will You make the land bloom again for the people of Earth?

Priestess of Demeter [as Demeter]:

I fear that I have no will to make the land green again
Without the Blossoming Maiden.
We know not yet what can be done.
Still, knowing of the love between You and Plouton,
I do confer my blessings upon Your Sacred Marriage.
And so, be joyful in your union with the Lord Plouton;
Together, learn from the gifts of Aphrodite, Gaea,
Dionysus, and Hecate.

And now . . . here are my gifts,
Come, receive them.
With these sheaves of grain [hands each a sheaf],
I bless You both with the powers of rebirth,
And this You may impart to the souls of the dead,
That they may be reborn to life on Earth again.
And so may remember, both in Death and in Life,
The joy of their eternal souls.

I also bring the pelanos, cakes of wheat and barley.
Let us break bread together, so that Life and Death
May sit at the table and be at peace.
And I bring ambrosia, and divine nectar.
Come, let us dine together in a great feast,
And celebrate the Sacred Marriage.

Priestess of Hecate [as Hecate]:

Look! Another comes into the Realm of Shades!
It is the Goddess Rhea!
Great Titan . . . Welcome!

Priestess of Rhea [Rhea]:

    I was upon my mountain in Phyrgia,
    When Zeus told me Your story.
    And so I drove with speed my harnessed lions
    To the very Gates of Tartarus.
    Immortals all, come and listen to my plan
    And You will have a feast in which all will truly rejoice.

    Let fair Persephone stay with the Lord Plouton
    From the time the grain is threshed and stored,
    To the time the seed is brought up for planting.
    This will be the season of the fallow time on Earth.
    Then, when it is time for the seed to be planted,
    May the Maiden appear at the Gates of Tartarus
    And be reunited with Holy Demeter.
    This will begin the Earth's season of growth and blooming.

    Have pity on the mortals above,
    For they cry out for the Verdant Goddess to return.
    They cry out for Demeter to return the fertility of the land.
    Have pity on them, else all will reside below, and none will
        live above.

    And so it may be, from planting to harvest,
    That the Holy Daughter will reside above.
    And from the time the seed grain is stored
    Until the time it is brought up for the planting,
    That She will reside below.
    Persephone, come and tell us what You think of this plan.

Hierophantid of Persephone [as Persephone]:

    Now that she who gave me birth has ceased weeping,
    So have I also ceased weeping.
    Rhea and all have so summed up my needs,
    That love has awakened in my heart again.
    Here are those I love . . . Beloved Mother, and Noble Lord.
    Yes Great Rhea, I will gladly abide by your plan.

    Rhea's wisdom has set my mind at peace.
    And the power of my Mother's understanding pours from
        my heart;
    May we all remember this power.

> I see that there is a Mystery that provides for me in times of
>> sorrow
> And is ready to bring me joy.

Priest of Plouton [as Plouton]:

> Persephone has grown into a great Queen,
> And I rejoice to see the Queen happy again.
> She has chosen, and I acknowledge the freedom She has,
> To yearly return to Her Mother above.
> Even when She is not with me, I will keep Her in my heart.
> I see that there is a Mystery that provides for me in times of
>> sorrow
> And is ready to bring me joy.
>
> Much praise to all, for my prayers are answered.
> And joy has returned to the heart of fair Persephone.
> Come, let us begin our feast.
> Before you return to Earth and High Olympus,
> Come and enjoy the splendors of the palace of Persephone and
>> Plouton!

Plouton and Persephone place their gifts into the cista mystica, and set it into the Anaktoron.

Priestesses Panagia [as the souls of the dead]:

> The road to Tartarus now taken
> By Demeter, who love has seen.
> A kiss gave She, unto the Holy Daughter,
> The kiss that healed Death's Noble Queen.
> And all the dead have in their joy awakened,
> Rejoicing with their King and Queen.

The sacred couple embrace, and all clergy and participants throw rose petals over them. Hecate retrieves the pomegranate and hands it to Persephone. Persephone holds it out in one hand, as if offering it to all. She then places it into the cista mystica. The sacred couple embrace again. They reverently remove their myrtle crowns, and place them into the cista, divesting themselves of deity. The clergy are seated.

XVIII. Epilogue to the Dromena

Priestess of Plouton:

> With Plouton and Persephone's love for each other,
> All souls below awaken to a rebirth of life within the Land of
>> Death,

And to the beauty of the Eternal Mystery.
Bright purple flowers grow even at the banks of the River Styx,
And the Underworld glows with a mystic light of its own.
All souls dance and sing, celebrating the Sacred Marriage
And the power of love and passion,
These, placing the light and the dark into accord and Sacred
    Union.

This is the story of Life, Death, and Rebirth,
The Dromena of Holy Demeter and Royal Persephone.
May life bring us beauty, health and good fortune,
And may peace rest lightly upon us all!
So be it.

XIX. Rite of the Cista Mystica

Hierophantid of Demeter   [She stands and says]:
    Now we shall begin the Rite of the cista Mystica.
    The Hierophant will remove the cista from the Anaktoron
    And display the hiera.
    All stand to observe the rite.

Hierophant: Hierophant removes the cista mystica from the Anaktoron. He takes it to the main altar, and places it next to the altar. The following rite is performed by taking the objects (the hiera) out of the basket, one at a time. Each is placed at the front edge of the main altar. Each object is taken out and held up. The Priest states the symbolism and meaning of each object, and then sets it onto the altar for viewing. Remove the objects in the following order: the myrtle wreaths, the roses, the pine branch, the snake, the scented oil, the sheaves of wheat, and the pomegranate. The Hierophant performs the rite and describes the hiera.

Priestesses Panagia:
    These are the hiera . . .

Hierophant:
    The myrtle wreaths, the first gift of Aphrodite . . .
    These are the symbols of the Sacred Marriage.
    The Sacred Marriage is ever-present
    Between you and spirit.
    It is the truest form of love
    That calls you to your heart's desire.

Honoring this love brings fulfillment and deep contentment.
The wise soul chooses to be wedded to those things
That are the true loves of the heart.
Follow this path.

Know also that your spirit is wedded to the eternal,
That you are a part of the Divine Source of all.
It is the knowledge and memory of this,
That brings light and joy to the spirit.

The red roses, the second gift of Aphrodite . . .
Roses were given to Persephone and Plouton
As a blessing upon Their union.
With this gift, the Sacred Couple were blessed
With the knowledge that Their love was pure and
        true.
When we begin an endeavor
And we come upon hardships or obstacles,
We must remember the love and good intent
With which that endeavor was founded.
We must also remember the love that we need
And so be gentle with our own self, and our own
        heart.

The pine branch, the gift of Dionysus . . .
As the pine that grows in the wild mountains
Remains ever green throughout all seasons,
So may the God of fiery passion and joy
Bring His sustaining blessings into your life.

The God of the vine is present
Not only in the autumn vintage,
But also in the wild mountains and the untamed dance of
        nature.
May your spirits be lifted
With His renewing passion and inspiration,
As is your need.

The serpent, the gift of Gaea . . .
The primeval and undulating snake
Is connected to the deepest part of the Earth.
It sheds its skin and changes, yet it remains the same.

The snake carries the deep voice of the Earth,
And a part of us which is wild and primeval
Also carries that voice.

If we listen to, and honor Gaea's serpent,
We will be strong during times of change,
And in wisdom will we perceive life
As an ever-changing and divine drama,
Sanctified by the primeval forces of nature

The saffron-and-rose scented oil, the gift of Hecate. . .
This is the symbol of the understanding and
    acceptance
That is given to us by the immortals.

As Hecate anointed the Sacred Couple
And blessed Their desire to be together,
So do the immortals bless us with loving
    understanding
As we journey down paths that are difficult
Or paths that others do not tread.
There are many paths that lead toward the good.
By the symbol of the scented oil,
May we learn to listen with true wisdom,
As we anoint ourselves and others
With the very same divine understanding
That is given to us from on high.

The grain, the gift of Demeter . . .
The seed has supported and sustained great
    civilizations,
Its cultivation and storage preventing famine
And providing time for the voice of the Muse.

The seed grows and flowers,
As does the Maiden Daughter.
Being cut at the harvest, it dies,
But in the dried and golden sheaf
Is the seed of its own regeneration.
So too are we born, do we flourish and mature
And later depart unto the Land of Death.

Though the body passes away, the soul continues
In the eternal dance of Creation.

To the feast of the immortals,
Demeter brought the pelanos.
At the table of Tartarus bread was broken
And this became a sign of peace.
Then, compassion and concord arose
Between Demeter, Persephone, and the Lord of
    Tartarus,
And so between all the powers of Life and Death.
And when we sit at table with friends and loved ones,
We may celebrate, remembering this divine accord.
We are twice-blessed, in life and in death.
Through the Holy Mother and Her Daughter Persephone,
The Land of Death has become a place of light and peaceful
    accord,
And when the anointed soul arrives in the veiled Realms Beyond,
There is only joy and light and celebration.

The pomegranate, the gift of Persephone . . .
As the spirit journeys from life to death
The tree of the sacred grove flowers.
The soul meets the Queen of Elysium,
And the budding branch bears fruit.

Red is Her fertile power;
Full of love, Her royal countenance.
The Queen receives you,
For the dead descend, but not to die.
And the scarlet fruit bears witness
To the powers of Death in Life,
And Life in Death.

Priestesses Panagia:
These are the hiera:
The myrtle crown, the rose,
The pine branch,
The saffron-and-rose scented oil,
The serpent, the sacred seed
And the pomegranate.

Hierophantid of Demeter:
>Initiates, in silence come to the altar
>To view the Hiera,
>And then be seated.

You may want to play soft meditation music. The initiates come to the main altar to view the hiera. After the hiera are viewed, the initiates return to their seats. The Hierophant returns the hiera to the purple cloth in the cista. The cloth around the hiera is tied and the bag is censed.

XX. Thanatos Rite

Hierophantid of Persephone:
>Now we will begin the Thanatos Rite.
>When the Priestess comes for you,
>Take your himation.
>Follow her directions, and after,
>Remain in silence.

Priestesses Panagia: Begin meditation music, the best being a soft, low, steady drum. Two Priestesses of Panagia at a time (or more) may perform the rite, one cleric to each initiate. Each Priestess lights a votive candle from the flame of an Anaktoron candle. She places the candle in a votive holder. Holding the candle, each priestess goes to an initiate, inviting the initiate to follow. The initiates are directed to lay their himations down near the Anaktoron. Each lays down on their himation.

Each Priestess Panagia sets her candle down. A small pillow is placed under each initiate's head. The Priestess covers the initiate with a black cloth from shoulder to foot. A band of black cloth is set over the initiates eyes. The votive candle is passed over the initiate's body, up and down. Then, it is drawn back and forth, across the covered eyes several times. The Priestess of Panagia says:
>Draw deeply down, down unto Persephone.

Even though the candle is in a votive holder, take great care when doing this to hold the candle even and steady. Then, set the candle down and blow it out.

The Priestess sits down near the initiate's head to speak the words of the Thanatos Rite. She speaks with gentle but sure voice, in unison with the other Priestess(es). Each Priestess directs her words and thoughts to the soul of the initiate, not to the name, form, or personality of the initiate:
>Bless-ed Initiate,
>You have entered the temple of the Two Goddesses.
>You have seen the sacred drama, and learned of the hiera.
>Now, clothed in darkness, you are prepared for death's rite.

Bless-ed One, I speak to your soul,
To you who are pure of heart.
Within thy body resides thy sacred soul,
O fair offspring of the Great Mother.

On the day when the Sun no longer shines
Upon thy sacred and earthly body,
And bread and wine are not taken again,
Then will you meet death upon the River of Memory.

Death, the great gatekeeper, will take thy hand,
And in a rush of thunder and wind,
You will hear the Sounds of Creation humming and flowing
As you move through the Great Song.

Shadows will shift and turn
Like the moving shadows of leaves over running water,
But hold tight to Death's hand,
As you move through Plouton's dark gate.

Have courage and look into the face of Death.
Then darkness will vanish and glory will be revealed,
For you will look into the face of the Holy Mother,
And light upon light will flood the face of beauty.

With loving care, She will guide you,
Seat you at the table of the immortals,
And fill your soul with the ecstasy of divine ambrosia.
Then, nourished thus, She will take you to the Holy Daughter.

Upon Her throne in fair Elysium,
Under the budding pomegranate tree,
In the center of the wide and flowering grove,
Reign Persephone and Her Great Beloved.

In love will Demeter greet Her Daughter,
And also the Lord of the Underworld.
The Mother will place your hand into that of Noble
    Persephone,
And in that moment, the budding pomegranate will bear fruit.

As Demeter gave you divine ambrosia to eat,
So shall Persephone give you a sacred drink
Made of the fruit of the pomegranate
And the waters of the Fountain of Memory.

Drink deeply of the Queen's gift,
And all of your lives will flow before thee.
The patterns that they make, beautiful and true,
Are the great songs of eternity.

It is then that thy soul will be unbound by time,
And life upon life will flow about thee.
Reveling in the great miracle, and in the light of Creation,
You will know thy divine and immortal soul.

Hail to thee who will live forever,
To the pure light of the Everlasting!
All honor unto you Holy One,
Just as it is given to the Mother and Daughter.

And so it is.

The black cloths are removed from the initiate. The initiate is instructed to stand. The white himation is picked up and set over one shoulder. The Priestess then bows in reverence to the initiate, guiding him or her to the place of crowning. (The whole process is experienced by each initiate.)

XXI. Crowning

The initiates are crowned with the myrtle or green leafy crown.

Priestess Panagia:
Peace be upon thy heart, now and forever more.

Initiates are then directed to their seats.

XXII. Closing Prayer

When all have been experienced the Thanatos Rite and Cowning, the initiates are directed to stand.

Priestesses Panagia:
Great Mother,
Through the journeys of Your Holy Daughter
Do we learn of the Sacred Marriage;
That Life is wedded to Death,
Each a part of the whole of being.

Blessed are Thee who has born us,
For as every woman gives birth to her child,
So You labored to bring us into being
And bestow upon us this gift of life.
You sustain us, and at the end of the drama,
Guide us in death's journey:
Through Plouton's gate,
To the table of the immortals,
And into the hands of Queen Persephone.

Panagia,
We have honored and praised You,
Lighting candles and fragrant incense,
Offering flowers and sweet fruit;
But it is the pure and sincere offerings of the heart
By whose devotion we may embrace Thee
And our inherited divinity.

Holy One,
Bless us with Thy wisdom,
And with a life that is just and full of bounty.
May the richness and beauty of Thy presence
Remain with us now and forevermore.

Hierophant and Priestess of Demeter:
The temple is prepared within,
For here does She reside,
Filling us with strength
And the power to create joy,

Healing the heart and the mind,
Embracing both the shadows and the sunny places
So that we may walk in grace
Throughout this life and into the next.

So do we honor
Both the Daughter and the Holy Mother
In this journey of life,
And so it is.

XXIII. Closing Song

Priestesses Panagia   [Chanting or singing]:

Here is Her wisdom,
For She is within.
Here is the Mystery
Where all life begins.
Hail, Hail, Hail.

XXIV. Closing Words

All Clergy:

These are the rites of the Greater Mysteries
Of Demeter and Persephone.
May you remain awake in the Mystery.

Her temple rites complete,
In grace and in joy,
May Her blessings proceed unto all,
And may you drink from the Queen's cup.[3]

RITES FOR THE DAY FOLLOWING THE GREATER MYSTERIES

I. Prayers for Departed Loved Ones

All light candles and say prayers for those loved ones who have passed on to the other side, as well as candles for Demeter, Persephone, and Plouton.

II. Placing the Hiera into the Megara

The contents of the cista mystica are placed in a chosen "Underworld cavern" location. If indoors, you may place the contents of the cista in another container or basket, but line the container with plastic. Place this in a dark place, or cover it with a black cloth, under an altar. Add to these contents the Demetrian fertility images of pigs as offerings, and images of snakes as guardians (see chapter 18). You may also use an outdoor megara (see chapter 18, "megara"). In this

---

[3]   Following this ritual is a light meal and a good night's rest. On the following morning, the offerings to Aphrodite are taken to the sea, or a nearby lake or river, and tossed into the water, followed by fresh flower petals.

case, take the hiera out of the basket and set the contents directly into the
megara. As you do this, say the following words:

These are the gifts given to Theos and Thea,
From the immortals.
May they reside in the Underworld.
May they become enchanted with the power and magic
Of the Sacred Lovers, and of the Hieros Gamos.
All honor to the Lord and Lady
Of the lands that lie below;
And so it is.

Then seal the megara, if outdoors, or cover the container or basket, if indoors.
There in the "Underworld," the hiera will remain until the Thesmophoria festivals. During the Rites of Arkichronia (see chapter 9) the megara will be opened
and the remains of the hiera will be used.

PART V

Establishing a Temple of Demeter

The Temple of the Solitary Devotee

*The devotee is mysteriously drawn to the deity
as if drawn to a lover. During prayer and ritual practice, the
heart opens and love flows not only to the deity, but from
the deity. It is in these sacred moments that the
love of the infinite fills the chalice of the heart.*

The private devotions of solitary worship can fill the heart with loving emotion, a kind of inner magical elixir that those in India call *bhava*. This arises from the devotee, and is returned manyfold from the Goddess. The solitary devotee is free to worship in both structured and unstructured ways, making changes spontaneously as need arises.

Demeter's religion is a form of *Shaktism,* of Goddess-focused religion. The basic theology of Demetrian Paganism is that, from the body of the Great Mother, life is born. The Mother is sacred and holy, and as a part of her, we are also sacred and holy. The body of Earth reflects the Goddess' many faces and powers. Her seasonal cycles teach us of our eternal nature and of our divinity. We are born of her, and return to her, in the spiraling cycle of life, death, and rebirth.

As an individual devotee, it is important to remember that there are many kinds of personalities in the world that require different forms of religion. This version of Demetrian Paganism arose to be of service. There are bound to be adaptations needed, however, because of natural human differences. For some, this may be a point from which to take off. If there are elements of this version that do not work for you, then a personal adaptation is in order. There are many ways one can celebrate divinity.

Overzealous religious missionaries have, in the past, justified violence by their cause. These are sad situations, because, at their best, religions are here to guide us to live a better life, one with honesty, integrity, and nonviolence at its core. Religion reminds us that the world is sacred. It can reconcile life's seeming misfortunes, create an understanding about death, provide rites of celebration, and bring us into a state of spiritual bliss.

As the myth and the theology provide the groundwork for the practices, it will be helpful to become familiar with them. The ideas within chapters 3 and 4 are woven throughout the seasonal festivals and mysteries. These rites connect the movements of the agricultural year with the religion's transcendent themes. Through experiencing the festivals and the mysteries, transcendent concepts become deep, transcendent experiences.

BUILDING YOUR TEMPLE

If you are to worship alone, you'll need to prepare an altar. Chapter 7 provides ideas for altar building. For this altar consecration you will need a Demeter icon (see chapter 18, "Icons"), two white taper candles on either side of the icon, a votive candle in front of the icon, a candle or oil lamp for Hestia, offerings of fruit and flowers for Demeter, offerings of food and drink for Hestia, incense (such as sandalwood, or frankincense and myrrh), and a censer and a censer coal if you are using pure sandalwood or the resins. Also get a bowl or large scallop shell, filled with water.

When you have finished setting up your altar, consecrate it with a blessing and a ritual. Light the incense and, standing in front of your altar, move the censer around your body three times, in a clockwise direction, by passing it hand to hand. Then trace the smoke around your altar three times.

Invocation of Hestia: Next, invoke Hestia and light Her candle/lamp.

I call Hestia,
Goddess of hearth and temple fire,
Of the spiritual center of our world,
And of all sacred places.
Hestia, beloved Goddess of the spiritual flame,
Come, and enter this temple.
Make all that is here holy and sacred in Your
          name.
Bring to us the peace and sureness
Of that place which is home and hearth.
Bring Your purity and beauty to this place,
As I honor You,
Who are the center of the spiritual flame.
So be it.

Offer Hestia food and drink, saying:

Hail Hestia!

Carry the smoking censer around your living space, going through each room in a clockwise direction. Feel purification and peace come into your home.

The Rite of Lustration: Next, return to your altar and do some visioning work. First, purify the space using the words and actions of the Rite of Lustration (chapter 7):

1   Dipping the fingers of your right hand into the lustration bowl, bring the fingers to the center of your forehead and say:

Eye of spirit where wisdom enters,

2   Extend your right arm out to the right, say:

May Her good enter from the right hand,

3   Extend your left arm toward the left, say:

May Her good enter from the left hand,

4   Bring both hands to your heart (mid-chest), and say:

For She dwells within . . .

5   Bring your forearms down, palms up, and say:

And without,

6   Bring your hands again to your heart, as before, and say:
     In beauty . . .

7   Bow your head and say:
     And honor,

8   Raise your arms up and say:
     Hail!

Visioning work: Envision the goddess in all of nature: in the air you breathe, the water you drink, and in the earth below you. Breathe her energy up from the earth. See it as a sparkling light flowing into your body. Breathe the light in. See it extend out to the tips of your fingers, down to your toes, and up to the top of your head. Radiate her light. When you are filled with it, send this light above, below, and around you. Flood your altar with this light. Continue to breathe in her light. Send it into every corner of the room.

Chanting and prayer: Light the taper candles to the right and left of Demeter's icon, saying:
     Hail Demeter! Hail Persephone!

Chant the following; establish a repetitive rhythm and/or melody:
     Dea Mystica . . . shine within me,.
     Holy Mother in . . . perfect beauty,
     Come, come to me!

Read the Prayer to Demeter Panagia aloud or silently (see chapter 5):
     All Holy Demeter,
     Pure luminous Mother of Creation,
     With Your great powers
     You turn barren lands into fields rich with wheat and barley.
     You entice orchards to grow lush and green,
     And to bear their weight of sweet fruit.
     In Your name, meadowlands are covered with brilliant flowers,
     As in its time, the patient ewe gives milk for the lamb.

     Panagia,
     Come to me, shining Your beauty upon my heart,
     Goddess of ever more than harvesttime,
     But of all life's seasons,
     O hear my prayer.

Beautiful Goddess,
Bring rapture into my heart,
Rising as divine ecstasy,
And I become Thine.
Let Thy radiance flow upon me,
Until my heart is full of light.

May Your blessings flow upon my body,
My soul, my house and my life,
Hail Panagia!
Hail!

Light the candle in front of her icon. Offer her fruit and flowers. Open your heart to Her. Ask inwardly that she be with you in your devotions. End by saying:
This temple rite complete, in grace and in joy.

Place some of the Goddess' offerings outside. Then, returning to your altar, partake of some of the food and drink offerings, sharing a repast with divinity.

OBSERVING THE GODDESSES IN NATURE

Set aside time to be outdoors, observing Demeter and her Daughter in nature. You can see them in both the city and the countryside, in every living thing that grows. In many ways, the Mother and Daughter overlap and can be viewed as aspects of the same deity. Earth is the Mother: the mountains, meadows, fields, gardens, etc. What grows from Earth is the Daughter. Both Demeter Chloaia and Kore are green Goddesses. All that grows to maturity and is ready to drop seed can be seen as both. For example, ripe fruit and dried seed can be seen as the Goddess of the Harvest, and also as the Maiden matured and ready to make her transition to Queen.

Leaves that have dropped to the ground and are decaying are as Persephone in her descent. It is this aspect of death that enriches Earth. Demeter Melaina, the black sorrowing Goddess, is also this same aspect. These double aspects are seen repeatedly, as Mother and Daughter follow both verdant and dark cycles. While it is not logical for two things (or two Goddesses) to be both different and yet one, they are. They are the Creatress and the Created. There is a level at which you are also the Creatress and the Created.

Observe nature, your place and connection to it. Though our spirit is eternal, physically, we are bound by the laws of time. As nature exists within time, we can learn from it. Our body has a cycle: it is born and it dies. The natural outcome of the fruited vine is to drop seed. From this, new life is born and new expressions are created. The fallow period, whether it is a harsh winter or an arid summer, follows maturity. The land rests and absorbs the nutrients of the previous cycle. Then it may make use of the seed. So, we may praise the moments in our lives that appear fallow, just as we praise the productive moments. We may view the end of a soul's physical life as a natural process.

This ending is also a beginning, a point in the natural cycle that makes possible the soul's new life to come. The concept of the eternal cycle is demonstrated in the Lesser Mysteries during the rite of Lighting the Wheel. In this rite, a circle of candles is created, each candle representing a point in the yearly cycle of the seasons. One holy day is connected to the next. In addition, while the wheel appears to be a circle, it is actually a spiral. This is created by the fact that the circle exists within time, and time moves forward.

Observe the natural cycles of the countryside that surrounds the city in which you live. If you are able, visit a forest during different seasons. Gardening is also a wonderful way to observe and interact with nature and her spiraling seasons.

EXPLORING ALL OF THE MYTH'S DIVINITIES

In Appendix 2, you will find a complete deity listing. An awareness of all of the divinities as sacred aspects of life and nature will increase your understanding of the myth. This will also further enrich your experience of the festivals and mysteries.

IDEAS FOR A SOLITARY PRACTICE

Weekly Rite and the Seven Demeter Prayers: After reading the myth and theology contained in chapters 3 and 4, perform the initial rite as outlined in the beginning of this chapter. Do this ritual once a week. Use different prayers from chapters 5 and 6 each week. This is a good way to explore the different names and aspects of the Goddesses. You may also want to vary the chant (see chapter 5 for chants).

The Rite of Lustration: Practice the Rite of Lustration daily for the first month, and then continue as you wish. It may become part of your morning preparations before you go out. I have also practiced this silently in various situations when I am away from home. I close my eyes and say the words mentally, while I envision the corresponding actions.

The New Moon Ceremony: On the next New Moon, try the New Moon Ceremony from chapter 7. After you have begun the seasonal festivals, you may find this useful, particularly in the months in which there are no seasonal festivals.

Making Crafts and Preparing for the Seasonal Rites: During the first few months, begin making any craft items you may need for your first seasonal ritual.

The Seasonal Festivals: After the first months, you might begin practicing your first solitary adaptation of a seasonal festival (see chapters 9–12). Be aware of the festival's place in the myth. The more background information and understanding you bring to your experience, the richer each festival will be for you.

The festivals of Proerosia (preplowing rites), Thargelia (harvest), and Kalamaia (threshing) are concerned with the planted grain, although adaptations may always be made that exclude planting in a field or harvesting field-grown grain. If you do not have a large enough space outdoors in which to plant grain, you may plant it quite successfully in a large pot. Grain is easy to grow (see chapter 19). If you are beginning your festival celebrations in the fall, when there is a heavy schedule of rituals, you may opt to do only some of the rites (such as Thesmophoria and Nestia-Kalligenia) at first, and the full schedule of rites in the following year.

The Lesser Mysteries: After you have begun the seasonal festivals, you may want to consider the Lesser Mysteries (see chapter 14), which include a consecration to Demeter. The Lesser Mysteries may be performed in early spring (the beginning of the verdant period). They may also be celebrated in late summer (the end of the fallow period), when they were repeated, in ancient times, every fourth year.

The Greater Mysteries: When you have experienced the seasonal festivals and the Lesser Mysteries, then it is time for the Greater Mysteries (see chapter 15). Although they require a good deal of preparation, they will reward you in many ways. While most initiates probably experienced this rite only once, it may become a part of your yearly celebrations.

SOLITARY ADAPTATIONS OF THE FESTIVALS

Chapter 8 gives you an overview of the Demetrian Wheel of the Year. The liturgy for the seasonal festivals is presented in chapters 9 through 12. Before the liturgy for each of the festivals and the mysteries, you will find a paragraph titled "Ritual Outline." As a solitary devotee, you may use the same outline and, in most cases, the same liturgy. The difference is that you take all clergy roles.

Occasionally some of the actions in the rituals will need to be a little different. In cases where there are instructions for one individual to anoint another, you can anoint yourself. Ritual garlands or wreath crowns can be placed by you on yourself. Instead of a group circle dance, you can dance and chant on your own. These are the kinds of adaptations that can be made.

Below are some examples of the Wheel of the Year Festivals, adapted for solitary celebrations. As explained in chapter 8, if your local climate is very different from a Mediterranean climate, you may need to shift the timing of the Wheel of the Year.

The Rites of Proerosia: In the Instructions of Triptolemos (see p. 85), Demeter crowns Triptolemos. In a solitary celebration, keep both the crown of grain and the green leafy crown on your altar (this may simply be a makeshift altar near your planting area). As Demeter speaks, you may lay your hand upon her crown. At Triptolemos' crowning, and when he speaks, lay your hand upon his crown. In the Closing Blessing (see p. 88), simply omit the staging instructions for the Hierophant and the Priestess of Demeter. Do the water blessings of each, individually. In all other portions of this rite you may perform the parts as presented.

The Rites of Chloaia: For the Song and Circle Dance (p. 152), you may choose to chant or sing the words standing at your altar or moving in a circular dance. For honoring Dionysus, the same can apply. In Rite for the Heart's Desire (p. 156), you can bless your garland and placing it over your own head. In all other portions of this rite, you may perform the parts as presented.

The Rites of the Skira Festival: You will need to wear a white himation that can be removed in the Maiden's Descent (see pp. 184–186). In the Dance on the Plains of Nysa (p. 181), you may choose to chant or sing the words while at your altar, or you may have previously tape-recorded them. You may simply sway to the rhythm of the words, or dance or move in a circle. In the Maiden's Descent, you will need to remove the white himation, scatter the red flower petals over yourself, drape the black himation onto yourself, and then take up the urn of seed as described. As Persephone, you will follow the staging directions for the descent into Tartarus, drink from the chalice of water, and then place the crown on your own head. The embrace with the God of the Underworld can be envisioned as an embrace with a passionate lover (p. 185). In all other portions of the rite, you may perform the parts as presented.

The Rites of the Lesser Mysteries: In Lighting the Wheel (pp. 209–211), you can light all the candles for the holidays. In the Rite of Consecration (pp. 214–215), you can use the same words, but anointing yourself. In the Crowning (pp. 215–216), you can state the meanings of the colors, twist the cloths together, and place the crown on your own head. In all other portions of this rite, you may perform the parts as presented.

Group Worship— The Temple of Devotees

*As a group, you may look beyond the surface
experiences of everyday life to see the sacred patterns
of nature and spirit. With this spiritual family,
group energies are raised, as magic and homage
to deity become a shared experienced.*

To celebrate religious rituals with a like-minded group is an
expression of family and of community, as all acknowledge
their mutual divinity together. Many times, when a religious
group begins, it is because an individual or small group was moti-
vated to found it. This is the natural beginning of a *hierarchy.*
"Hierarchy" is not, in and of itself, a bad word. In my experience of
Goddess religion, those at the top of the hierarchy take the greater
responsibility in order to present the rites for others.

The hierarchy of a religious group is defined by the various pro-
gressive ranks of clergy who govern the religious body. This is particularly required when a group is so large that all of the administrative and
sacred functions need to be organized into various positions. The nega-
tive connotations of the word "hierarchy" in religion are due to groups
who have dictated inordinate restrictions to lifestyle or worship, or who
perpetrate violence. In its simplest form, hierarchy represents the structure of an organization, ideally with the most experienced at the top.

When a group is small, it can function on a consensus model. Even in a consensus model, however, there seems to be one or a few people who spend the most energy organizing and motivating others. A large consensus group may require a leader in order to keep discussions moving. The leadership role may change from one person to another, rotating throughout the group.

Regarding clergy and taking roles in rituals, there is a lot of room for modification in the rites. I have celebrated rituals with a group, and, on occasion, I have celebrated the festivals with only one other person. With this "group" of two, the rituals were performed with great success. Each of us took many clerical roles. Regarding the gender of clergy, changes in the choice of priest or priestess (as the liturgy is written) may be needed or desired.

People can have differences of opinion, or change their opinion about their religion, as time moves on. Its always good to be prepared for that. A participant may leave the original group and create an offshoot group with adaptations in myth or theology. As far as this interpretation of the myth goes, I remember one participant having difficulty with Demeter's anger, and another with the closeness of Mother and Daughter. The closeness of the Mother-Daughter relationship contributes to the emotional intensity of the drama. Demeter's anger leads to a crisis. The crisis in the sacred drama leads to the development of a resolution. These changing emotional aspects parallel nature and agriculture. It is not always springtime; relationships change; life experiences can get tough. Some people experience freezing, barren winters, while others experience dry, barren summers. Joy comes after the resolution of a crisis. Myth helps us move through the difficult times, and celebrate the joyful times. The barren time passes. Life is renewed and the fertile season begins again. There are many ways that modern pagans can, and do, portray the myth of Demeter and Persephone.

Demeter's myth has been perceived in many ways. The version of Demeter's religion presented in this book has been influenced by many of the myths and their variants. A most important source has been the observation of the archetypes in nature. This is the original source of the myth. The resulting religion presents a system of beliefs that sees the soul and the natural world, whether cultivated or wild, as precious and holy. These, having risen from a divine source, are a part of the sacred drama of life. The poetic images within the rites and festivals illustrate this set of beliefs. One may ride on these images into the mystic experience, beyond form and beyond name.

Each group participant will benefit from the practices of the solitary devotee. I suggest that each participant first practice as a solitary, to provide a resource of personal experience. This will establish a relationship with Demeter and Persephone and their mythology. When you come together to discuss the myth, you may then make any initial adaptations. As you review the ritual you plan to do, discuss responsibilities and clerical positions. Taking a clerical role, helping to create altars, having rituals in your living space, or helping to create craft items such as wreaths, are all ways of enjoying your participation in group ritual.

Group worship can be a wonderful path into the mystic experience. Through the practice of Demeter's festivals, you can experience the natural world, and each other, as sacred. As you move through the rites of the festivals and mysteries, the Great Mother will reach out to you and fill your heart, as you reawaken her ancient temple.

Costumes, Oil Lamps, and Other Ritual Accouterments

*Her chiton edged in soft gold, her veil white
and sheer as starlight, her hair adorned
with a ring of roses, sometimes violets, sometimes ivy
as the season dictates; here is her priestess.
The bright flute calls,
its sound inviting her to join the procession.
She has made ready, and will attend the Great Festival.*

While Demeter's myth and theology are the primary components from which the rites were born, the manner in which they are presented provides the style. In taking on the style of early Greek culture through the use of costumes, wreaths, oil lamps, and so on, you empower yourself to journey back in time. Each ritual is very much like a theater piece in which actors, stage settings, and props are a part of the performance. Indeed, the history of theater seems to show that as a performance medium, plays were originally born from religious ritual. The origins of Greek drama, which included masked actors and a chorus, are attributed to the god Dionysus. The art of drama developed in his honor and the line between dramatic festivals and ritual festivals, early on, may have been rather obscure. I encourage you to re-create the style, flavor, and feeling of this ancient culture, which enliven and enhance your rituals. To this end, I have provided many suggestions for making ritual accouterments for use in performance of the rites. In addition to these suggestions, you may find yourself adding many creative flairs of your own.

BAUBO STATUE

This statue can be made of either clay or plasticene. Both materials may be purchased in a terra-cotta, reddish-brown color at a local craft or art supply store. If you use plasticene, it can be baked in an oven as directed on the packaging. If you use clay, you will need to take it to a commercial kiln for firing. Use low-fire clay. The form for this sculpture needs to have a pointed lower half, so that it can be set into a bowl of earth for the Stenia ritual. This Baubo has arms at her sides, legs together forming the point at the bottom that can be inserted into the earth so that the image can stand. Her legs will be completely imbedded in the soil (this needs to be damp). The image may have large breasts and buttocks to show her aspects of primal fertility. Particularly important is the smiling face you carve on her belly.

If you use clay, you may "antique" the image by painting it, when dry and hardened, with an off-white underglaze before firing. Before the underglaze dries, wipe off the excess with a wet sponge, leaving the off-white color in the indentations and crevices. The same principal may be used for plasticene, but you will apply your off-white latex acrylic paint after the image is baked, rather than before. To make the "antiquing" permanent on the plasticene, spray or paint it with a clear acrylic matte finish. When ready to use the statue in ritual, insert it into your large pot of earth and surround it with white household candles, as directed in the liturgy for the Stenia festival.

CISTA MYSTICA

For the cista mystica, you may use a basket with a detached lid. Traditionally, the cista was tied with red ribbons. Tie the lid to the basket with a $1^1/_2$ foot length of 1-to-2-inch wide red ribbon. Repeat this on the opposite side of the lid. When the cista is being used, one of the ribbons is untied and the lid lifted. Inside the cista place a large piece of purple fabric in which the hiera (sacred objects) will be placed during the Greater Mysteries (see chapter 15). There is also a ribbon to tie the purple cloth into a bag, once the objects are inside.

CROWNS (HEAD WREATHS)

Crown Base: For most of the following crowns, you will be making a crown base. For the base, you will need a length of 18-gauge floral coil wire, 18–20 inches long. This is sometimes called floral stem wire. You will also need $1/_2$-inch wide floral tape (sometimes called stem wrap tape). The tape is stretchy and sticky, and comes on a roll. These can be purchased at a craft store or from some florist shops. Bend the wire to fit around your head and make two small loops at the ends. You will later thread ribbon through these. After the wire is shaped, cover it with the stem wrap tape by winding it around the wire, pulling and stretch the tape gently as you go. Omit putting stem wrap tape on the loop ends. Press the beginning and ending points of the pieces of tape down on the wire as you go.

Cloth Crown: The cloth crown is made by the Priestess of Demeter for the initiates at the Lesser Mysteries. The initiate prepares three $1^1/_4$-yard strips of fabric, one each of red, yellow, and green. The initiate will sew the strips of cloth together at one spot, about 10 inches from one end. This will be done prior to the ritual. During the Lesser Mysteries, the pieces of cloth will be twisted into a crown.

Consider the red cloth as red pomegranates, poppies, menses, and all signs of fertility (Demeter and Persephone). Consider the green cloth as the verdant aspects of the Goddess, meadows, fields, and the season of flowering (Demeter and Kore). Consider the yellow cloth as harvesttime; as Demeter of the Harvest, as Hecate's sickle, and as the Maiden about to descend.

Dried or Artificial Flower Crown: Use the "crown base." Shorten the stems of the flowers you have chosen. Beginning at one end of the crown base, use the stem wrap tape to fasten each flower to the base. Set the flower onto the base, with its stem somewhat lined up with the base. Gently pull and wind the tape around the base and the flower you are attaching. Continue to lay flowers onto the wire, attaching them with tape, until you have covered the wire. Tie ribbons to the loops at the ends of the crown. Some may be long and hang downward. Others are used to tie the crown on the initiate's head.

Fresh Flower Crown: Use the same method as described above for the dried or artificial flower crown. This may be made a day ahead of use. Place it in a box, cover the box with clear plastic wrap, and refrigerate. Before use, attach ribbons to the loop ends.

Green Leafy Crown: Use the same method as described above for the dried or artificial flower crown. Or, if you find narrow, pliable green leafy branches (such as the ends of myrtle or bay), you may simply wind 16-gauge wire through them to create your crown. Or, you can use 18-gauge wire as a crown base, and then use 16-gauge wire to wind the branches to the base. Attach the ribbons at the loop ends.

Wheat or Barley Crown: Use the same method as described above for the dried or artificial flower crown.

FERTILITY TALISMANS

These talismans are made during the rites of Arkichronia, one of the fall festivals. They are dispensed at Kalligenia. If you begin to celebrate the festivals of the Demetrian Wheel at Thesmophoria Proper (or at Nestia-Kalligenia), you will need to make the talismans. They are made with a an 8-inch circle or square of cloth. Since the talismans are intended as a gift from the Holy Daughter to help bring on the period of growth, you may want to use green colored fabric. Inside the cloth, place rose petals, pine needles, wheat seeds, and myrtle. Sprinkle it with a few drops of saffron-and-rose anointing oil (see "Saffron-and-Rose Annointing Oil," p. 280). Tie each talisman together with a 12-inch length of ribbon. Place them into a bowl or basket on top of a clay or sculpy image of a snake.

FIRE ALTAR (See color insert between pp. 144–145.)

The fire altar is assembled on the floor. You may adapt the following, always keeping safety in mind. First place a round or square piece of 1-inch-thick wood on the floor. I painted mine with a red-brown latex paint. Then I covered the wood with a single layer of terra-cotta brick. On top of the brick, I set a deep cast-iron (or stainless-steel) pot. If the pot is not actually a cauldron with little feet, create an air space below the pot by placing two bricks beneath it. On the bottom of the pot, place a 2-inch layer of sand. Onto the sand, place a smaller pot of brass or stainless steel. You will need flammable alcohol (90–91 proof). Pour the alcohol just before the ritual. *Never* place liquid fuel onto a burning fire. Use only dry fuel. Small pieces of wood may be added, if the altar is outdoors (wood will cause smoking). For decoration, around the outside of the pot, you may place rocks to give the look of an outdoor firepit. If outdoors, a wood fire may be created, using an altar of tile, brick, and stone.

GARLANDS

Garlands are used in the spring festival of Chloaia. Greenery and flowers are tied together to make a long floral necklace. This can be done simply by tying small branches of greenery into a necklace and then tying flowers to it with twine for embellishment. After making the garland, cover it lightly with plastic wrap and refrigerate it until you are ready for the festival. (Do not make the garland more than 24 hours ahead of the celebration.)

GREEK COSTUME (See color insert between pp. 144–145)

Doric Chiton: Two large rectangles of cloth, pinned or sewn across the shoulders, create the basic classical dress. The width of each rectangle from selvage edge to selvage edge should be approximately 45 inches. The length of each rectangle should approximate your combined measurement from the top of your shoulder to your ankle, plus 8–12 inches to allow blousing when chiton is tied, plus 2 inches for hemming, plus 6–12 inches for an (optional) top "collar." (The top edge may be folded over as a collar, and then pinned on the fold at the shoulder.) The chiton may be stitched together down the sides. I have opted to stitch mine together across the shoulder at intervals as well, and then sewn decorative buttons over the stitching at the same intervals. The edging decorations can range from none to elaborate.

The chiton traditionally fell to the knees for young and active men and for women exercising in the gymnasium. It was otherwise worn long to the ankles by women and older men, and by all at formal occasions. It was tied under the breast, or girdled at the waist or hip. Generally it was made of linen or wool. I like using drapy synthetic or cotton-synthetic-blend fabrics.

Ionic Chiton: This garment was made of very fine linen or silk with many small vertical pleats added across the top edges (across the shoulder and the top of the arm). This enhanced a gathered, draping appearance when belted. It was influenced by Eastern dress.

Himation: This was a shawl-like garment that was draped over the chiton in various ways. Draping himations of varying lengths became a fine art. The himation could range from silk to light diaphanous linen. A version of it in heavy wool was used as a cloak for outdoor wear. I like using drapy silk-like synthetics, georgette, or Indian cotton gauze ($2^1/_2$–4 yards may be used for the himation).

Peplos: Classical dress.

Chlamys: A short form of the himation, this was used by young and active men. It was drawn below one arm, and then up at an angle, from hip to opposing shoulder. It was fastened at that shoulder, leaving one arm free ($2^1/_2$ yards of fabric will suffice for the chlamys).

Decoration: The front and back of the chiton were two separate rectangles of fabric pieces clasped together by simple or highly decorative pins. These could be set at intervals across the shoulder and arm. Jewelry clasps or decorative metal buttons or beads may be used. The sides, top, and bottom edges of the chiton were sometimes decorated with embroidery, woven ribbon, or paint-stamped designs. Himation edges could be decorated in similar ways. Sometimes, edging decorations were woven into the fabric itself. The draping himation can be fastened with a decorative pin or broach, or hang freely over one shoulder.

ICONS

An icon is a picture, statue, or other form that represents deity to you. There are photographs of Greek Demeter and Roman Ceres in books and encyclopedias on mythology. They can be used as inspiration for a three-dimensional form. I have made some good laser copies of some of the photographs. I have an icon that is a copy of a photograph of Demeter of Cnidus that I have placed in a gilt, Italian standing frame.

You can make a statue or flat tablet-style image out of clay or plasticene. These materials can be purchased at craft stores. For plasticene statues, follow package directions, baking your piece in your kitchen oven. For clay pieces, I suggest low-fire earthenware clay. Firing can be done in a small home kiln, or in a commercial kiln.

LIBATION BOWL OR TROUGH

Any bowl that is at least 6 inches in depth will suffice. When pouring libations indoors, you may want to have a piece of fabric or other covering on your floor to catch any drops of wine or juice that may splatter out of the bowl. A libation trough may be made out of low-fire clay (fired in a home or commercial kiln). It may also be made out of terra-cotta-colored plasticene (following package directions). Make the trough from 12–16 inches in length and about 5–6 inches wide. Build the sides nearly straight up, and slope the ends gradually outward. Suggested designs for use around the inner and/or outer top edges are spirals, Greek key designs, grapes and grape leaves, or ivy. See "Oil Lamps," p. 279 regarding firing clay pieces.

MASKS (See color insert between pp. 144–145)

The following description of mask making uses plaster gauze. This material is similar to that used by physicians to make casts for broken bones. Craft stores sell dry-plaster gauze for mask making and other art projects. You will need a roll of plaster gauze, a mirror, scissors, a bowl of water, face cream, lotion, oil, or Vaseline, gesso or white acrylic paint, assorted colors of acrylic paint, a $1/_2$-to 2-inch brush and a few small brushes (# 0, # 1 and # 2), ribbon or cord to tie the mask on, and any additional decorations (acrylic paints, costume jewels, beads, trims, etc.).

Sit at a table with the plaster gauze, mirror, bowl of water, scissors, and face cream in front of you. Prop the mirror up so that you can see into it. Pull all your hair back away from your face. Put on a generous amount of face cream or lotion. You will be cutting 2- to 3-inch pieces of gauze from the roll, wetting them, and applying them to your face, piece by piece. As you apply each piece, dunk it into the water. First cover the bridge of your nose with one narrow 2-inch-long strip. Then fill in the area of your forehead, connecting the area to the strip of gauze that covers the bridge of your nose. Do not cover your eyebrows. Next, cover your nose with pieces of gauze, leaving the nostril area open. Then cover your cheeks and cheekbone areas. Cover the areas outside the eyes, next to the hairline. Do not cover the area under your eyes. Then cover the area around your mouth. Leave the mouth itself uncovered, particularly if you are making a Plouton or Persephone mask, as you will need to speak while wearing the mask. You may cover the mouth if you are making a Dionysus mask, as it will not be worn, but will only be set on an altar.

Now cover the rest of the face with dampened plaster gauze pieces, down to your jawbone. Cover your chin. By this time, the top half of the mask will be drying. Repeat the process, by covering all areas with a second layer of plaster gauze. When the two coats have hardened somewhat, move your facial muscles under the mask. This will begin to loosen it. Move your mouth around a bit. Lift your eyebrows. Every movement will loosen the mask a little. Wedge your fingers under the forehead or chin area of the mask and work at moving it until you can lift it away.

After you remove the mask, set it aside and wash your face. Then return to your work area. Using strips of dampened plaster gauze, create a finished edge around the outside of the mask and around the inside of the eye and mouth holes. You may make the mask thicker by adding another layer of gauze if you like.

Air-dry the mask overnight, or heat it for 30 seconds at a time in a microwave oven, until dry. When the mask is completely dry, paint it with a coat of gesso or white acrylic paint, using your large brush. When the first coat is dry, add a second coat. When the second coat is dry, begin painting your mask. I suggest painting it with one solid background color. Then add color where you wish, painting it around the eyes, the mouth, and other areas.

Symbols of the deities for which you are making the mask may be painted on the forehead or cheek areas: pomegranates for Persephone, or grape leaves for Dionysus. Artificial flowers, leaves, jewels, or beads may be glued at the top of the forehead areas. Fabrics or ribbons may be glued to the outside of the mask. One half of the mask can be different from the other half. There are endless possibilities. To tie the mask on, glue an 18-inch piece of ribbon or cord to the area next to each cheekbone, just on the inside of the mask.

MEGARA

The megara was a pit or below-ground enclosure from which remnants of earlier offerings were drawn up during Thesmophoria. From these remnants, fertility talismans were made to bless the new planting season. It is a mythic location that is a connection to the Underworld. The megara is used in the Greater Mysteries and in the rites of Arkichronia. A lidded basket lined with black fabric will suffice for an "indoor megara." Place the basket in a location that will remain undisturbed.

For an outdoor megara, you can dig a square or rectangular pit and line it with slabs of stone or brick. Place it in a corner of your yard in which there will be little traffic. Make it a minimum of 12 x 18 inches square. Or, you may purchase a very large terra-cotta pot and bury it in the earth, with just a small edge above the ground. The megara will need a cover, and this may be a slab of stone, or lacquered or painted wood. A stone top is heavy enough to remain in place. A wood top will need to be secured by a weight, such as a small pile of stones.

Oil Lamps

A one-wick Greek-style clay oil lamp is quite simple in design. Use low-fire earthenware clay. Mine is approximately 5 inches wide and 3 inches deep. It is basically a small bowl with a flat top, a "wick spout," and a handle. There is a small hole in the center of the top, into which you can pour oil. The loop handle extends from the place where the top joins the side, and attaches to the side of the bowl approximately $1^{1}/_{2}$ inches down. On the opposite side of the handle is the opening for the wick. (See figure 4, p. 280.)

If you do not have a potter's wheel, you can make a bowl in the following way. Find a small bowl and lay cotton fabric in it. Roll the clay out on a board and set the clay into the bowl. Smooth out the inside and even the thickness of the walls. Level the top edge. You can make the opening for the wick by using slight pressure with the finger on the edge of the bowl to create a "spout." Roll out and cut to shape the clay for the lid. The lid will dry faster than the top, so make the bowl a day ahead, or cover the lid with damp fabric if it is drying out too quickly. Move the lid once while drying to prevent sticking. Attach the lid to the bowl when the clay is leather-hard (still damp, yet holds its shape). Rough up the edges with a tool and add slip (very wet clay) to the rough surfaces. Attach the top to the bowl and smooth over any rough areas.

Let the lamp dry for one week and fire it in a home or commercial kiln at 04. After the first firing, glaze the inside of the lamp by pouring a little diluted clear or matte glaze into the center hole. Tilt the lamp around to coat the inside. Pour the rest out through the wick hole, and then clean up any excess glaze on the outside. Let the lamp dry at least 24 hours and fire at 06.

You can purchase lamp wick in a sporting goods store, hardware store, or boat shop. You will probably need to cut the wick, making it more narrow. Cut a 6-inch length and insert it into the wick hole. If the hole seems too narrow, use copper wire as a needle. Twist it around the end of the wick, in through the oil hole, and push it out the wick spout. Leave about 1 inch of wick coming out the spout. Fill the lamp with olive oil. Coat the wick coming out of the lamp with oil. Light the wick. As it burns, it will have to be pulled up every so often with small pliers.

PERSEPHONE'S VESTMENTS

Crown: I have made Persephone's crown out of artificial purple flowers, with red satin ribbons running through it. I have also made a crown from ornate, woven silver trim, 1 inch wide. The length of ribbon is sewn to fit around the head and then embellished with sewn-on jewels and gold and silver beads. Two strands of florist wire shaped into two circles, are glued to the inside, with a covering of seam or hemming ribbon on the inner side of the crown, to cover the wire.

Diaphanous Veil: For this veil, I suggest $2^1/_2$–3 yards of sheer draping black fabric. Black netting or black nylon chiffon are the best, as these are somewhat see-through. The edges may be trimmed with silver or embroidered ribbon, or small black tassels can be sewn to the corners.

Black Himation: Make the himation out of 5–6 yards of drapy black fabric. You may find black fabric with silver designs woven into it. Trimming an area at the ends of a plain black himation with silver trim works well. Tiny silver sequins or sewn-on costume jewels are additional possibilities. You may also create designs with glue and then sprinkle silver glitter over the glue designs.

PLOUTON'S VESTMENTS

Crown: See above for Persephone's crown.
Black Himation: See above for Persephone's himation.

SAFFRON-AND-ROSE ANOINTING OIL

This scented oil is used by Hecate to anoint the sacred couple during the Greater Mysteries. To 2 tablespoons of sesame, safflower, or light high-quality olive oil, add a pinch of saffron and 2 tablespoons of rose oil. Place into a small glass bottle and shake.

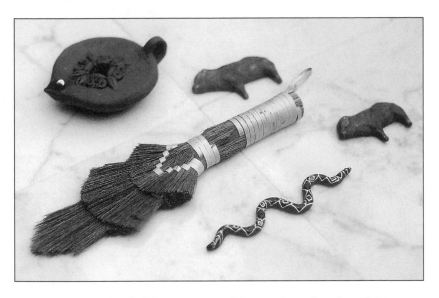

Figure 4. Ritual objects: spurge, oil lamp, pig and snake effigies.
Spurge found and cut, all other objects by author.
Photograph by Jery Stier, 1999.

SNAKE AND PIG EFFIGIES

Make these images out of low-fire clay or plasticene. Encyclopedias or other books can provide image ideas. If you use plasticene, follow the package directions and, after they have been baked, paint the images with acrylic paints. After this is dry, you may want to add a final coat of clear acrylic paint. If you use clay, incise any designs when the images are leather-hard. When dry, paint with underglaze colors. Complete the first firing in a home or commercial kiln, then glaze and fire according to glaze jar or package directions. (See figure 4.)

SPURGE

The word "spurge" is used to refer to the instrument for water blessings. It comes from the Latin word *expurgare*, which means "to purge." Any small leafy branch will suffice for a spurge. Simply dip it into a bowl of water and anoint as directed in the rite. Pine leaves will produce smaller droplets. Bound straw works well. I have used a straw fan that was bound to a handle. I cut the outer edges into a design with scissors. (See figure 4.)

THESMOI

Thesmoi Scroll: The thesmoi are used in the rites for Thesmophoria Proper. Use two wooden dowels, 1–1$^1/_2$ inches wide, and cut to about 20 inches in length. You may want to finish the ends of the dowels by gluing wood or metal knobs to them, and/or finish the wood with a stain or varnish. Copy the ten thesmoi (see chapter 9) on an 8$^1/_2$ x 11-inch piece of paper. Make two extra copies for the small scrolls (see below.) You may want to decorate the scroll with a border. I used parchment-like paper. Attach with glue, two pieces (same size) to the right and two pieces to the left of the thesmoi. This will make one (approximately) 11 x 43-inch piece of paper. Stitch the corners of the joined paper together, by hand, for added reinforcement.

Glue the two ends of the 40-inch length of paper to the two dowels. (The thesmoi will be in the center.) You may want to tape them down as well with a narrow strip of paper packing tape. Let the scroll dry for 24 hours. Roll the dowels inward toward the thesmoi. Tie them together at the center with a strip of fabric, or velvet or satin ribbon.

Thesmoi Cover: You may want to make both an inner and an outer cover. The inner cover may be white cotton, bordered with gold. This is basically a white bag, perhaps a small pillowcase that fits lightly over the scroll. The outer cover may be of more elaborate fabric. Mine is burgundy velvet, bordered with gold. It is also tied across the middle with the same fabric.

Small Scrolls: The small scrolls are used by clergy in Thesmophoria Proper. These are copies of the thesmoi, rolled up and tied.

TORCHES

For those rites in which torches can be used, you may always use a 2- or 3-inch-wide-pillar candle in a holder instead. It is advised that torches only be used in rituals that are done outdoors. Inexpensive torches meant for beach use can be purchased in some areas. These are fueled by lamp oil, or are long sticks with candles on the ends. To create a torch, wooden dowels or heavy branches stripped of twigs may be used. The ends of these are wrapped in cotton cloth, and alternately dipped in hot wax and sawdust until several layers have been built up.

On Raising Grain
The Temple Field

Then the goddess of fertility yoked her two dragons
to her (chariot) . . . and rode away through the ai r. . .
until she came at last to (Athena's) city.
Here she gave her fleet (chariot) to Triptolemus,
and bade him scatter the seeds of grain . . .
in fields that had long lain fallow.[1]

By 6000 B.C.E., durum, emmer, and einkhorn varieties of wheat were being grown throughout Greece and in southeastern Europe. Emmer was the most popular variety cultivated in Thessaly and Macedonia. In these locations, some of the earliest examples of clay ovens for bread baking are also found. Barley, "believed to be man's oldest cultivated grain," was the favored grain crop in the coastal city-states of Greece and in the Aegean islands.[2] Requiring less water, it had a higher yield than wheat in the Med-iterranean climate.

I received my first instructions for raising grain from Mr. Michael DeHart, horticulturist of the J. Paul Getty museums in Malibu and Brentwood, California. The museum building in Malibu

---

1   Ovid, *Metamorphoses,* vol. I, Frank Miller, trans. (London: William Heinemann; New York: G. P. Putnam's Sons, 1921), p. 283.
2   Sara Pitzer, *Whole Grains* (Charlotte, VT: Garden Way Publishing, 1981), p. 75.

is a reconstruction of a Roman villa in Herculaneum. It houses a wonderful art collection and is surrounded by several gardens. It was in the villa's kitchen garden that I first saw wheat, barley, and oats growing. Varieties such as Excelsior barley, and black-bearded wheat rose on either side of the path at the garden entrance. Adjacent to them were pomegranate trees and beds of herbs.

Pear, quince, apricot, fig, olive trees, and gallica roses also flourish in this lovely Roman garden, along with other flowers. The drifts of deep blue larkspur, behind which rose-multicolored fragrant sweetpeas abound, were a joy to behold. There were artichokes, chard, other green leafy vegetables, and such a great variety of herbs that one had to summon enormous strength not to touch and taste.

Planting: Mr. DeHart explained the seasonal timing and the planting style he used for grain. He confirmed what I had read in sources such as Hesiod and Brumfield that, in a Mediterranean climate, grain is planted in the fall. Mr. DeHart employs an ornamental style of planting for grain. This is the style that I have used in my own past four seasons of planting, using it for spaces ranging from 12 x 15 feet, to 3 x 4 feet.

To prepare the soil, weed the area thoroughly and turn the soil over. Do this again over the next two weeks, wetting the ground between weedings. Break up any clods and rake the ground over. While grain needs some nitrogen, too much nitrogen-heavy fertilizer can cause problems, and will not increase the size of the seed. The grain will grow very fast, with tall stalks. Tall stalks, however, run the risk of *lodging*, or falling over at the base. The formation of the seed and the strength of the stalks can benefit from the addition of gypsum or bonemeal to the soil. After the harvest, to replenish nitrogen taken from the soil during the growing season, try growing nitrogen-building crops such as beans, other legumes, clover, or alfalfa. Then turn them under after maturation.

If you do not have an outdoor space available, then planting in a pot is an option. Choose a light-colored pot. A terra-cotta pot will work, if the inside is glazed. Or, if you like the look of terra-cotta, place a plastic pot inside. The roots of the plants need to stay cool, and plain unglazed terra-cotta absorbs both heat and moisture. A pot that is cylindrical or box-shaped is a good choice and will give the roots more space. If you are going to fill your pot with commercial potting soil, add a little bonemeal and a little manure to the mix, and water two or three times a week for several weeks to prepare the soil.

For ornamental-style planting, use a narrow stick or your finger to dig holes 1–1$^1/_2$ inches deep in the soil. Place 3 or 4 seeds into each hole and cover the seed with soil. Create a row of seeds planted in this way, with holes about 4 inches apart. Leave a space of 4 inches between rows. Adjust the spacing of the second row so that its holes are below the open spaces of the holes of the first row. In this way, as you continue, the holes and seeds of the first, third, and fifth rows will line up, while the holes for the second, fourth, and sixth rows will line up. Leave some rows unplanted, so that you will have space to walk and room to weed. When you are done planting, water.

Broadcasting the seed is another way to plant your grain. Hand broadcast your seed and then rake it in, to a depth of about 1$^1/_2$–2 inches. Stamp the ground down a little with your feet, then water. Broadcast in rows, leaving space to walk and to weed.

I plant red winter wheat in November. Hesiod advised planting prior to Winter Solstice, and wrote that any later planting would produce a meager crop. For those in winter-freeze climates who will be altering the timing of the Wheel of the Year, spring wheat should be planted as soon as the ground is warm enough to be worked.

Cross-hatching and Irrigating the Field: Before planting, dig 4–5 inch deep trenches approximately every 4 feet. Press the soil of the sides of the trenches firmly, compacting it soil with your hands or feet. During the rainy season, when the seedlings are small, these trenches keep the seedlings from drowning. Later in the year, you can use the trenches to irrigate if the ground is drying out too quickly. Once or twice during the growing season, the trenches need to be weeded and repaired. If the rains are not consistent, be sure that the crop gets water twice a week in the early stages, and then water once a week, until the grain has flowered and the seed matured. Do not water from above when the grain is turning from green to yellow.

Flowering and Weeding: Fall-planted grain begins to flower in late February and takes about forty days to mature and ripen. When the grain is still green, you can see the little bits of pollen on the flower heads, just before the seed sets. Weeds steal moisture from the grain, so weed about once a month.

Harvesting: About seven weeks after the grain has flowered, stop any irrigation (and hope for continuing dry days.) In a Mediterranean climate, April begins to get hot, and sunscreen and wide-brimmed hats become the thing to wear. The grain may be ready to harvest anywhere from May through early June. It can be cut when the heads are golden. When the wheat is ready, the heads will begin to bend over a bit, but it can be harvested a little early.

When the cut grain is drying in the field, unseasonable rain can cause a variety of molds that can make the seed unusable. The first year, we planted a field of half wheat and half barley. The barley I had procured had a very large beard, and this held moisture. When the grain was drying in the field, there were some unusually heavy rains at the end of April. This caused the barley to mold, and it had to be discarded. I did not use this variety of grain again, but used the red winter wheat. It had a small beard and was very successful.

Regarding harvesting, if you do not have a large quantity of grain, you can harvest with sharp scissors. You may also use a sickle, but I found this a little more difficult. Grab a bunch of grain at the bottom of the stalks and cut with the other hand. Lay bunches down on top of each other, with the heads pointing the same way. When you have several bunches, bind them together into a sheaf using twine. Eight to twelve sheaves, standing piled together, are called a shock. If the weather is dry, you may leave a shock in the field to cure (dry), for ten days or so. I bring my relatively small amount of grain into a loft storage area in my garage to cure.

Threshing and Winnowing: There are several ways to separate the seed from the straw and chaff. You can place the grain on a designated threshing floor and beat the heads with a wooden flail. This is evidently an arduous task that I have never tried. I, and patient friends, have separated the wheat from the chaff by hand in small bowls, rubbing the grain heads between our fingers. We then tilted the bowl and gently blow sending the chaff over the side of the bowl. I have found this a lot of fun, but it is only feasible for a relatively small amount of grain.

We also tried placing the heads of grain into a child's swimming pool. Two people at a time stepped in and crushed the grain heads with a twisting motion of their feet. Then, the grain and chaff was scooped up and slowly dropped, while a leaf blower blew the chaff over the side.

This method of winnowing was very successful. Be careful, however, when using the leaf blower. Let the stream of air hit the inside of the pool and then ricochet to the falling seed. Too much air flow, and your grain will go over the side with the chaff. Some have used an electric fan to winnow. Pour the seed from one container into the other, the air from the fan substituting for a good strong breeze (that is, unless you actually have a good strong breeze!).

Storage of Seed: Place the seed in large zip-seal freezer bags. I add a dried bay leaf to each bag, something that my granny did with her grain and flour. To kill any possible pests, place the grain in the freezer for 30 days. It may then be removed, left in the zip-seal bags, and stored as you wish.

Ordering Seed: I found a farming supply company by first contacting a large nursery chain. They told me what farming supply company to contact for a catalog. I chose an organic seed supply company. I knew that all their seed was open-pollinated, which means that unlike most modern hybrid seed, they are able to reproduce true to variety under natural conditions, and that I could replant from my previous year's seed with success.[3]

Growing Companion Flowers: Flowers and herbs, such as rosemary, mint, and pennyroyal, are used in some of the rituals. They are lovely additions and you may want to add them to your garden as well. Lemon thyme is a wonderfully fragrant herb. Dried, it was burned as incense in Greek temples. I have used a combination of dried mint, lemon thyme, and rosemary, placed on a censer coal as incense.

Growing red poppies beside the wheat completes a part of the myth. Red poppies grow naturally in the open fields and grain fields of Europe and the Mediterranean. While there are actual Greek varieties, I have used the European variety called "Flander's poppy." I have always planted them at the outer edges of the grain field. You may plant them in separate pots, if you are using pots for your grain. Be patient with them. They grow slowly, from very tiny seed. They do not flower until the grain is ripening.

Fall crocus and narcissus begin to come up when the grain is sprouting. They are the perfect symbol of the Maiden. Narcissus and daffodils can be used at the Haloa festival. Lilies, hyacinth, larkspur, and delphiniums can be used in the Chloaia festival. Some of the

---

[3]   One source from which to procure seed grain and other open-pollinated seed is Peaceful Valley Farming Supply, P.O. Box 2209, Grass Valley, CA 95945, (888) 784-1722, http://www.groworganic.com.

rites call for roses or rose petals. Growing roses is a wonderful experience. I recommend it highly. There are many books and videos on the subject. Contact your local nursery. They can tell you about garden catalogs for bulbs, herbs, and roses. All of these can be grown in pots, if necessary, in a community garden (contact your local Chamber of Commerce for information), or in your yard.

Ritual Foods

Sweetened Pansperma (the many-seed offering)

1 cup wheat

$^1/_2$ cup barley

$^1/_4$ cup pistachios

2 Tbs. poppy seeds

$^3/_4$ cup broken almonds

1 Tbs. cooking oil

$^1/_4$ cup black mission figs

$^1/_2$ cup raisins

$^1/_4$ cup diced apple

1 tsp. cinnamon

$^1/_4$ cup brown sugar

$^1/_4$ cup apple juice

Make this 24 hours in advance. Place wheat into a pot with $4^1/_2$ cups water and 1 Tbs. cooking oil. Stir and then bring to a boil. Cover, reduce heat, and simmer slowly for two hours. Add the barley and simmer for one more hour. When the "pilaf" is done, drain, if necessary, and pour it into a large bowl. Add the almonds, pistachios, raisins, diced apple, figs, and juice. Mix. Combine the brown sugar with the cinnamon. Add sugar and cinnamon to the mixture. During the following 24 hours, turn over and mix a few times. When ready to use, pour into a round serving bowl. Sprinkle the top with poppy seeds. Serves 8.

The Pelanos Offering Loaf

$^3/_4$ cup warm water

1 package active dry yeast

3 Tbs. sugar

$^3/_4$ cup lukewarm milk

2 Tbs. olive oil

$1^1/_2$ tsp. salt

1 Tbs. sesame seeds

1 Tbs. anise seed

2 to $2^3/_4$ cups unbleached white flour

1 cup whole wheat flour

cornmeal or finely ground

    cracked wheat (couscous)

Into a mixing bowl place the $^3/_4$ cup warm water. Stir in and dissolve the yeast. Add the sugar. Stir and let stand for 10 minutes. Combine 1 $^1/_2$ cups of the unbleached flour, the whole wheat flour, and the salt in another bowl. Blend these thoroughly. Add the milk, oil, sesame, and anise seed to the yeast mixture. A cup at a time, add the flour mixture to the yeast mixture. Use the rest of the reserved unbleached flour as required, to form a stiff dough. Knead on a lightly floured board for 10–15 minutes, until smooth and elastic. Dough may be a little sticky. Add flour as required, for kneading.

Round up into a ball. Lightly oil a mixing bowl. Place the ball of dough into the bowl and lightly oil the top. Cover with a damp cloth and let rise $1^1/_2$ hours in a warm place. Punch down. Cover with a damp cloth. Let rise 1 hour. Punch down and shape the dough into a slightly flattened round loaf. Sprinkle a baking sheet with cornmeal or fine couscous. Place the loaf on the baking sheet. Cover with a damp cloth. Let rise 1 hour.

Preheat the oven to 375 degrees. Spinkle the top of the loaf with an equal mixture of sesame and cornmeal (or fine couscous). Bake at 375 degrees for about 30–35 minutes. Remove and let cool on a rack. Do not cut until cool. (Recipe makes one 8–9-inch round loaf.)

Stenia Butter Cookies

1 cup butter	5 cups flour
2 cups sugar	4 tsp. orange juice
2 eggs	2 tsp. vanilla
4 tsp. baking powder	dried fruit, nuts, and chocolate for decoration

Cream the butter and sugar together until smooth. Add the eggs and mix until smooth. Separately, mix the flour and baking powder. Slowly, add the flour mix, orange juice, and vanilla to the creamed mixture. Chill for at least one hour, or you may keep overnight.

Preheat the oven to 375 degrees. Participants may each take a portion of the dough and work it in their hands if it has become a little too cold. The pastries are then shaped into their licentious Stenia images: Decorate with dried fruit, nuts, and chocolate as desired. Make your creations $1/_3$ to 1 inch thick. Bake 20 to 25 minutes, or until lightly browned. Pastries thicker than $1/_2$ inch may need to remain in the oven a little longer. After all these serious instructions, I have just one thing to say: Have fun!

Stenia Marzipan Candy

You can purchase premixed marzipan made of almond paste and sugar. It is available in Greek, Mideastern, or Italian markets. Simply take it out of the packaging and form candies as described above in the cookie recipe. Taste the marzipan first, however. Some find it too sweet.

Deities

Aphrodite: Goddess who rose from the sea, a Goddess of love, passion, and sexuality. In human perception, the mother of Eros is seen to bring blessings or challenges. She relates to the idea of fate, in that she governs all human relations that relate to love, sexuality, and birth. She brings her blessings to Persephone and Plouton during the Greater Mysteries and crowns them with myrtle wreaths. She is associated with myrtle, roses, seashells, and doves.

Baubo: Eleusinian wife of Dysaules, the mother of Triptolemos, Euboleus, and Eumolpos. She invited the disguised and grieving Demeter into her home, where she lightened the goddess' heart with hospitality, as well as a bawdy and sensual dance. Prior to her encounter with Demeter, she had honored the Great Mother with lunar rites. Her family line became demi-gods and the mythic founders of Demeter's religion in Eleusis.

Daira: Sea Goddess related to an early aspect of Demeter (Demeter is pictured on Eleusinian coins with dolphins). Daira symbolizes the plenty and the resources that we derive from the sea. She was extremely important to the coastal and island cities of Greece. Not much is known about the Sacrifices to Daira that were part of the Eleusinian religious calendar.

Demeter: Dia Mater, the Great Mother Goddess who gives birth to creation, both physical and spiritual. Her powers of creation are seen in nature and are illustrated, in particular, by the growth cycle of the grain. Her seasonal myth provides an example of the cycle of life, death, and rebirth, as experienced by the soul on Earth. She gives birth to the Holy Maiden, who works with her in the process of creation. Her Daughter is in some ways emblematic of all who are born, because all are the offspring of divinity. Demeter's seasonal festivals teach the ideas of honest labor, preparation, cultivation, caretaking, and compassion. Through her rites and mysteries, we learn to honor the Great Creatress who sustains us during our sojourn on Earth.

Demeter's mysteries teach the initiate that all souls are of divine origin. To understand her mysteries brings knowledge and ecstasy. Through the holy objects that are a part of her mysteries, initiates are shown concepts that guide them and teach them about the art of living. Her mysteries prepare us for the transition of death, and for the new life to come. Her primary symbols are poppies, sheaves of grain, and the snake.

Demeter Antaia, Besought by Prayers; Demeter Chloaia, The Verdant One; Demeter Chthonia, Of Below, Of the Underworld and the Deepest Forces of Earth; Demeter Evalosia, Of the Good Harvest; Demeter Erinys, Angry One; Demeter Melaina, The Black Goddess; Demeter Panagia, All-Holy One; Demeter Thesmophoros, Of the Sacred Laws; Demeter Mystica, Of the Mysteries.

Dionysus: God of the vine, of grapes and wine, of wild mountains, of dancing and ecstasy. He enters into Demeter's religion, not only through the use of wine in some of the rites, but also as a deity of joy and celebration. The sacraments of bread and wine are harmonious and in sympathy with one another. Like Demeter, Dionysus had his own mysteries of life, death, and rebirth, and a seasonal cycle that followed the growth and maturation of the grape vine. He brings his blessings to Persephone and Plouton during the Greater Mysteries. His symbols are grapes, the grape vine, ivy, and pine.

Dysaules: Eleusinian farmer, husband of Baubo, and father of Triptolemos, Euboleus, and Eumolpos. As a farmer, he exemplifies the spiritual values of honest labor, and the ability to work in harmony with the Great Mother. His family line became demi-gods, and the mythic founders of Demeter's religion in Eleusis.

Euboleus: Son of Baubo and Dysaules whose name means "good counsel." A swineherd, he was tending his pigs when he observed Kore and Plouton descend into the Underworld. After Demeter searched for her daughter for nine days, she encountered Euboleus, who told her what he had seen.

Eumolpos: Son of Baubo and Dysaules whose name means "he who sings beautifully." A shepherd. From his line, the Hierophants of Demeter's temple descended. Singing the holy songs was one of the responsibilities of the High Priest of Eleusis. Many of the other Eleusinian clergy also came from the family of Eumolpidae.

Gaea: Also known as Ge (Earth). She had many children with Uranus (Sky), among them the Titans Rhea and Kronos. Rhea and Kronos gave birth to some of the Olympian deities: Hestia, Demeter, Poseidon, Zeus, and Plouton. As the great-grandmother of Persephone, Gaea brings the gift of the snake to the sacred couple during the Greater Mysteries. Her snake teaches of life's ever-changing and primordial nature.

Hecate: Goddess of magic, associated with the moon, caverns, the sickle, and crossroads. She is the blade that cuts the wheat at harvesttime, ending one season and beginning the next. Following the harvest, Hecate guides the Holy Maiden toward her destiny as Queen Persephone. She also assists in the performance of the sacred marriage in Tartarus, between Persephone and Plouton.

Helios: God of the Sun, brings both heat and light to Earth. In Mediterranean climates, his gentle spring days encourage growth and blooming, while his days of intense summer heat signal the end of the growing season. (In Northern European climates, the Sun warms Earth after a cold winter and provides pleasant summer days.) Day is created as he drives his flaming chariot through the sky, rising at the eastern horizon and descending in the west.

Hestia: Goddess of the home and the hearth fire and of temples and the spiritual flame. Lighting a lamp or candle for her at the beginning of a rite invokes a high spiritual focus. She is light, and spiritual purity.

Kore: Lovely and virgin Kore is a verdant Goddess, and the aspect of the Holy Daughter as she appears on Earth. As the seed, she is planted in the body of the Mother, in Earth. All that sprouts and grows is Kore. Together with her Mother, Demeter, she brings life to Earth. The beauty of all that is green and flowering, and of returning life, is attributed to the united powers of Demeter and her Maiden Daughter.

Persephone: Queenly aspect of the Holy Daughter as she expresses her powers in the Underworld. Her transition to an Underworld Goddess is made through the maturing powers of love and passion, that draw her to her beloved, Plouton. Overcoming the fears of her transition, she summons divine strength and courage. To the Underworld, she brings flowering beauty, justice, and an awareness of eternity to the dead. The characteristics of royalty and nobility arise within her through her desire to serve the dead, her mother,

Demeter, and the people of Earth. Her powers are needed in both worlds, but serving in two worlds entails sacrifice. It is through her compassion that each year, she leaves Plouton and the Underworld to return to Earth. Her symbols are her crown, the grain (stored below after threshing), and the pomegranate.

Plouton: God of the Underworld, son of Rhea and Kronos. He holds Tartarus and Elysium as parts of his domain. His is the doorway, the cavern entrance known as the dark gates, the Ploutonian cave of Eleusis. Called "the Host of the Dead" and "the Unseen One," Plouton falls in love with Kore, the Maiden of Earth. He appears to steal her for marriage (klepsigamia), but her passion is as strong as his; She enters into Tartarus' chariot, making the choice of her own free will.

When the powers of the God of the Dark combine with those of the Holy Daughter, a new kind of life begins in the Underworld. The fertile union between Plouton and Persephone brings flowering beauty to the lands below. Their combined powers also preserve and keep fertile the seed grain, stored underground to await the next planting. Plouton's symbols are his crown, precious jewels, and his mask.

Rhea: Titan who appears in the sacred drama of the Greater Mysteries where she creates a contract, the means by which Kore-Persephone can fulfill her destiny. She is the final catalyst that harmonizes the conflicts within the sacred drama. At her suggestion, the Holy Daughter agrees to spend part of the year with Demeter and part with Plouton. Through her contract of compromise and the Holy Daughter's desire to serve, the cycle of life is reborn and moves forward again. An early Earth Mother, Rhea is sometimes associated with Phyrgian Cybele and her lion-drawn chariot.

Triptolemos: Son of Baubo and Dysaules who becomes the teacher and demi-god of plowing, sowing, threshing, and the art of cultivation. When Kore returns to Earth, Triptolemos is sent by Demeter to shower seed across the Earth. His name means "thrice-plowed," referring to his part in the ritual triple plowing of the sacred field at the beginning of the planting season. He was worshiped by farmers on the plains of Thessaly; and threshing floors were dedicated to him. He is associated with Demeter's winged chariot, with the plow, and with the activities of planting and threshing.

Zeus: Son of Rhea and Kronos, Zeus is the ruler of Olympus, the heavenly dwelling place of the deities referred to as the Olympian Twelve. However, in myth, the forces of the Twelve often vie for supremacy. While he is a ruler in many myths, his part in Demeter's religion is primarily that of a Rain God. Dark cloudy skies, bright lightning, thunder, and fructifying rains are associated with Zeus. He is particularly important at the preplowing rites of Proerosia, when rain is invoked. In the form of precious showers, Zeus unites with Demeter so that the seed (Kore) sprouts and the green of the land returns. Zeus Epakrios, Of the Heights; Zeus Meilichios, The Kindly One, Zeus Olympios, Of Mount Olympus, the Sky, and the Heavens.

Demeter-Persephone Myths from Ancient Authors

APOLLODORUS

Apollodorus, "The Library; Book I, Ch.. V." [1]: Translator J. G. Frazer, discusses the probability of Apollodorus living some time from the middle of the first century B.C.E., *to the second century* C.E.

According to Apollodorus, Pluto fell in love with Persephone and Zeus assisted Him. "He (Pluto) carried her off secretly."[2] Demeter searched for her Daughter, until she finally arrived in Eleusis in the guise of a mortal woman. The Goddess sat down at the Laughless Rock (Mirthless Stone) beside the Well of Fair Dances (Callechoron Well). Then she went to the house of Celeus, King of Eleusis, where the crone Iambe joked with her, and was able to make her smile (Apollodorus comments that this is why women joke at the Thesmophoria).

To the child of Celeus and Metanira, Demeter became a nurse. Each night she set their son in a fire in order to make him immortal. One night this action was observed by Praxithea (perhaps a daughter of Celeus and Metanira), who cried out. Demeter then revealed her true form, but the child was consumed by the fire. Demeter set

---

[1] Apollodorus. Sir James George Frazer, trans. *Apollodorus, The Library, vol. 1* (London: William Heinemann: New York: G. P. Putnam's Sons, 1921), pp. 35–41.
[2] Apollodorus, *The Library*, p. 127.
[3] Apollodorus, *The Library*, p. 39.

Matanira's oldest son, Triptolemos, in her winged chariot and sent him to sow seed across Earth.

Finally Zeus orders Pluto to return the Maiden to Demeter. But before he does this, Pluto gives Persephone a pomegranate seed in order that she "might not tarry long"[3] with Demeter. Because of this, Persephone must remain one-third of the year below the earth, and the remainder of the year above.

CALLIMACHUS

Callimachus, "Hymn VI; To Demeter"[4]: Callimachus lived during the time of Ptolemy (who reigned from 285–247 B.C.E.). His probable birth date is thought to be 310 B.C.E.

In Callimachus, Demeter is a Grain Mother who wanders in search of her stolen daughter. During her search, she sits three times at the fountain Callechoron (the Callechoron Well of Eleusis). The author says that he does not want to "speak of that which brought the tear to Holy Deo!"[5] He continues saying that Demeter was the first to harvest and thresh grain, and that she "taught the good craft to Triptolemus."[6] Then his story abruptly shifts to another focus—one concerning Demeter's sacred grove.

Demeter loved the land of Dotium (in Thessaly) where there was pine, elm, pear, and apple trees. There was a grove of trees that belonged to her, in which there was a giant poplar where nymphs would play at noon. Erysichthon and his men went into the Goddess' sacred grove with axes, in order to use the wood to build a dwelling place and a banquet hall. Demeter's anger was "beyond telling."[7] She told him to go ahead and build his house and have his banquet.

But the Goddess laid upon him a hunger for food and wine that would not cease. (Callimachus says that what angers Demeter also angers Dionysus.) Erysichthon ate his family out of house and home, but still he wasted away. Finally he was cast out of his parents' house and became a beggar. In the end, he learned to honor Demeter and praise her blessings upon humankind. There is no further mention of Demeter's Daughter.

---

4   *Callimachus and Lycophron—Aratus,* A. W. Mair and G. R. Mair, trans. (London: William Heinemann, New York: G. P. Putnam's Sons, 1921), pp. 125–135.

5   *Callimachus and Lycophron—Aratus,* p. 127.

6   *Callimachus and Lycophron—Aratus,* p. 127.

7   *Callimachus and Lycophron—Aratus,* p. 129.

CLEMENT OF ALEXANDRIA

Clement of Alexandria, "Exhortation to the Greeks; Section II: Description of the Greek Mysteries"[8]*: Titus Flavius Clemens was born in the mid-second century* C.E. *A Roman citizen living in Alexandria, Egypt, he was a church leader in the Christian community. In Alexandria an area called "'the district of Eleusis" may have been where Clement experienced the myth and rites of Alexandrian Eleusis, or he may have learned about them secondhand because there was no rule of secrecy for the Mysteries of Alexandria. In his work "Exhortation to the Greeks," he rages against various pagan rites, myths and beliefs, including Demeter's Mysteries.*

In his initial discussions of the Greek Mysteries, Clement focuses on ideas such as the "lascivious orgies of Aphrodite."[9] He calls the Festivals of Demeter "godless legends and deadly daemon-worship."[10] Regarding Demeter's Mysteries, Clement states that those who worship Demeter, celebrate "with torches the rape of the Daughter and the sorrowful wandering of the Mother."[11]

He tells the brief story of Zeus having intercourse with Demeter. (Clement says he doesn't know whether to call her mother or wife.) Demeter gives birth to a daughter, who also has intercourse with Zeus. From this union Persephone bears a child.

The author writes of an alternate version (closer to Homer), one in which Persephone is abducted by Hades while picking flowers. A chasm opens and Persephone and Hades fall in, along with the swineherd Euboleus and his pigs. (Clement says that this is why pigs are thrown into the cavern at the Thesmophoria Festival.)

Demeter wanders into Eleusis, searching for her Daughter. She sits at a well and grieves. In Eleusis live Baubo, her husband Dysaules, and her sons Triptolemos, Eumolpos, and Euboleus. Demeter becomes Baubo's guest, and is offered "a draught of wine and meal."[12] Because of her grief, the Goddess declines. Clement writes that "Baubo is deeply hurt"[13] by this refusal of hospitality and thinking that Demeter has insulted her, "uncovers her sacred parts and exhibits them to the goddess."[14] This turns out to please Demeter, and so she partakes of the drink. This is the point at which he ends his account.

---

[8]   Titus Flavius Clemens, *Clement of Alexandria: The Exhortation to the Greeks, The Rich Man's Salvation, and To the Newly Baptized*, G. W. Butterworth, trans. (London: William Heinemann, New York: G. P. Putnam's Sons, 1919), pp. 28–47.

[9]   Clemens, *Clement of Alexandria*, p. 33.

[10]   Clemens, *Clement of Alexandria*, p. 33.

[11]   Clemens, *Clement of Alexandria*, p. 41.

[12]   Clemens, *Clement of Alexandria*, p. 43.

[13]   Clemens, *Clement of Alexandria*, p. 43.

[14]   Clemens, *Clement of Alexandria*, p. 43.

Clement makes no connection between agriculture, the divinity of Earth, and the myth of Demeter and Persephone.

HOMER

Homer, "Hymn to Demeter"[15]: *While this hymn is attributed to the blind poet Homer, various translators have placed its creation anywhere between the ninth and seventh centuries* B.C.E. *The writer's myth is presented in a beautiful, lyric, and flowing style. It, and its abduction theme, most probably are the lineage source for the many other versions that followed through the centuries. The hymn ends with an explanation of the origin of Demeter's Mysteries.*

Demeter's Daughter was picking flowers with the daughters of Oceanus when she discovered a special narcissus. This had been planted as a trap by Gaea, according to Zeus' plan, as a favor to Hades. As the Maiden reached out to pick it, she was abducted by the God of the Underworld, Plouton. (The word "rape" was not used by the author, but is implied.)

For nine days, Demeter searched for her Daughter, wandering Earth. Hecate and Demeter also search together for the Maiden. Finally the Sun God Helios tells Demeter that the Maiden has descended in Plouton's chariot. Demeter is seized by grief and anger. In disguise as an old woman, she arrives at the well in the city of Eleusis. There she meets the daughters of King Keleos, and tells them that she has just arrived from Crete. Demeter is invited to come and be a nurse for their newborn brother.

Arriving at the house of King Keleos and Queen Metaniera, Demeter is invited by the Queen to be seated. Iambe, the serving maid, sets out a stool covered with white fleece for the Goddess. Demeter is sorrowful and will not speak, eat, or drink, so Iambe tries to lighten her heart. She makes jests until the Goddess smiles and laughs. Demeter is offered sweet wine, but refuses, asking instead for a drink of barley groats mixed with mint.

Demeter receives Demophon, Metaniera's son. The author writes that the child "grew like a god," though he did not eat or drink. Each night Demeter anointed him with divine ambrosia and placed him into the fire. One night Metaniera saw this rite of fire, and screamed

---

[15]   R. Gordon Wasson, A. P. Ruck, and Albert Hofmann, *The Road to Eleusis*, Danny Staples, trans. (New York: Harcourt Brace Javanovich, 1978), pp. 59–73; Marvin Meyer, ed., *The Ancient Mysteries: A Sourcebook*, David Rice and John Stambaugh, trans. (San Francisco: HarperSanFrancisco, 1986), pp. 21–30; Helene Foley (hymn trans. and commentary), *The Homeric Hymn to Demeter* (Princeton, NJ: Princeton University Press, 1993), pp. 2–26.

in fear for her son's injury. At this, Demeter withdrew the boy from the fire and shouted that mortals are fools. She announced that she was the Goddess Demeter and appeared in her divine beauty, and in an aura of light. The Goddess demanded that the people of Eleusis build her a temple.

Her temple built, there she came to reside, still grieving for her Daughter. In her sorrow, she caused the land to become barren. Zeus sent the Goddess Iris to implore Demeter to relent and return to Olympus, but she would not relent. Zeus then sent Hermes to the Underworld to bring Persephone back to her Mother. Hades (Plouton), told Persephone to return to her Mother, adding that he felt that he was actually an appropriate husband. Hermes took Persephone to Demeter, who waited in front of her temple. Joyfully, Demeter ran to meet her Daughter. She asked Persephone if she had eaten anything in the Underworld, saying that if she had, she must remain there a third part of each year. Persephone stated that Hades had forced her to taste a pomegranate seed.

Zeus then sent the Goddess Rhea to tell Demeter that he would give her whatever honors she would choose to have among the Gods, and that the Daughter might spend one-third of the year below, and two-thirds above. Demeter accepted, returning first to Olympus and then going to the Rarian Plain. There she created a green field of grain that soon became ready to harvest. She filled the land with green growth, and with fruit and flowers.

Demeter went to Triptolemos, Diokles, Eumolpus, and King Keleos, and showed them her secret and holy rites, which make those who know them blessed. Then the Goddess returned to Olympus. Toward the end of the hymn, the author says that those who love the Gods will have wealth (Ploutos) upon their hearths.

OVID

Ovid, "The Metamorphoses; Book V, Death and Proserpina"[16]*: Publius Ovidius Naso (43 B.C.E.–17 C.E.) completed his work, "The Metamorphoses" in Rome in 8 C.E. Thought to be a corrupting influence on Roman youth, Ovid was banished from Rome by Emperor Augustus. However, this and other of his works have lived on, to be read and become an influence upon authors such as Shakespeare, Chaucer, and Spenser.*

---

[16] Ovid, *The Metamorphoses*, Mary M. Innes, trans. (London: Penguin Books, 1955), pp. 125–133; Ovid, *The Metamorphoses*, Horace Gregory, trans. (New York: Viking Press, Inc., 1960), pp. 149–159; Ovid, *Metamorphoses, Vol. I, The Loeb Classical Library*, Frank J. Miller, trans. (New York: G. P. Putnam's Sons, 1921).

This myth begins in Sicily with the giant Typhoeus, who has been trapped by the land itself, and who eventually succeeds in becoming free. All this cracking and groaning of Earth under the weight of the giant sends fear even into the heart of the God of the Underworld.

Venus (Aphrodite) looks down on the Underworld God, and suddenly suggests to Cupid (Eros) that love should conquer Hades (Plouton). She suggests that Cupid should marry Ceres' (Demeter) Daughter, otherwise Proserpina (Persephone) would remain a "virgin till she dies."[17] So, Cupid pierces the heart of the God of Death with his arrow.

The story continues: Ceres' Daughter is picking lilies and violets by a lake in a place where it is always springtime. Death abducts her and rapes her while she screams in terror. (The author specifically speaks of her loss of virginity.) Death then takes off with Proserpina. They pass by a bay where the nymph Cyane lives. She tries to stop Death, descrying his use of force, but Death and Proserpina descend into Hades. Cyane grieves.

In the meantime Ceres is looking for her Daughter. She searches day and night, throughout the world. She eventually comes to a cottage where an old woman lives, who gives her barley water to drink.

Ceres continues to wander in search of her Daughter. Cyane tosses the belt, which the Daughter had dropped, into the Mother's path. When Ceres finds this, her grief becomes madness. She crushes the farmer's plows, causes crops to die at birth, and weeds to flourish. Then Arethusa, a water nymph, rises and asks the Mother to forgive, saying that the countryside is innocent. She says that she had seen Ceres' Daughter, who, though in tears, was still a regal Queen.

Ceres flies in her chariot to plead her case before Jupiter (Zeus). Jupiter states that the Daughter has not been hurt, but is loved by a worthy husband. He further states that the Daughter may return if she has not eaten anything in the Underworld. But Proserpina had innocently eaten of a pomegranate and so, according to Jupiter, must remain half of each year in Hades and half the year above.

The story switches to Arethusa, who explains to Ceres how she came to be a water nymph. When Arethusa ends her story, Ceres flies through the skies in her winged chariot to Athens. There she gives her chariot to an Athenian boy named Triptolemus, and orders him to rain seeds across Earth. This, she says, will bring a good harvest without weeds or thorns.

---

17   Ovid, *The Metamorphoses*, Horace Gregory, trans. (New York: Viking Press, Inc., 1960), p. 150.

Demeter and Persephone in Modern Experience

Many thanks to the following women who provided their views and personal insights into the myth. Their discerning and thoughtful contributions enrich us, bringing even greater awareness and understanding to the subject. They show us that this is a myth which can be (and will continue to be) seen and used in many powerful ways.

SUSAN GRAY & STARR GOODE: "NEMESIS AND DEMETER: FATE AND THE CYCLES OF LIFE"

Susan Gray and Starr Goode are a part of Nemesis Coven that began in 1985, in Los Angeles, with seven feminist women artists. They work together, using their combined skills as artists and writers, to educate the public about Feminist Craft. They have exhibited Goddess art, done performances, created videos, produced lecture series and newsletters, held summer camp, and taught Craft. They have also had a regular TV show: "The Goddess in Art," and have written books: "Lady of the Northern Light: A Feminist Guide to the Runes," *and* "Expanding Circles: Women, Art and Community." *Nemesis seeks to create ritual, and to ease their life transitions, making the practice of their craft the basis of their lives together. Susan and Starr relay their experiences with the Demeter and Persephone myth as it has been used in their coven. They have used it at their Autumn Equinox ritual, for healing purposes, and for life transition rites.*

Nemesis uses what may be regarded as the standard elements of the myth; but there are no gods or elements of abduction in our version. We refer to the Mother and Daughter (who we also see as parts of one Triple Goddess) as Demeter and Persephone. We also call Demeter Grain Mother, and Persephone Queen of the Dead, and Goddess of the Underworld. We view the Daughter's descent as a part of the cyclic process of the seasons, and of life, death, and rebirth. Her descent represents the inner journey of the subconscious. As Persephone, she represents the dark aspects of each of us, the shadow self, and also implacable, impersonal mortality.

We have used the myth in our Equinox celebrations, where the use of bread is an important aspect. We have baked bread shaped like the Goddess, and filled her with seeds. Another year we kneaded our intentions into the bread and then each ate a bite, taking home the rest to use to inspire our work.

We have also used the myth in memorial services for family members of Covensisters. In those instances we took the coven member on a journey to the Underworld, where, like Persephone, they could communicate with a dead family member for healing purposes and final farewells.

Our use of the myth is Pre-Hellenic, calling forth a more ancient version of the Goddess. She represents the Great Goddess as cyclic seasons, and as the source of life, death, and rebirth.

JUDITH TOLLEY: "MAIDEN, MOTHER, CRONE: PSYCHOLOGICAL ARCHETYPES FOR WOMEN"

Judith Tolley is a long-time woman's activist, artist, and ritualist, living in Long Beach, California, who has fulfilled her dream of becoming a licensed M.F.C.C. as a second career. She loves cats, the ocean, and silence. In the following, Judith relays her experience in creating a public Demeter ritual. The ritual she describes explores aspects of the Mother-Daughter relationship as well as the three archetypal faces of the Goddess as phases of a woman's life.

Format: The Demeter and Persephone Ritual that I cowrote with Laura Hines-Jurgens, and produced in 1987, had two specific parts: the dramatization of the myth of Persephone's journey into the Underworld and Demeter's search for her, and an exploration into contemporary women's role/relationship with their natural mothers during the breaking away period as they entered womanhood. The latter was experienced in dyad format (one-on-one personal dialogue), with everyone experiencing the drama as audience/observer.

There was no preparation given to the 40 attendees, except when breaking into dyads. They were to explore their relationship with their mother (Demeter), with respect to how they broke away to find themselves as women (Persephone). There was also a look at whether or not they received intergenerational support (examining the Crone role). This was shared with their partner who listened for five minutes without conversation. They exchanged roles, and the listener became the talker for five minutes. There was a short time allocated for processing the experience with each other, then feedback was solicited from the group before the ritual was ended.

Goals of Ritual: In my vision of the ritual, the participants were expected to be affected by observing the drama of the myth being acted out, using actors and a storyteller. It was expected that, by observing the drama, their psychological recollection of the archetypes—Maiden, Mother, and Crone—would be triggered. Since each person carries a unique interpersonal history, no two archetypes will be manifested the same way in a personality. But, there are certain prerequisites that an archetype has to possess to be true to type; universality is one criteria. Recognizing the archetypes—Maiden, Mother and Crone—led directly into forming a dyad. As a dyad, the participants discussed the personalized story of each woman as Persephone struggling into womanhood, and separating from a mother similar to Demeter. Therefore the goals were realized when participators were able to apply features of the myth and the archetypes to their internal archetypes and personal story.

Three Faces of the Goddess: At all times, the ritual presentation of the story of Persephone was considered to be about the Divine Female—the GREAT Goddess—that has been worshiped on Earth from the beginning of our species. Her attributes and powers are modified and embellished from era to era, but there remain three salient identities when addressing the archetype. The Goddess is the living example of womanhood manifested into the three major life periods during one's life as female—maidenhood (presexual and pubescent), motherhood (sexual and fertile), and finally, cronehood (wise blood age).

All three aspects are represented in the story, which leads me to speculate that this myth is ancient and prepatriarchal in origin—it strikes me as an initiation into womanhood ritual that evolved into a myth about the Goddess Demeter, her Daughter Kore/Persephone and the Crone Hecate. This in turn can be interpreted as the three physical stages of womanhood—menarche, pregnancy, and menopause.

Kore is usually viewed as the virginal preadolescent (premenarche), with Persephone being possibly sexual (postmenarche) but not with-child or married. There are psychological stages also that correspond to the physical changes in a woman's body as it regulates her passage through life's stages.

By examining the archetypes and comparing their experience to our personal experience, especially when viewing how we carry the archetype in relation to others, we can learn about ourselves and benefit from the comparison. Each woman will create and carry her own interpretations of the archetypes, and it will look different during different phases in her life cycle, but it will be some combination of the three archetypes—Maiden, Mother, and Crone.

MARYSCARLETT AMARIS:
"CONFESSIONS OF A MODERN-DAY DEMETER"

MaryScarlett Amaris is a writer and a teacher who lives in Long Beach, California, with her 17-year-old son and 12-year-old daughter. For the past ten years, she has been involved in her local Goddess community, serving as witch and priestess. MaryScarlett relays her experiences with the Demeter and Persephone myth first as a child, and second as a mother. As a child, she questioned the victim aspect of the classic version of the myth. As an adult, she discovered a pre-Hellenic nonviolent Demeter-Persephone myth, to which she could relate. Also, as a modern-day Demeter, MaryScarlett shares her very personal experiences as Demeter, the mother of a young Persephone.

Seventh grade English—Mrs. Nettleton—was she your teacher, too? You remember: gray flip, cat-eyed glasses, sweaterclip—standing vigil next to her overhead projector, tapping her mini-baseball bat against the desk of any sleepy-headed student (my desk was actually dented from her wake-up taps!). She had two reasons for living: to indoctrinate students into the world of sentence diagramming, and to open young minds to the world of mythology.

At age 12, under the auspices of Mrs. N., I first learned of Demeter and Persephone. While I don't remember everything about that initial meeting, I remember learning the explanation for winter and spring, Demeter's sorrow, and the haplessness of Persephone. As I recall, even though she was central to the myth, Persephone, herself, was more of a plot device than a real figure. Even then, however, this struck me as strange. I was curious about her—her point of view. Did she view herself as a victim? Was she curious, adventurous? Why did she continue to honor her promise to return to the Underworld, pomegranates or no? She was a Goddess after all.

My teen and early adult years whirled by. Mrs. Nettleton faded away, as did every other teacher, book, lesson. I emerged into the fullness of womanhood detached from myth, from history, from politics, from economics. I finally learned to attach myself to the world through both feminism and the Goddess.

Some eighteen years after we were first introduced, I re-acquainted myself with the woman figures of mythology—Athena, Artemis, Aphrodite, and of course, Demeter and Persephone. This time my guides were my emerging sense of woman-self, my mature intellect, and Charlene Spretnak's *Lost Goddesses of Early Greece*, 1984. Spretnak retells the myth from a pre-Hellenic, prepatriarchal stand-point. The Gods and Goddesses of pre-Hellenic mythology are not the vengeful ones of "classical" mythology; they did not throw down lightening bolts and curses from Mount Olympus, like the God of Christian mythology does in the Old Testament. Instead, the pre-Hellenic pantheon can be characterized as more reflective of a time when the socio-political climate was one in which no one sex oppressed another, when the contributions and attributes of mascu-line and feminine deity worked together in order to create a balance within the world.

I feel like I need to note here that I do not necessarily believe that there was a time, pre-Hellenic or "classical," when Goddesses and Gods roamed Earth. Mythology was created (and is still created today) as metaphor, begun from an oral tradition, in order for people to make sense of a world that, quite frankly, never really makes any sense.

The pre-Hellenic Persephone chose to make her first foray to the Underworld in order to learn the ways of the dead. They appear to her in the fields, asking for her guidance—a people in need of a Queen. Naturally, Demeter did not want Persephone to travel far from home, but the Daughter was drawn to the Underworld and its lost souls. While Persephone inhabited the Underworld, Demeter mourned, and brought winter to the land. After a time, Persephone returned, and as to rejoice, Demeter filled the lands with flowers and life. Mother and Daughter were reunited, and the cycle of life continued.

This telling was not at all like the one that I learned all those years ago. There was not a victim, but a Maiden becoming woman, finding her role in the world. There was a mother who wanted to protect her daughter, but who was, at last, willing to accept the daughter's choice. Mrs. Nettleton's Persephone was not mythology to me—for in order for mythology to have its power, it must work on a deep-subconscious level, archetype, collective soul—Spretnak's Persephone and Demeter resonated deep within. This myth I could take to heart; I could use to heal. The "classical myth" did not resonate within me because I do not see myself or other women as victims. This is not to say that victimization does not occur, but that woman-as-victim is not an archetypal, mythological role: it is a prescribed or chosen role.

This Persephone made sense to me—she answered some of my 12-year-old's questions. This myth felt right. Persephone is not just a hapless plot device, she is a young woman of power making a choice. Like Inanna of Sumerian lore, Persephone chooses to explore the world below in order to understand the world above. And whether she is renewing the dead, learning the ancient ways from Grandmother Hecate, eating pomegranates with Hades, or reigning as the Queen of Hell, she is fulfilling the function of daring. Each woman must dare to face the Underworld: her own personal demons, fears; that which oppresses her, her sisters, her children, if she is to emerge whole and strong, if she is to free herself from socialization, politicization, and any familial or religious indoctrination designed to keep her down.

But the political, feminist overtones of the Demeter and Persephone myth have been replaced by the archetypal dynamic of "Mother and Daughter." Where before I found affinity for Persephone most strong, I am now coming to know, more personally, the Goddess Demeter.

My 12-year-old daughter, Caitlin, the same age as I when I learned of the myth, has become Persephone to my Demeter. She is choosing a path for herself that, for now, is illuminated by the light of halftruth. Like Persephone, she must choose the Underworld, but my daughter's underworld lives above ground—it is not the souls of the dead that she seeks to ease, but the dead soul of the living she is drawn to—the MTV world that deifies objectification, that displays sexuality. And I stand like Demeter, howling, with mother-soul's mourning, waiting for her to emerge.

The knowledge that my Persephone is destined to choose her own path, that she must know the dark to come into the light, is of little consequence or comfort. In waiting for springtime, my Demeter self rages, hurts, longs for mother-daughter reunion, communion, aching for the connection I felt to my daughter when she and I were one. I remember my own mother, and remember my own Persephone self. When a girl-child was born to me, I was ecstatic. I could be the mother that my mother could not.

Yet Persephone chooses to deny me this right, rejecting—as all daughters must—my advice, my efforts to teach and train, my experience as a woman in this world. The Goddess was lucky: she could count on a season of sorrow followed by a season of joy. Modern-day Demeter and Persephone can experience four seasons in a day. The mercurial nature of our temperaments shuttles us both back and forth between winter and spring. The slam of the door signifies her absence.

There is an actual physical presence to contend with, as well. Three days out of seven, my Persephone chooses to live with the man who broke apart her family, who broke her mother's heart. This is another place of half-light, where joy is suspect, denial embraced. Demeter mourns each absence, feeling betrayed. Each return is difficult because Demeter is always aware that she must prepare for the next leaving. Persephone is torn between love and duty, she struggles to please—an impossible task. The energy of that under/other world encircles Persephone in attitude, in anger, disrupting any possible springtime harmony between mother and daughter.

I live this myth. I struggle to have compassion for myself as I live it. Demeter struggled years and years before she was finally able to accept Persephone's chosen path. As much as she wanted to bind Persephone to her forever, to shield her from darkness, hurt, experience, she could not. Persephone's spirit, defiant, loving, adventurous, wild, demanded that she must find out for herself. This myth teaches me about love, trust, and surrender. I must love my daughter no matter what she chooses, or what she becomes. I must trust in the wisdom of time, and in the belief that each is here to walk a path of her own choosing. I must surrender my fear, my guilt, my anger—I must surrender to the cycle of life. Demeter and Persephone, please guide me.

JANE R. WHEATLEY "MYSTERIES OF INITIATION: ANCIENT AND MODERN"

Jane R. Wheatley, M.S.W., is a Licensed Clinical Social Worker in private practice in Santa Monica, California. She has been working with individuals, couples, and groups for over 25 years. With a background in Jungian and Kleinian analysis, family therapy, and gestalt, she also brings to this subject her personal experience with soulwork, the process by which she was led through dreamwork into writing songs. Jane relays her experience with the Demeter and Persephone myth as she uses it in her therapy practice. She sees those in psychotherapy as initiates moving through various aspects of the myth.

As a Jungian-oriented psychotherapist, I have found the myth of Demeter and Persephone to be an ongoing source of sustenance and inspiration. Timeless feminine wisdom permeates this mother/daughter story in which seasonal changes remind us of the cyclic nature of all human experience. Over the years I have come to view this myth and its ritual expression in the Eleusinian Mysteries as a paradigm for depth psychotherapy.

Rooted in the prehistoric religion of the Mother Goddess, this myth deals with themes of death, birth, and immortality. It was so important to the ancient Greeks that it was celebrated for over 2,000 years as the centerpiece of their religion, the Eleusinian Mysteries. Aristotle said that the purpose of initiation into these Mysteries was not intellectual learning but rather "to suffer an experience and be moved." For men and women alike in ancient Greece, to be initiated into the Mysteries at Eleusis was to become one with the sacred Mother and Daughter who were worshiped there. As the Goddesses were separated through death, as they endured and survived this experience of suffering and were transformed, so were the initiates.

Like the initiates in the ancient mysteries, those who enter depth psychotherapy embark upon a modern-day ritual of initiation. Through this process individuals learn to "suffer. . .and be moved" by the powerful archetypal experiences in which they find themselves. Rather than trying to get rid of their suffering, people learn to accept it for what it is—a symptom that carries a sacred message. Gradually, as modern day initiates decipher the messages within their suffering, they are transformed. What follows will illustrate this ancient/modern parallel.

While Persephone was being seduced by the overpowering scent of the narcissus, Eleusinian initiates identified with her innocence, her fascination with the pleasures of the unknown. With her they took their first steps out into the world on their own, away from home. When the Maiden Goddess was swept suddenly away by the God of the Underworld, initiates in the Mysteries suffered with Persephone the terror of her descent into darkness. As her terror was transformed into love for her Dionysian husband, as she embraced the physical pleasures of their marriage, the initiates likewise transformed their own suffering into wholeness.

Similarly, modern-day initiates become caught by the lure of addictions, political or spiritual causes, depression or illness—even unrequited love. During this descent into the winter of their own unconscious, they seek the help of depth psychotherapy. While searching for the message within their obsessions or projections, they often discover that the psyche is asking them to "die" to one part of their lives as presently lived. By bringing the light of consciousness into their darkness, they find healing.

With respect to Demeter's role in the myth, after Persephone's abduction her Mother was overcome with shock, betrayal, depression, and rage. Heartsick with yearning for her beloved Daughter and their lost closeness, Demeter was unaware of her possessive reluctance to let her Daughter grow up. When she was no longer able to tolerate the barrenness caused by the loss of her daughter and her own lost youth, this golden-haired Goddess of the Grain grew vengeful. Blaming her brother Zeus for his part in Persephone's abduction, Demeter refused to allow Earth to flower again with the bounty of springtime, until he arranged for Persephone to return from the underworld.

Likewise, modern-day initiates in psychotherapy may end up in a depression after the loss of a significant relationship, a sudden change of circumstance, or a shift in personal or professional identity. When people are unable or unwilling to bear the pain that results, they often blame others for their suffering. In psychotherapy these initiates discover that anger functions as a defense to guard against the danger of being vulnerable. In learning to work more cooperatively with their defenses, they learn to identify what has provoked their need for protection. When the fear, or hurt, or loneliness hidden beneath the anger can be allowed its expression, eventually the energy trapped within the emotion is released and rechanneled into other areas of growth.

Returning to the myth, out of death Persephone was ultimately born once again, though her life had been irrevocably altered. No longer a maiden, she had emerged into the fullness of her own womanhood. Each year she divided her time between the two worlds, returning to the underworld following harvesttime, where she lived with her husband for the winter, serving as Queen of the Dead. When it came time for new seeds to sprout forth in spring, she returned to the upper world to be reunited with her mother.

Though a mother never wants to let her daughter go, Demeter was moved by Persephone's sadness over her separation from her husband. Recognizing in her daughter's loss the echo of her own, Demeter released her possessive hold on the past and accepted her daughter's marriage. The loss itself had created an emptiness inside the Mother of Grain, into which her own maidenly aspect was born anew. Thus, her barrenness passed, and she was once again able to send forth fruits from the fertile fields. As she did so the two Goddesses again were reunited, becoming Mother and Maiden in one.

As with all creative cycles, Demeter and Persephone had learned not only to accept but to embrace the emptiness and uncertainty of the fallow season, out of which the fullness of a new season of growth emerges. When Eleusinian initiates experienced Persephone's birth out of death, and the resolution of the Goddesses' suffering, they gained reassuring insights into the nature of their own death. Similarly, modern initiates in depth psychotherapy learn to accept the "death" of change and loss as a natural part of life. As they learn to differentiate those aspects of their lives over which they do and do not have control, they begin to accept their helplessness to undo the loss. Gradually, they develop skill in rechanneling the energy of their anger into more effective limit-setting. Ultimately, as they endure and survive their suffering, these initiates learn to decipher the sacred message carried within it—letting go. Only after this release does the springtime of new opportunity follow.

Moving through and beyond suffering, honoring the mystery of death giving birth to new life, these humble initiates become one with the ever-turning Great Round, the cycle of seasons that never winds down. In so doing they are blessed, as were those at Eleusis, with a glimpse into Eternity.

Sacred Words
and Symbols

Anaktoron: small room inside Demeter's temple, the Telesterion. This room remained in the same place throughout the centuries as the temple was enlarged and embellished. From classical times to the Roman period, the Anaktoron was located toward the center of the temple. [1] Its dimensions were approximately $47^1/_2$ x $11^1/_2$ feet. Inside was a natural projection of rock rising from the sanctuary floor. Because of a light that is known to have emanated from the center of the temple roof during the night of the Greater Mysteries, it is believed that a fire was lit upon this rock. The name Anaktoron means palace, or holy of holies. One of its purposes was as a storage place for the hiera (holy objects), which were used during the Greater Mysteries. The Anaktoron was also known as the Megaron or Chamber of Demeter.

cista mystica: sometimes transliterated as kista mystica, kista being the Latin form. Its meaning may relate to the word "cistern," a holding place. This was the sacred mystery basket that held the heira (holy objects). The virgin priestesses were responsible for its care and safekeeping. Some speculate that there may have been many cistas; however, there is no evidence whether there was one or many. The cista was an important part of the Greater Mysteries, where it was brought out from the Anaktoron and its sacred objects used in the rites.

---

[1]   By 146 B.C.E., the Romans were in power in Greece.

In the Roman period, there was an inner gateway to the sanctuary grounds called the Lesser Propylaia. This gateway was flanked by two caryatids (statue columns) of priestesses. On each priestess' head was balanced a cista mystica. A remnant of one of the figures (from the waist up) is preserved today in the Museum of Eleusis, and another is in Cambridge, England.

crocus and narcissus: flowers that, in a Mediterranean cycle, bloom in late fall and early winter, respectively. After the barren season of dry summer, the fall and winter rains return the green to both wild nature and cultivated field. The rains replenish the land, and crocus and narcissus are seen as the symbols of the Maiden Goddess and the sign of her return. In their beauty we see joy and new beginnings.

Epopteia: the moment during the Greater Mysteries when the secret of Eleusis was revealed to initiates. Carl Kerényi describes it as a beatific vision.[2] We can never really know exactly what it was, but only do our best to surmise. It was a sublime experience, brought about through sacred ritual and the sacred drink.

fire: a symbol of transformation though dangerous and often uncontrollable. Used wisely, it benefits us. It cooks our food, warms our homes, and sends fragrant smoke up into the skies. In the myth, fire clears the field after the harvest, creating rich and fertile ash that will benefit next year's crop. After the harvest, Hecate ignites the field with flame before the Holy Daughter crosses over to Tartarus. In the crucible of human transformation, fire is that unbridled energy that sweeps away all that has gone before, in order to create a place for a new kind of life.

grain: symbol of life and regeneration. We eat its seed to live. We save some of its seed and replant new crops in the new season. We harvest the grain; in the death of the plant comes the essence of continuation. Our spirit is as the seed; in our own cyclic births, changes, and deaths, it is our continuation.

hiera: the holy objects inside the cista mystica. Used during the rite of the Greater Mysteries, we cannot be completely certain what they were. If we take cues from the exterior of the cista mystica of the Eleusinian caryatids, we can assume that what was sculpted on the

---

2   Carl Kerényi, *Eleusis: Archetypal Image of Mother and Daughter* (Princeton, NJ: Princeton University Press, 1991), p. 95.

outside represented what was on the inside: poppy rosettes, poppy pods laid out on leaves, wheat sheaves, myrtle, and a vessel for the sacred drink.

Iacchos: *Iacchos!* was the celebratory cry of joy that rang out as the prospective initiates began their journey from Athens to Eleusis for the Greater Mysteries. The image of Iacchos was one of a young Dionysus, long-haired, and myrtle-crowned. He represents the initiates' joy at being able to participate in Demeter's Mysteries.

kernos: vessel for food offerings, a pot with many little cups around its edge. In the cups were placed some of the Goddess' gifts: grain, pomegranate seeds, poppy seeds, milk, spun wool, sage, peas, beans, honey, oil, egg, and wine. The empty center of the pot was thought to be used for either incense or fire, most probably incense.

korai: the name given to young plants, whether in the cultivated field or wild nature. Having been born from the mother's body, they are as Kore, the holy maiden.

kykeon: the sacred drink. It may have been made of mint, barley, honey, and a psychotropic agent. This was ingested only at the Greater Mysteries. There have been many discussions as to its contents by authors Carl Kerényi, Albert Hofmann, and Terrence McKenna, but there is no absolute evidence.

light and the dark: symbols that relate to the marriage of Persephone and Plouton, and the reconciliation of Demeter and Persephone. These pivotal moments of the drama bring the light and the dark into balance. The meaning extends deep into human consciousness, and I do not want to limit it by one explanation, but would rather let the general metaphor speak for itself.

Through the passage of time, the light of life has become divided. The child (maiden) of light challenges the Mother of light. The child descends into the dark, the unknown. The Maiden, light of the Above, unites with the Princely dark of the Below. Balance and beauty are achieved in the Underworld, but this is not yet permanent. Soon the Mother of life, in love and compassion, brings her light below. Mother and Daughter, light and light, are reconciled. Beauty and balance are reestablished in both worlds. The Mother returns to her domain above. In the Great Cycle, the child of life will journey both above and below, her movement creating now discord, now balance, but always resulting in knowledge, and in the continuation of life.

megara: chamber used during a part of the Rites of Thesmophoria. From this chamber, women drew up contents left from previous offerings. During the rites, these remains were mixed with some of the sacred seed from the temple's Rharian Field. This fertility charm was dispensed to farmers to mix with their own seed for the planting of wheat and barley.

mystagogos: sponsor of the prospective initiate into Demeter's Greater Mysteries. The sponsor prepared the prospective initiate in the week prior to the event and accompanied the initiate as far as the journey to Eleusis. One had to have this sponsor in order to consider initiation.

mystai: means "initiates" and is the name given to those who had been prepared for the Greater Mysteries. The term was used, not only to describe prospective initiates into Demeter's Mysteries, but also for those being initiated into the mysteries of Dionysus, Cybele and Attis, Mithras, and Orpheus. Our word "mystery" comes from the Greek word *mustes,* meaning closed lips, or one vowed to silence. Those initiated into the various mysteries were ordered not to reveal the rites.

pelanos: sacred first-baked loaf of bread from the harvest, given to Demeter as a thanks offering. In modern form, it is still given today in Eleusis at the Christian chapel above the old temple site. It is offered to Mary, The Lady inside the Seed.

pig: hardy and prolific symbol of abundance and fertility. Easy to raise, it produces many offspring in a relatively short period of time. The pig was a common offering to Demeter and Persephone.

pomegranate: in a Mediterranean climate, a tree that flowers as Persephone descends into the Underworld. It bears fruit between the time of the Greater Mysteries and her return at the Kalligenia portion of the Thesmophoria holidays. It is symbolic of the land of death (the pomegranate groves of Elysium), but also of the fertile womb of both woman and Goddess. The fruit, having many seeds and a blood-red juice, is a sign of both life and death.

poppy: blood-red flower that, as the grain matures, shows brightly in the field, in contrast to the yellow gold color of the grain. The Maiden has achieved fertility. The red grain-field poppy is thus a sign of her maturing and transforming state, and also of Demeter's coming harvest. The Maiden is ready to become Queen. Poppies are near the end of their blooming cycle at this time, which is also the time of the Maiden's descent. This is the red *papaver rhoeas*. The opium poppy is quite a different variety than the grain-field poppy. Poppy pods are imaged on the cista mystica of the caryatids of the Lesser Propylaia as oblong-shaped pods of *papaver rhoeas*, rather than the rounded shape of *papaver orientalis* pods.

sanctuary: site of the temple of Demeter, rebuilt many times. By the Roman period, there were many buildings on the Eleusinian Acropolis: temples, courtyards, gateways, granaries, living quarters, and more. The sanctuary consisted of all of the buildings and structures that surrounded and the Telesterion.

sexuality: the sacred aspect of life that keeps the wheel of life moving. Without it, there is no fertility, no birth. Its energies are those of passion and creativity. The sacred lovers, Persephone and Plouton, make the Underworld bloom through their love. Above, when Demeter returns to fertility after the barren time, she receives the rains of Zeus and makes the land fruitful again.

snakes: images that appear in the rites of Arkichronia. In these rites, fertility talismans are made and snake effigies guard the elements that are used. Snakes also appear on reliefs of initiate purifications, where they reside beside the throne of Demeter. They are an aspect of the Goddess with which the initiate must come into accord. Snakes are a symbol of change and of cyclic rebirth, as they periodically shed their skin and are renewed. They have been imaged with Hecate as well as with many other deities. In addition, their flowing and slithering movements are seen as sensual and primeval, suggesting creative, fertile sexuality.

Telesterion: Demeter's temple in the Eleusinian sanctuary. It was where the rites of the Greater Mysteries took place. The temple was approximately 58 x 58 yards, within which was the Anaktoron as described above. With its 42 columns, peaked roof, and tiers of inner seats against its walls, the Hall of Mysteries dates from the fifth century B.C.E.

Telete: final rite of the Greater Mysteries. Taking place in the Telesterion, it is related to the word *telos*, meaning "to initiate."

thunder: sound (made by a great resonating gong), heard during the night of the Greater Mysteries, according to Clement of Alexandria. However, the rites he observed were a later version in Alexandria, rather than in Eleusis. According to Kerényi, the great gong, or *echeion,* was used in Greek theater, this influence perhaps having come from an archaic cult of the dead.[3]

thymiateria: vessel used for fragrant smoke offerings. It had little handles and a design of openings in the lid, from which the incense smoke emerged.

3   Carl Kerényi, *Eleusis: Archetypal Image of Mother and Daughter* (Princeton, NJ: Princeton University Press, 1991), p. 84.

BIBLIOGRAPHY

Apollodorus. *Apollodorus: The Library,* vol. I and II. James G. Frazer, trans. Cambridge, MA: Harvard University Press, 1946.

Aristophanes. *Aristophanes: Five Comedies.* n. trans. Cleveland: World Publishing Company, 1948.

———. *The Eleven Comedies.* n. trans. New York: Horace Liveright, 1930.

Athanassakis, Apostolos N. *The Orphic Hymns: Text, Translation, and Notes.* Atlanta, GA: Scholars Press, 1988.

Bowra, C. M. and Editors of Time-Life Books. *Classical Greece.* New York: Time-Life Books, 1965.

Brumfield, Allaire Chandor. *The Attic Festivals of Demeter and their Relation to the Agricultural Year.* Salem, NH: Arno Press, 1981.

Caldwell, Taylor. *The Glory and the Lightning.* Garden City, NY: Doubleday, 1974.

Callimachus. *Callimachus and Lycophoron—Aratus.* A. W. Mair, trans. London: William Heinemann; New York: G. P. Putnam's Sons, 1921.

Cavendish, Richard (ed.). *Mythology: An Illustrated Encyclopedia.* New York: Rizzoli/Orbis Publishing, Ltd., 1980.

Clemens, Titus Flavius. *Clement of Alexandria: The Exortation to the Greeks.* G. W. Butterworth, trans. London: William Heinemann; New York: G. P. Putnam's Sons, 1919.

Clinton, Kevin. *The Sacred Officials of the Eleusinian Mysteries.* Philadelphia: American Philosophical Society, 1974.

Coxhead, Nona. *The Relevance of Bliss.* New York: St. Martin's Press, 1985.

Cunninghan, Scott. *Cunningham's Encyclopedia of Magical Herbs.* St. Paul, MN: Llewellyn Publications, 1990.

Deiss, Joseph Jay. *Herculaneum: Italy's Buried Treasure.* New York: HarperCollins, 1985.

Durant, Will. *The Life of Greece.* New York: Simon and Schuster, 1939.

Eisler, Riane. *The Chalice and the Blade.* Cambridge, MA: Harper Collins, 1987.

Eliade, Mircea. *Rites and Symbols of Initiation: The Mysteries of Birth and Rebirth.* New York: Harper & Row Publishers, 1958.

Estés, Clarissa Pinkola. *Women Who Run with the Wolves.* New York: Ballantine Books, 1992.

Farrar, Janet and Stuart. *Eight Sabbats for Witches.* London: Robert Hale Limited, 1981.

Fleming, William. *Arts & Ideas,* Seventh Edition. Philidelphia: Holt, Rinehart & Winston, 1986.

Foley, Helene P. (ed.). *The Homeric Hymn to Demeter: Translation, Commentary, and Interpretive Essays.* Princeton, NJ: Princeton University Press, 1993.

Fontenrose, Joseph. *Python: A Study of Delphic Myth and Its Origins.* Berkeley: University of California Press, 1980.

Graves, Robert. *The Greek Myths.* 2 vols. New York: Viking/Penguin Books, 1986.

Griffith, F. & Herbert Thompson (eds.). *The Leyden Papyrus.* New York: Dover Publications, 1974.

Hades, Moses and Editors of Time-Life Books. *Imperial Rome.* New York: Time-Life Books, 1965.

Healey, Robert F. and Sterling Dow. *A Sacred Calendar of Eleusis.* Cambridge, MA: Harvard University Press, 1965.

Hesiod. *Hesiod.* C. A. Elton, trans. London: George Routledge & Sons, 1894.

———. *Hesiod—Theogony, Works and Days.* M. L. West, trans., intro. and notes. Oxford, England: Oxford University Press, 1988.

———. *Hesiod and Theognis.* Dorothea Wender, trans. and intro. London: Penguin, 1973.

Hoeller, Stephan A. *Jung and the Lost Gospels.* Wheaton, IL: Theosophical Publishing House, 1989.

Homer. For sources of the Homeric Hymn to Demeter, see the following listings: Wasson, Hofmann, and Ruck, *The Road to Eleusis;* Meyer, Marvin, *The Ancient Mysteries: A Sourcebook;* Foley, Helene, *The Homeric Hymn to Demeter.*

James, E. O., *The Cult of the Mother Goddess.* New York: Barnes and Noble Books, 1994.

Kanta, Katherine G. *Eleusis: Myth, Mysteries, History, Museum.* W. W. Phelps, trans. Athens: n.p., 1979.

Kerényi, Karl. *Athene: Virgin and Mother in Greek Religion.* Dallas, TX: Spring Publications, 1978.

———. Carl. *Eleusis: Archetypal Image of Mother and Daughter.* Princeton, NJ: Princeton University Press, 1991.

Knipe, Rita. *The Water of Life.* Honolulu: University of Hawaii Press, 1989.

Leek, Sybil. *The Complete Art of Witchcraft.* New York: New American Library, 1973.

Luck, George. *Arcana Mundi*. Baltimore: Johns Hopkins University Press, 1985.

McDaniel, June. *The Madness of the Saints: Ecstatic Religion in Bengal.* Chicago: University of Chicago Press, 1989.

———. "Shaktism" in *Hinduism Today*. Kawaa, HI: Himalayan Academy, Dec. 1991 issue.

McKenna, Terence. *Food of the Gods*. New York: Bantam Books, 1992.

Marinatos, Dr. Nanno. *Art and Religion in Thera: Reconstructing a Bronze Age Society.* Athens: D & I Mathioulakis, 1984.

Meyer, Marvin W. (ed.). *The Ancient Mysteries: A Sourcebook.* San Francisco: HarperSanFrancisco, 1987.

Metropolitan Museum of Art. *Prehistory and Early Greek Art.* New York: Metropolitan Museum of Art, 1996.

Mikalson, Jon D. *Athenian Popular Religion*. Chapel Hill, NC: University of North Carolina Press, 1983.

Moyers, Bill, interview with Joseph Campbell, *Joseph Campbell and the Power of Myth;* vol. VI, *Masks of Eternity.* New York: Mystic Fire Video in assoc. with *Parabola Magazine*, 1988, videocassette.

Murray, Liz and Colin. *The Celtic Tree Oracle*. New York: St. Martin's Press, 1991.

Mylonas, George E. *Eleusis and the Eleusinian Mysteries.* Princeton, NJ: Princeton University Press, 1962.

Nilsson, Martin. *Greek Folk Religion*. New York: Harper & Row, 1961.

Oates, Whitney and Charles Murphy. *Greek Literature in Translation.* New York: Longman, Green and Co., 1945.

Otto, Walter F. *Dionysus: Myth and Cult.* Dallas, TX: Spring Publications, 1989.

Ovid (Publins Ovidus Naso). *The Metamorphoses*. Horace Gregory, trans. New York: Viking Press, 1960.

———. *The Metamorphoses*, Mary M. Innes, trans. New York: Penguin Books, 1955.

———. *Metamorphoses,* vol. I. Loeb Classical Library. Frank J. Miller, trans. London: William Heinemann; New York: G. P. Putnam's Sons, 1921.

Pausanias. *Pausanius Description of Greece*. vol. I. W. H. S. Jones, trans. London: W. Heinemann; New York: G.P. Putnam's Sons, 1918.

Pindar. *The Odes of Pindar (Fragments).* Sir John Sandys, trans. Cambridge: Harvard University Press; London: Heinemann, 1923.

Plato. See listing: Oates and Murphy. *Greek Literature in Translation.*

Plutarch. *Plutarch's Moralia,* vol. I. Loeb Classical Library, Frank Cole Babbitt, trans. London: William Heinemann; New York: G. P. Putnam's Sons, 1925.

Spretnak, Charlene. *Lost Goddesses of Early Greece.* Berkeley, CA: Moon Books, 1978.

Starhawk. *The Spiral Dance.* San Francisco: HarperSanFrancisco, 1979.

Stone, Merlin. *Ancient Mirrors of Womanhood.* Boston: Beacon Press: 1990.

Taylor, Thomas. *The Eleusinian and Bacchic Mysteries.* New York: J. W. Bouton Publishers, 1875; Mokelumne Hill, CA: Health Research, 1971 (reprint).

Walker, Barbara G. *The Women's Encyclopedia of Myths and Secrets.* San Francisco: HarperSanFrancisco, 1983.

Wasson, R. Gordon, Albert Hofmann, and A. P. Ruck. *The Road to Eleusis: Unveiling the Secret of the Mysteries.* New York: Harcourt Brace Jovanovich, 1978.

Westbrook, Joel. *Greece: A Moment of Excellence.* Joel Westbrook, Jason Williams, and Jenny Barraclough, producers. Alexandria, VA: Time-Life Video and Television, 1995, videocassette.

Williams, Hector. "Secret Rites of Lesbos" in *Archaeology Magazine,* New York: Archaeological Institute of America, July-August 1994.

Wolfert, Paula. *Couscous and Other Good Food from Morocco.* New York: HarperCollins, 1973.

Wood, Michael. *The Sacred Way* (Travel Series). Rebecca Dobbs for WNET, producer. New York: 1991, videocassette.

Wright, Dudley. *The Eleusinian Mysteries and Rites.* Santa Fe, NM: Sun Publishing, 1992.

Zuntz, Gunther. *Persephone.* Oxford, England: Oxford University Press, 1971.

I N D E X

Photograph by Michelle Hart, 1999

Jennifer Reif, artist, poet and musician, has studied the relationships between nature, ancient cultures and their mythologies since 1983. In 1986 she began teaching classes on the Wiccan Religion. She has taught classes on Wicca and Goddess Religion in the Los Angeles area through Memosyne Arts and Studies, Long Beach Woman-Spirit, the Pallas Society, and Circle of Aradia. She also founded the Temple of Demeter and its newsletter *Mystica*. In 1992, she released an album of original Goddess-Pagan songs titled "Mysteries of Earth," distributed by Serpentine Music. She lives in Venice, California.